THE DYING MAN LIVES

---∞---

BIBLICAL HOPE FOR CONFRONTING CANCER AND THE END OF LIFE

BRIAN ZIMMERMAN

Edited by
PIERCE TAYLOR HIBBS

THE DYING MAN LIVES

Copyright © 2025 by Karen Johnson Zimmerman

All rights reserved.

No portion of this book may be reproduced in any form without written permission from the publisher or author, except as permitted by U.S. copyright law.

Paperback ISBN: 979-8-3485-2847-8

CONTENTS

Foreword: Reflections of a Friend   1

Introduction   5

1. When the Bell Tolls   9
2. How It All Happened   13
3. Why Are We Surprised?   23
4. Experiencing Death   25
5. Dealing with Denial   29
6. Fear of Death and the Conquering Christ   33
7. Are You Ready?   37
8. Christmas Eve   41
9. A Positive View of Death, Part 1   45
10. A Positive View of Death, Part 2   49
11. Comfort for Those Left Behind   53
12. Gratitude in Deliverance   57
13. Paul's Advice for Facing Death   61
14. Accepting Death   65
15. The Value of Courage   69

16.	Death and the Discipline of God	73
17.	Death and Our Plans for Life	77
18.	Death and Forgiveness	81
19.	Death and the Right to Cause It	85
20.	Death and Modern Medicine	89
21.	Death and Hospitality	93
22.	Death and the Trajectory	97
23.	Death as a Shepherd	101
24.	Death and Wisdom	105
25.	Learning How To Die Properly	109
26.	Cremation or Burial?	113
27.	Living as Sojourners	117
28.	Death and Resurrection	121
29.	A Long Dying Is a Blessing	123
30.	No Grumbling about Death	125
31.	Do You Believe Him?	127
32.	Death and Joy	129
33.	Death and Life in the World	133
34.	Death and Vaccines	137
35.	Death and Judgment	141
36.	Death and Its Power	145
37.	Death and the Breath of Life	149
38.	Death and Our Frailty	151
39.	Clemency for Brevity	153

40.	Shortness of Life and the Length of God's Years	157
41.	Mercy for Frailty and Faithfulness	163
42.	The Blessing of Life Everlasting	167
43.	The Fragility of Our Lives	171
44.	Our Lives Are Written	173
45.	Why Hope in Mortal Man?	175
46.	The Bleakness of Hell	177
47.	The Cure for Anxiety	179
48.	Come, Sweet Death	181
49.	The Whole Community	185
50.	The Greater Treasure	189
51.	Our Refuge	191
52.	Emily Dickinson and Flies Buzzing	193
53.	Which Is Better?	197
54.	Authority over Our Day	199
55.	The Removal of All Death	201
56.	The Earth Gives Birth	205
57.	The Covenant with Death	207
58.	What Abides Forever	209
59.	The Mighty Stubble	213
60.	Why Be Afraid?	215
61.	Courage in Dying	219
62.	What Happens When We Die?	223
63.	Death Could Not Hold Him	225

64.	The Prince of Life	227
65.	Lord of the Dead and the Living	229
66.	Paul's Poignant Statement	231
67.	The Last Enemy	233
68.	Tomorrow We Die	235
69.	The Hope of Handel	237
70.	Death Is Swallowed Up	241
71.	Carrying about Death	245
72.	Death Has Been Abolished	249
73.	The Hope of Revelation	251
74.	Marriage and Death	255
75.	The End	259
76.	Treatment Continues	263
77.	What Season Is It?	271
78.	Watch the Sunrises	275
79.	Content with Weaknesses	277
80.	Be of Good Courage	279
81.	In Whatever Circumstances	281
82.	Final Updates and Parting Words	283
83.	Appendix 1: On Healing	293
84.	Appendix 2: Reflections on Cancer Treatment	325
85.	Appendix 3: A Sermon for Brian's Memorial	343

FOREWORD: REFLECTIONS OF A FRIEND

Richard L. Pratt

You may not have known or heard of Brian Zimmerman, the author of *The Dying Man Lives*. You may have occasionally nodded as you passed him in the neighborhood or in some hallway. Perhaps you worked with him. Maybe you are one of his treasured children or grandchildren. I am one of Brian's many friends.

Everyone who was close to Brian knows that this book is his gift to Karen, his precious wife of more than fifty years. How could it be otherwise? More than any other, she was with him through his years of battling cancer—consulting with doctors, enduring the next round of chemotherapy, exercising with him, remembering the past, planning for what was coming, and praying about it all. She was at Brian's side with laughter and tears every day, until he took his last breath and left this world.

But at the same time, this book is also Brian's gift to *you*, whoever you may be. So, let me tell you a little about him.

I only knew Brian at a distance in high school. Everyone saw that he was smart, far too smart for me. So, I stayed away. He devoured books, remembered nearly everything he heard, and loved to talk about everything with anyone who would listen. You'll get a taste of that in this book. You'll see that he was a man who knew a lot and reflected deeply on life.

But you're also going to read the words of a changed man. And that's where our lifelong friendship began, one evening when Brian was transformed from the inside out. While on break from his university studies, he showed up at a high school Bible study that I happened to be leading. To my surprise, he stayed afterwards to talk.

"Do you really believe those things?" he asked. "You know, what you said about following Jesus and receiving forgiveness and eternal life."

After I awkwardly offered a feeble response, Brian looked down and spoke with firm resolve, "Ok. Starting today, I'm going to follow Jesus, too."

And just like that, Brian became a new person, and it showed for the rest of his life. He freely forgave when others disappointed him. He was a generous and a delightful friend. Over the years, he became a true husband, then a caring father and grandfather. He had purpose in all that he did. Despite his imperfections, Brian always stood out from the crowd, and it never took much conversation with him to find out why. He loved to tell others that he followed Jesus through it all.

So, why did Brian give you the gift of this book? I asked him that question on one of our visits. Why did he spend so much time writing for others when most people in his circumstance would be consumed with thinking only about themselves? I'll never forget his answer.

"The most certain thing about living is that we're all going to die," he quipped. Then he added, "I want everyone to know that I'm forgiven. I'm not afraid to die. I will live again with Jesus."

This is why Brian wrote *The Dying Man Lives* for you. He hoped that you will be able to say those words, too. You do not need to be afraid to die. Jesus died so that you can be forgiven. He was raised from the dead so that you can live again with him. All you have to do is follow Jesus. This book is the sure testimony of a dying man who knew that Jesus told the truth when he said, "I am the way, the truth and the life. No one comes to the Father except through me" (John 14:6).

January 2025

INTRODUCTION

Pierce Taylor Hibbs

Words have gravity. They weigh something in our hearts and hands. But not all words weigh the same. Some words are light and airy. They blow away in the breeze of our conversations and experience, and we forget them. Others—like grains of wheat in the biblical image of a threshing floor—fall down into us through the whipping wind. They meet the soil of the soul and silently take root. There they grow from seedlings to saplings, and they begin giving us life as we remember them—by leaf and bough. Such are the words you hold now: weighted grains of wheat ready to be planted. The question is whether your heart-soil is ready to receive them.

I was not privileged to have known Brian Zimmerman on this side of eternity. But I do know him now through his words. Brian had the rare experience of being a Christian who looked long and hard at the face of his own death . . . and he saw *through* it. His faith in the resurrected Christ was put to the ultimate test. And so he lifted up the words of Scripture that had taught him his faith. And as cancer assaulted his body, the words of his God held true. They remained. And that is what enabled Brian to teach his friends and family not just how to *live* well but how to *die* well. And yet, even in his death, he lives, just as Jesus promised (John 11:26)—hence the title for the book: *The Dying Man Lives*.

Much of what you find in these pages are reflections based on biblical meditation. They are snapshots from an earnest Christian who stared right through his own death at the glory on the other side, the glory of his risen Savior. And because of that, this has been one of the most hopeful and encouraging books I have read in a long time.

I thought about why this was the case. Why is this book such an uplifting testament? And it dawned on me that we have such trouble *trusting* another person's words, don't we? This is especially the case when it comes to death. Lots of people can wax eloquently about life after death and the eternity of the soul, especially Christians. But until death is put right in front of them, until their words are tested, we remain a bit skeptical. *Do they really believe that?*

I can assure you that Brian really believed what he wrote. And that's because he didn't just understand the words he expressed; he lived them. He clutched the promises of God in his own two hands amidst the harrowing destruction of cancer. Nausea, weakness, brain fog, and a host of other physical symptoms gave him little rest. And yet he saw God's *goodness* even there. He saw God's mercy. He saw God's patience. He saw God's loving discipline for his own soul. Even in the darkest of places, Brian found and focused on the ever-present light of God: the candle of the risen Christ.

That is so deeply encouraging to me. I watched my father die of cancer when I was eighteen, and that left a hole in my heart. It would take years for God's promises to line that hole like ivy, covering over the absence. But now, years later as I read Brian's words, I said to myself, "Wow. He sees death for what it is. His vision is crystal clear. He looks right through the smog of death and picks Christ out of the crowd. And he's helping me stare at the same Christ." There can be no better work for a Christian to leave behind for his brothers and sisters.

As you explore the chapters that follow, it may help to read one a day. Read them devotionally and slowly. Do not rush. Remember: these are weighted words. They are worth pondering and praying over as you consider your own death in a world that tries to get you to think about anything *but* death. Don't be fooled. Staring at your own death, as Brian knew well, is the key to unlocking true and lasting life—both now and in eternity.

Lastly, there are several places where Brian provides medical updates. Brian's journey with terminal cancer was a long one. His cancer symptoms began in December 2020, with a diagnosis in April 2021, and his death was not until September 5, 2024. He wanted to teach others as much as he could about what the experience was like. This included his symptoms from medications and chemo treatments. While these could be off-putting to some readers, I found them helpful in two ways: (1) they kept nothing shrouded in mystery. As Brian writes, we often prefer "the devil we know to the one we don't." It can be helpful to know more about what dealing with cancer is like—not just for our own potential experience but for our ability to encourage and care for others who are battling cancer. (2) These updates are part of Brian's personal story. The more you read of them, the more access you gain to him as a genuine person, someone battling pain and suffering like the rest of us, and yet one who stares at God in the midst of that suffering.

Ultimately, I believe Brian would want every reader to walk away from this book with two things: *a certainty of hope in the face of death* and *a biblically measured sense of what is important right now*. If you can leave this book with those things in hand, that alone is a momentous victory in the kingdom of God—something worth celebrating. May your reading of Brian's story drive you closer to Jesus Christ and the people of his pasture. It is to him—and to his resurrected people—that we all look in the midst of a passing world. Wherever you stand right now, your life is a cloud drifting on the skyline. Never forget to keep your face set towards the sun that burns behind it.

When the Bell Tolls

Getting a Terminal Diagnosis

> Send not to know
> For whom the bell tolls,
> It tolls for thee.
>
> — John Donne

My name is Brian Zimmerman, and this is my first entry in an account about my experience of dying. My intention is to document my thoughts and encounter with the event of dying. This is not a discussion of political news or cultural problems, though I may occasionally allude to such things if they're appropriate. I'm mainly concerned to try to help anyone who's been diagnosed with a terminal illness, or is concerned about death and dying, or may have a parent or child or friend or neighbor who's going through this process.

I may sometimes provide a quote at the beginning of a chapter because it's related to what I'm going to write about, or maybe just because it's a quote concerning dying that I have found helpful. The Donne quote at the beginning of this chapter is an example. It may seem from the quote I gave that he's simply saying that we all have to face death at some point. But, if you google the poem and read it in its entirety (it's not very long), you'll see that his real point is that we all as humans are affected by each other's death. This is the poem that begins with the familiar line: "No man is an island…" We're not islands, but a part of the continent of humanity, and so are affected by others, especially in death. So, though I write as a Christian, I also write as a part of humanity in our common experience of death.

My friends requested I do this to help them understand my and perhaps their preparation for death. But I also have a medical background: a bachelor's degree in medical technology (nowadays clinical laboratory science), and I even taught clinical chemistry in a school where seniors in affiliated colleges would come for a 12-month program to learn how to perform hospital laboratory tests. I also have a doctorate in physical therapy (I graduated in 2010). In between those two careers, I worked for Hewlett-Packard for almost twenty-one years on the service side in the field, and took early retirement at age 55 in 2007 to move to another city with my wife to enter the doctor of physical therapy program. I practiced as a PT in a number of settings: acute care (hospital), spinal cord injury (rehab and a special pressure ulcer wound care program), outpatient, then finally in home health physical therapy for the past six years. My wife is an RN who worked for many years in surgery. So, I've had a fair amount of medical experience and educated a lot of patients on PT principles, but also on more general medical ideas that I thought would help them understand what they were going through. So, I'll try to explain PT ideas, but also more general medical issues (such as lab tests) and terms in language that I think most people can understand.

CANCER IN MY LUNGS

So, now I'm sixty-nine years old, and have been diagnosed with esophageal cancer, that is, cancer of the tube running from your mouth to your stomach. Mine is just before the esophagus enters the stomach. That tiny spot of cancer *metastasized* (meaning some cells from this original spot of cancer, called the primary tumor, traveled somewhere else). In my case, they went to my lungs and grew like gangbusters. So, now my lungs are full of cancer. It's not lung cancer, but cancer *in* my lungs. There's a difference. What's in my lungs is actually a GI (gastrointestinal, meaning from your gut) cancer, not lung cancer. It's stage IV (we'll talk more about staging and prognosis later), treatable, but not curable. So, I'm on two kinds of chemotherapy (one oral, one IV), and another IV treatment in a clinical trial called immunotherapy, which is designed to attack my type of cancer (in my gut and in my lungs). That's what I'll be talking about during the rest of this book: my faith and medical experience of what it's like to be diagnosed with a disease that's going to kill you and the medical work to try to extend your life as long as possible. To learn the details of how I got here, turn the page.

How it All Happened

August 5, 2021

> Come now, you who say, "Today or tomorrow we will go to such and such a city, and spend a year there and engage in business and make a profit." Yet you do not know what your life will be like tomorrow. You are just a vapor that appears for a little while and then vanishes away. Instead, you ought to say, "If the Lord wills, we will live and also do this or that."
>
> James 4:13–15

It started somewhere around the end of December of 2020 during the time when the COVID vaccines were being first administered. I had gotten my first shot at the main hospital of the system I work for, and had a bad bout of night sweats, muscle aches, and a little soreness, but nothing terrible, and it lasted only about twenty-four hours. But, before I received the second shot in January (2021), I noticed one day that when I ran up the basement stairs in our home from the family room to the kitchen, I was briefly short of breath. *Huh. That's odd*, I thought, but then thought nothing more of it.

I was still working full time (though only thirty-two hours a week) in home health physical therapy, and so was busy with work and chores and the rest of life as it happens. My wife and I had dropped our gym membership, as there were so many restrictions in using the gym, and decided to lift weights in the garage in the basement of our home. I noticed over the course of weeks that it became harder and harder for me to perform a workout. We weren't doing anything that strenuous, but at the end of a workout I was doing lunges holding two 45 lb. dumbbells. At each workout, I became progressively more short of breath after performing that exercise until finally I started panting when I finished. At that point, one day after such an experience, I called the primary care physician (PCP) office, and requested a visit on a Wednesday because that was my weekly day off.

"It'll be a month before we can schedule you a visit."

"Yeah, but I'm really short of breath. Something is seriously wrong."

"That's the first appointment on Wednesday we have available."

So, I was stuck with that. I guess you might think I should have gone to one of the offices that take walk-ins for the same day, or even to the emergency department (ED) or had sense enough to schedule it on a different day, but I doubted the ED would want to waste time on someone working full time who was still lifting weights, and I figured the same day office would in effect tell me to go see my PCP, and I hated taking a day for something that I figured was some minor problem. I may have been wrong and made a bad choice, but hindsight is 20/20, right?

Seeing My Primary Care Physician (PCP)

I did finally see my PCP, who listened to my story and told me that it was likely one of three causes: medical (e.g., anemia), heart (most likely), or lungs (very bad if that was the case). So, he would order some blood work to check for things like anemia, do an EKG, schedule a visit with a cardiologist, and get a chest x-ray. They did the EKG (normal), drew the blood work (all normal), and did the chest x-ray. The tech who shot the x-rays told me to have a seat and that she would be right back. I sat down in the empty x-ray room, not really thinking anything about it, and checked email on my phone, texted my wife, poked around on the internet and waited.

In a few minutes, I saw a pair of feet appear in front of me. Lifting my head, I saw it was the PCP. He said that the tech virtually never came to get him because of an x-ray but had this time.

"We know why you're short of breath," he said. "Come and look."

I thought that sounded like good news. Maybe he'd give me some pill like an antibiotic for a lung infection, or a drug for some weirdo fungal infection, or for inflammation or a severe allergic reaction. Then I could get back to work.

"You've seen a chest x-ray before, right?" I nodded yes. "X-rays are blocked by dense tissue like bone, which show up white, but soft tissue is dark. Look at your x-ray."

My lungs were white in the x-ray with little bright spots scattered around.

"What is that?" I said.

"I don't really know," he mused. "I've never seen anything like it before. What I think it probably is is scarring of some type, like idiopathic pulmonary fibrosis (IPF)." IPF is a condition whose name pretty much says it all: scarring (fibrosis) of the lungs (pulmonary) for unknown reasons (idiopathic)).

"I'll order a CAT scan of your chest, and see what it tells us, but there's no good treatment for IPF."

I was stunned. "What am I going to tell my wife?" I exclaimed. "What's the prognosis?"

"Three to five years," he said.

I was numb by this point, wondering how I was going to break this news to my wife. As it turned out, the PCP was wildly optimistic about my prognosis.

Telling My Wife and the First ED Visit

I told my wife, who took it well and with her characteristic good sense observed that we didn't really know what was wrong and that it was better to wait on the CAT scan before jumping to conclusions. I agreed but didn't feel very hopeful. Meanwhile, I continued to live fairly normally, working each day, until one day I started coughing as I left my home to see patients and continued to cough, and couldn't stop. I had to pull my car over to the side of the road until I could get control of my breath. I was gasping for air, and finally called my patients to cancel my visits, and my supervisor to let him know that I wouldn't be working that day. Fortunately, he was very understanding as I had already shared with him the PCP's assessment. My wife said I should go home and rest, but I disagreed and felt if I was taking a day off for this illness, whatever it was, then I should I go to the ED and see what they had to say.

It was pretty much a wasted trip, as I had suspected it would be a month ago, when this event had started. The ED MD was a fairly young guy who basically said what the PCP said.

"I have no idea what's wrong with your lungs, but they look like people's lungs who have suffered some serious damage from COVID. I'm going to have you tested for COVID."

"But, I've had the vaccine."

"I know, but it's not 100% effective, only 90–95%."

No argument there, so they tested me, but it was negative.

"Also," he explained, "I can't justify admitting you to the hospital. Your O2 saturation readings are too high, and you're just in too good a health. It would be more risky for you to be in the hospital than at home. Go home and wait for the CAT scan." (This visit to the ED was on a Monday and the CAT scan was on Wednesday). So, I went home and waited. I had received a message on MyChart (the software that my hospital system used to communicate with patients) from my PCP, who said he had showed my X-ray to the other MDs in the practice, and they all agreed: we have no idea.

THE SECOND ED VISIT

So, on Wednesday I went to have the CAT scan, and read the results from the radiologist that afternoon. It was a laundry list of possibilities, including fungal infection, IPF, metastatic carcinoma, etc. Pretty much the same reading that had come from the PCP's office after my chest x-ray. In other words: we have no idea. Meanwhile, the PCP had made me a pulmonology appointment for further work up, but that visit wasn't for another month! I was not very happy but didn't see what I could do about it.

But, as it happened, on Friday night of the following week (by this point, it was April 2, Good Friday), I went to bed early as I was exhausted from work, but woke up after an hour of sleep gasping for breath. I told my wife that I was sorry but I really felt the need to go to the ED. She agreed and took me there but couldn't stay because of COVID restrictions. I went to the ED not just because of the symptoms, but also because I was hoping there was a chance I could short circuit the system by getting admitted and speeding up this very slow diagnostic process of seeing a physician and having a test, then seeing another physician and having another test, etc. As it turned out, I was very blessed to been seen by an ED doctor who had the same thought: we can't wait.

"I'm admitting you and we're going to get to the bottom of this now," he said. So, I spent the weekend having a CAT scan again, an MRI, and finally on Monday, a biopsy where they punched a needle into my chest to get a tissue sample. After that I went home and waited.

The Verdict

On Thursday morning, I received a call from one of the hospitalists. A hospitalist is a physician who works for the hospital and sort of acts as a general contractor for the other physicians who are specialists that come to see you while you're admitted. When you leave the hospital, they turn you over to your PCP. If you don't have one, you're on your own. So, my advice is if you don't have a PCP, even if you don't think you need one, go get one. I've seen patients without a PCP who went into the hospital, and when they went home, they were scrambling trying to arrange appointments with other MDs, interpret the hospital tests, etc. Trust me, it is not a good experience. Get a PCP.

"Mr. Zimmerman, we received the pathology report back about your lung tissue sample, and I'm sorry to have to tell you, but your lungs are full of cancer."

It's hard to know how to respond to that kind of statement, but I finally asked what was next.

"Well, you'll go back to your PCP for a follow up this Friday." So, while waiting, I called one of my best friends about the news.

"You need to get someone else involved," he said. My friend was on the board of several charitable organizations with one of the most prominent oncologists in the city. "I'm going to call him and ask for his help and advice." So, he did, and Friday morning while I was shaving, getting ready for the PCP visit, the oncologist called. I told him my story, and he said that I needed two things: an immediate visit with an oncologist, and a PET scan, and if I didn't have those scheduled within the coming week, to call him. So, when I went to the PCP, I apologized for involving another doctor, but stated that these were his suggestions. The PCP said he could set up the oncology appointment, but couldn't order the PET scan. I was surprised.

"Why not?" I asked.

"Because," he said, "the hospital system has told PCPs we do not have the right to order PET scans, so you'll have to get the oncologist to order the PET scan." I assumed it was a money thing because of Medicare, but who knows.

HELP ARRIVES

Monday morning I didn't see any sign of an oncology visit scheduled in MyChart, so I called the oncologist who had spoken with me the previous Friday.

"I will have you an oncology visit and a PET scan scheduled this week," he reported. And he did. So, I had a PET scan, which I'll discuss more in another chapter, and went to see the oncologist, who said I needed to start chemo, like right now (and as short of breath as I was by this point, he got no argument from me). So, he scheduled an IV chemo appointment for the next Friday, but before that I had to have Porta Cath installed that Wednesday (two days before the IV chemo session). A Porta Cath, at least the kind I have, is a sort of tough plastic bubble they install under your skin just below your neck in the front. They then threaded a tube up through my neck and inserted it into a vein and ran it down near the right atrium of the heart. The oncologist told me it was because the chemo drug was toxic and could cause serious problems if they were administering it by IV in a vein in my arm and the needle came out of the vein. So, now they insert my IV needle into the bubble through the skin. Easy peasy. And, because the PET scan lit up near my stomach, the oncologist scheduled an EGD (basically an endoscopy procedure where they admit you to the hospital and put a tube down your throat to look at your esophagus/stomach, and in the intestinal tract beyond the stomach). The following Monday I had that done. After it was over, the gastroenterologist came back to my room where my wife and I were waiting. He told me I was a mystery patient as the spot that lit up near the end of my esophagus didn't look like cancer. They had even used an ultrasound (I think) to look inside the lining of the esophagus and didn't see anything.

"It looked irritated, so maybe the reason it showed up in the PET scan was inflammation." But he said he had also taken several biopsies and would send them off for analysis.

The tissue analysis (from that needle biopsy) showed that it was cancer in my lung, but that it was not lung cancer, i.e., the cancer that was growing in my lungs was not lung tissue. Instead the tissue markers showed that it was GI cancer; in other words, there was another tumor—the primary one had to be somewhere in my gut. They needed to find it, or it would continue to grow and dump cancer cells in my system and grow tumors at other sites. That was why the EGD was necessary.

Nailed It

I couldn't see that report in MyChart, but at my oncology visit for IV chemo treatment, he told me that the esophageal site was indeed cancerous. And, because of tumor markers, it was determined that it was the exact same cancer that was in my lungs. In other words, I had cancer in my lungs, but it wasn't lung cancer; it was GI cancer. *Nice*, I thought. *Only I would have some tiny place that didn't appear cancerous but metastasized to my lungs and filled them up. Go figure.* But, at least we knew where the primary tumor was (the esophagus) and that by treating the cancer in the lung we'd also treat the esophageal cancer. That's a twofer, and I'm all for it. Neither of the CAT scans or PET scan (or the EGD) showed any sign of other metastases.

So, that's how it all happened. But, let me close by noting that the quote from the book of James at the beginning of this chapter nails it: you really don't know what your life will be like tomorrow—good, bad, or ugly. I went from being short of breath briefly while still working full time to being out of work in less than four months. Hard to believe. As a friend of mine said: "Nobody gets out of here alive," and it is reckless to pretend otherwise. Still, we all seem surprised by our own death. But that's for the next chapter.

WHY ARE WE SURPRISED?

August 2, 2021

> We have finished our years like a sigh.
> As for the days of our life, they contain seventy years,
> Or if due to strength, eighty years,
> Yet their pride is but labor and sorrow;
> For soon it is gone and we fly away.
>
> Psalm 90:9–10

IT IS AMAZING TO me how surprised I was to get a diagnosis of impending death. I am a Christian and have read the Psalm quoted above many times, but somehow the words apparently didn't sink in. What part of "they contain seventy years, or if due to strength, eighty years" didn't I understand? (As mentioned, I'm now sixty-nine, only six months from that seventy year mark).

Apparently, though, in our American culture, it's a common problem now but wasn't always that way. I'm reading David McCullough's *The Pioneers* (one of about ten books as I love to read) and have been struck by the frequent occurrence of death in the lives of the people that he is chronicling—the people who left the east coast (especially Massachusetts) not long after the end of the war for independence (in the 1790s) and traveled to what was to become Ohio. They and their children died of many causes, sometimes just on the trip out west: disease, accidents, attacks from the natives. Though they were obviously sad and grieved, I don't get the impression that they were surprised or resentful (towards the world or God). For them, death was a constant though harsh companion and an event that was not a shock.

I Missed the Dying Part

My wife and I often pray from the *Book of Common Prayer* an evening prayer with this line: "And grant us grace always to live in such a state that we may never be afraid to die; so that, living and dying, we may be thine..." I think I caught the living part but missed the dying part. Now when we read it, I practically catch my breath as I am suddenly faced with what it was telling me to prepare for. As I mentioned at the outset, I worked in home health physical therapy for six years, and in all the hundreds of homes I entered, I encountered only the occasional person who didn't seem to be surprised or resentful or upset that they had contracted a serious illness, or suffered a serious injury, or had received a diagnosis of a terminal illness. I think as a culture we have done what we can to isolate ourselves from death, both ours and those around us. We have lost the urgency of preparing to die.

In the following chapters, I'll describe some of the cultural differences among people that I saw pretty consistently as families dealt with sickness/debility and dying. I'll also talk about denial and how intentional we need to be in preparing for death.

EXPERIENCING DEATH

August 3, 2021

> My mother is a fish.
> — William Faulkner, As I Lay Dying

Little Experience of Death

Before my diagnosis of a terminal disease, I had very limited experience of death and dying personally (except with my dad, who also died of cancer, though of a very different sort and in his 80s). Most of my experience was from my clinical work in the hospitals where I practiced acute care PT, but more importantly, in my home health job. I entered literally hundreds of homes over six years seeing people sick, or suffering from injuries or recovering from surgeries, or dying, and observed the many forms of family dynamics in responding to those circumstances. Sickness and dying/death are not experienced in a vacuum. I gave the quote above from one of my favorite authors about the death of a mother. The quote is from a chapter narrated by her young son, Vardaman, as he tries to make sense of her death. The reason I bring this quote in is that Vardaman's experience of his mother's death is in a context of what he has experienced of death. And I saw this phenomenon many times in home health.

The first time I realized how limited my cultural experience of sickness and dying was, I found myself in a hospital setting. I received a referral to go see an elderly black woman who was recovering from surgery. When I arrived at her room, I had difficulty entering because it was packed with her family: children, grandchildren, great-grandchildren were all in there. It sounded like a party or family holiday get together. I called her name—"Mrs. Smith?" and was told I was in the correct room and so pushed my way in with "Excuse me, excuse me" to reach her. When we discussed her discharge plans, she assured me she would have plenty of help. I believed her.

Almost literally right next door was an elderly white woman who was also recovering. But when I entered her room and called her name—"Mrs. Jones?"—it was like an echo in a cathedral. The room was empty except for her, and I saw no visitors any time I went to see her. When I asked about her discharge plans, she was very vague except to say she wanted to go home.

"Do you have any children?" I asked.

"Oh yes," she responded, but one lived in Maryland, another in Tennessee, etc.

"Okay, what about local family?" Well, there was a sister, but they didn't have much to do with each other. "Friends and neighbors?" Well, she had a neighbor who would check in occasionally. In other words, she was going home without being able to care for herself and having no expectation of any assistance from anyone else. She assured me she would be fine. I didn't believe her.

Death Care Requires More Than One Generation

So, what I saw over the course of years was that many middle-class white people live in multi-generation family situations for only a short time (for the length of their children's childhood), and then the parents were alone with a spouse for the rest of their lives. But many African American, Asian, and Hispanic families are multi-generational for many years. So, when grandma gets sick or injured or feeble, there's always someone there to help her. Trying to replace that family assistance with paid help is extraordinarily difficult and expensive. Maybe the idea that the end of life is an individual's problem and not anyone else's needs to re-thought by those of us who grew up in a family that scattered as soon as the children could leave and live on their own.

I'll close this chapter by mentioning Paul's discussion of familial responsibilities in 1 Timothy 5:

> Honor widows who are widows indeed; but if any widow has children or grandchildren, they must first learn to practice piety in regard to their own family and to make some return to their parents; for this is acceptable in the sight of God.
>
> 1 Tim. 5:3–4

Paul elsewhere makes clear the obvious responsibility that parents have for their children. But here he reverses the responsibility, an application I believe is true about one of the Ten Commandments: "Honor your father and mother." Honor initially is about obedience when we are young children, but what constitutes honor changes when we become adult children. We were cared for when young by our parents, but as they age, the roles should reverse: we honor them as we become the caregivers. And those parents or children who resist that responsibility have the worst experience of sickness or suffering or dying in my observation. The parent who obstinately refuses to accept help from her children causes them no end of worry and trouble. The child who refuses to accept that mom can't care for herself any longer just increases the mom's worries and suffering and dangers.

But, of course, that's only the problem situations I saw. There were also many families in which I saw people willing to change and accept the situation: a parent who was willing to move in with a child or even move from out of state to be near a child, and children who built rooms or even mother-in-law suites onto the house, or simply opened up a bedroom to a parent who moved in with the family. It often meant the child had to alter their work life, such as working from home or taking early retirement, but usually involving a loss of income that they accepted because they were willing to provide care for their mom or dad, or sometimes both. I had a lot of respect for that kind of sacrifice as they had no way of knowing exactly what it would involve or how long it would continue.

WHAT ABOUT THE CHURCH?

I can't let the church off the hook here as Paul makes it clear that widows who have no family to care for them are to be cared for by the church. How many churches are set up for that responsibility? "If any woman who is a believer has *dependent* widows, she must assist them and the church must not be burdened, so that it may assist those who are widows indeed."

As boomers age and as our culture fractures our familial bonds, I think this problem will only continue to grow. There's not enough caregivers, ALF's (assisted living facilities), and nursing homes to care for all these elderly people. Our idea of family needs to be more accepting and intentional in accommodating multi-generational responsibilities.

DEALING WITH DENIAL

August 4, 2021

> Therefore in that day the Lord God of hosts called you to weeping, to wailing, to shaving the head and to wearing sackcloth. Instead, there is gaiety and gladness, killing of cattle and slaughtering of sheep, eating of meat and drinking of wine: 'Let us eat and drink, for tomorrow we may die.'
>
> Isaiah 22:12–13

> 'Come,' they say, 'let us get wine, and let us drink heavily of strong drink; and tomorrow will be like today, only more so.'
>
> Isaiah 56:12

ONE OF THE GREATEST problems I saw in home health in dealing with debility, sickness, and dying was denial. As illustrated in the quote above, though disaster is predicted, people have a remarkable ability to convince themselves that it will never arrive, that "tomorrow will be like today, only more so." I mentioned this propensity before but in a more cultural respect.

But, it also shows itself with individuals and families quite often. I had parents (one of whom was the patient, though sometimes I had both partners as patients!) who insisted on living on their own despite the fact that they were falling and breaking bones and were doing ordinary daily tasks that were now dangerous for them, e.g., cooking. Or, they were experiencing sun downing, in which the patient becomes increasingly confused in the late afternoon and evening and may turn on the stove and leave it on, or wander out of the house with no idea where they are. Or, they may refuse to accept the fact that their single biggest problem is that they sit most of the day doing nothing but watching television, resulting in increasing weakness and deteriorating balance with resultant falls. On the other hand, children may request PT because they believe that their parent can be "fixed" if they are just exhorted enough to get up and move. The same attitude, of course, exists to what seems a greater degree when a terminal diagnosis is given. The patient, or sometimes only the family, want everything done that is possible to save the patient's life, though it's obvious that the 85 year old mom is highly unlikely to be cured or returned to a healthy, functioning state. So, instead of preparing for death, the family avoids the topic and process by constant MD appointments, frequent hospital admissions, home health visits, all with the idea that "tomorrow will be like today." And, of course, it isn't.

Preparing for Death Must be Intentional

This problem is not to deny that there are situations, of course, where medication or surgery can increase someone's likelihood of improved health or quality of life. Rather, it is to say that because people in our culture think so little of death, they are unprepared to deal with debility, sickness, and dying when those problems enter their or their parents' home. Preparations of that type need to be intentional, something thought of before the event occurs, like buying car insurance before you have the wreck, not afterwards. But I have seen often that as parents begin to reach the point where they are not safe to live alone or are in the process of dying, the child goes on looking for a fix to reverse the process instead of thinking, "What's plan B? What should we do if mom can't stay at home alone anymore? Or, what do we need to do to help her and us to prepare for her death?" There's not a fixed answer to that question. Could the parents stay in their home if they had some in home assistance with cooking, cleaning, bathing, and so on? Or, would they be better in an assisted living facility (ALF). Is it possible the child can have the parents move in with the child? Or, is it clear from the MD's assessment that the parent is dying and the family needs time to prepare her and themselves for that eventuality? In the latter case, we need other questions: Where is the will? Who's the executor? Are there funeral arrangements? All these questions need to be answered *before* mom is admitted yet again to the hospital but this time will not be released home as the hospital staff refuse to send her back to what is obvious to everyone but the family as a dangerous situation—before she dies "unexpectedly."

And, of course, the parents can make this whole process easier or harder by their acceptance of their limitations or terminal diagnosis. If they are willing to accept and discuss their situation and help find solutions, such as having an aide come in, or moving nearer the child, wherever they may be. In short, there are a lot of problems inherent to sickness, debility, and dying, but arguably the worst are those that are self-created.

FEAR OF DEATH AND THE CONQUERING CHRIST

December 9, 2021

> For to this end Christ died and lived again, that He might be Lord of the dead and of the living.
>
> Romans 14:9

Surprised by Death

As I mentioned before, I was surprised—*shocked* might be a better term—to learn that I had a terminal diagnosis. In fact, I was surprised to realize that I was surprised! And, as I've said before, I don't think I'm alone in this reaction—our whole culture is death aversive. We are all quite stunned to find out we are mortal. In my home health days, it was a rare person who was not speechless to discover that he or she was dying.

As the quote I gave at the beginning of this chapter implies, the Christian faith is one that should prepare us for death in a way that worldly cultures won't. This experience has been documented by many people over many centuries across many different ethnicities. I just finished reading David Zeisberger's book *History of the Northern American Indians*, a book about his experiences as a Moravian (i.e., a Brethren) missionary among North American Indians in the late 18th century. By that time the Indians had had contact with Europeans for a while, but the effects of that contact on their culture was still being resisted by them. Zeisberger notes that though Indians were generally a brave people, unafraid of pain, for instance, even in torture (which they practiced regularly), they were still generally terrified of death itself. And I think that most of us still are, despite the fact that we live in a civilization that is far more advanced in technology, science, and just about any other measure you can think of beyond theirs. But the Christian religion is built on the foundation of the belief that there has been a conquest of death: "He himself likewise partook of the same [flesh and blood] that through death he might render powerless him who had the power of death, that is, the devil, and free those who through fear of death were subject to slavery all their lives" (Heb. 2:14–15). Christians of all people should have no fear of death. To the extent that we do, there may be a lack in our faith that we have been unaware of. Perhaps meditation on the Hebrews passage would be helpful for those who still have that fear.

As our culture becomes more post-Christian—dare I say anti-Christian?—we see more of the fear that the Indians experienced 250 years ago—a fear of death itself. What happens when we die? Again, Christianity claims that there is one who has the answer, one who has returned from the grave and, in addition, will give that power to others as well. This is the ultimate question: was that claim true or not? I have been a Christian for almost 50 years and can now say that this question is more important for you than any other you will ever have to answer. We can avoid answering that question for many years in a culture like ours where people generally die out of sight, enabling us to delete the thought of death, but it doesn't change the fact of death's inevitability. It is an event we will all experience eventually, whether soon or late in our lives. But how we will face it is what is most important. Most of us are unprepared in any fashion, including even making a will or preparing for our own funeral and burial, which most of us would agree are wise things to do. I speak as one who had failed in that regard as well, and so, being given a terminal diagnosis but also given treatment so I could extend my life, I have been granted the opportunity to do those things I should have already completed. I'm almost finished with most of those preparations—making a will, arranging my funeral details, getting the finances in order, etc. But these were things I should have done at least by the time I was 50 years old, not when I'm almost 70. In our culture, however, most of us at that age (of 50) are so busy with everyday cares that large issues get delayed, even obscured. It's the problem of the "tyranny of the immediate," as I've heard it called. To me now, I see it as a dangerously risky habit. It matters not if the world goes out with a bang or a whimper; what matters is how *you* go out. My personal heresy is to believe that all the hysteria surrounding COVID-19 (and, maybe even climate change) is just another manifestation of this submerged fear of death in one form or another.

Are You Ready?

December 20, 2021

Are you ready to meet Jesus?
Are you where you ought to be?
Will He know you when He sees you
Or will He say, "Depart from me?"

When destruction cometh swiftly
And there's no time to say a fare-thee-well
Have you decided whether you want to be
In Heaven or in Hell?

Have you got some unfinished business?
Is there something holding you back?
Are you thinking for yourself
Or are you following the pack?

Are you ready for the judgment?
Are you ready for that terrible swift sword?
Are you ready for Armageddon?
Are you ready for the day of the Lord?

Are you ready? (Get ready!)

> I hope you're ready? (ready, are you ready?)
> (Are you ready? Get ready!)
> (Ready, are you ready?)
> — Bob Dylan, "Are You Ready?" (1980)

Death Is Not Value Neutral

I THINK FOR MOST people in the West who are not Christians, death tends to be seen as "value neutral," i.e., you just die and disappear, and your body decays, and that's that. Like a beautiful leaf falling from a sugar maple in the autumn, your time is over and you're done. No right or wrong or good or bad about it; it just is. But for the Christian death is an ethical event; it is value heavy, for it is then that we face an assessment that is not only complete, encompassing the entirety of our lives, not just the parts we want seen, but just as important, it is final. There is no appeal, no reprieve call from the governor, no do-over.

Death Is Value Full

The Christian, then, should lose the fear of death for the reason that death ushers in a true and perfect judgment, one that a genuine faith should welcome—not because Christians don't sin; we assuredly do. In fact, contra to "God is not Great," Christopher Hitchens's screed against all faiths, but especially Christianity, Christians are well aware and are embarrassed by the failure of the church to be holy as God is holy. But to use that as an argument against Christianity seems to be on the order of attending an AA meeting and being astonished that it's a meeting of a bunch of former drunks who sometimes fall off the wagon. It's a support group for sinners, not a slap-on-the-back group for all those who recognize their moral superiority. The Bible is a history of the Old Testament (OT) and New Testament (NT) church being full of people who fail to live out their faith, even—may be even especially—their leaders. Paul says, "I know that after my departure savage wolves will come in among you, not sparing the flock, and from among your own selves men will arise, speaking perverse things, to draw away the disciples after them" (Acts 20:29–30). Paul's goodbye address to the Ephesian elders was not exactly someone defending the perfection of the church, much less its leaders.

Why then would a Christian look forward to death? If his life isn't perfect, what hope is there? It is because of the death and resurrection of Jesus, whose death paid for our sins and whose resurrection gives us new life that has already begun. But I think whoever is a non-Christian knows in his heart, and his conscience accuses him, of his many failures over the course of a life time. He rightly, then, fears a full and true assessment because he is sure he will be found wanting. All attempts at avoidance and rationalization will end. There will be no more *pretending* death is the end, or just another step in our cosmic journey as some may hope. Instead, it is a revelation of all that has been hidden from others, or hidden in our hearts, or denied, justified, or even boasted of. The lives of Christians and non-Christians will alike be examined. Christians don't get a pass on judgment. But our faith is paramount, for the proof is in the existential pudding. Our lives will reflect that our faith was genuine and not a hypocritical statement or confession of word only.

What is the difference between the scrupulous obedience of true faith versus the hypocrisy of an attempt at self-righteousness? The hypocrite attempts perfect obedience out of a sense of duty, an attempt to earn the right to enter paradise, an effort doomed to failure. But the Christian strives to improve his obedience out of a sense of gratitude, a joy that he has been forgiven, and he wants to live in a way that honors the Savior who bought him forgiveness at such a high cost.

The Final Separation at Death

The Shepherd will be able to separate the sheep and goats in the church not based simply on words, but on looking at their lives (Matt. 25:32ff). For the Christian, then, death has a momentous significance because our journey will be finished, and we will finally know that Paul's statement was true: "For me to live is Christ, and to die is gain" (Phil. 1:21). There is a joy, then, that the Christian can have now in facing death, suffering, and pain, for we know that this life is not the end of life; it's a precursor, a trial that has meaning, allowing us to rejoice when God decides we have reached its conclusion. But for the non-Christian, death will be and should be a time of fear and worry; beyond death there is no hope. Still, even the thief on the cross found words of comfort from a Savior who was hanging on the same instrument of a very cruel death (Luke 23:42–43). It is never too late until death finally arrives. There is always hope if we will repent and believe, if we will change and submit in obedience to him, putting our life as well as our death in his hands.

CHRISTMAS EVE

December 24, 2021

Christmas and Death

In this chapter, I thought I would take a moment to reflect on the celebration of Christmas and its relation to death. You wouldn't think death would have much to do with Christmas, but I'm not talking about our celebration of Christmas, but what Christmas was. It always amazes me how many modern Christmas songs are all about what we did or do in our celebrations and family traditions and how little they are about Christmas itself, i.e., the birth of Jesus in Bethlehem.

When Jesus was born, his birth was heralded by heaven through the legions of the army of God (i.e., the angels). Now, for a moment, try to ignore the Renaissance paintings of angels, especially the cherubs pictured as chubby little babies. The first encounter we have with the cherubs in the Bible is in Genesis 3:24, where God stations them as guards with flaming swords to prevent Adam or Eve making it back into the Garden of Eden to reach the tree of life. That sounds more like Special Forces than pudgy infants. Why else when angels appear would they constantly have to say, "Don't be afraid"? Again, this sort of response makes it sound as if soldiers have appeared from nowhere, startling everyone. These were no light and whimsical fairy creatures. (Did Tinkerbell have to reassure the lost boys when she showed up?) Maybe the singing angels were like the West Point Choir.

There was also the worship of the nations coming to see the long expected king—the magi bearing gifts of great value: gold, frankincense, and myrrh. How did they know to show up? Where did they get that prophecy? (Probably from Jews in the Diaspora.) This is the version of Christmas we tell our children so as to not frighten them.

But there is a grown up side to Christmas as well. The world of Satan had a response to Jesus's birth too, and it was an orgy of death trying to destroy the gift of life. Herod, in his attempt to end the life of a possible rival king, murdered all male children in and around Bethlehem who were two years old and under. So while the angels, shepherds, and magi rejoiced at Christ's birth, there was a part of the world system that opposed him, and caused death to be its response to God's offer of life. The people of God were moved to lift up their voices not in praise but in great sorrow as a response to the first Christmas: "A voice was heard in Ramah, weeping and great mourning, Rachel weeping for her children; and she refused to be comforted, because they were no more" (Matt. 2:18).

And so the pattern has continued that had begun following the disobedience of Adam and Eve, their fall from innocence with one child murdering another (Cain against Abel), death attempting to end the gift of life. But with the birth of Jesus we have our greatest hope, for he came to rescue us from darkness and death, granting us light and life, the hope of peace with God and with one another.

Christmas and Life

We live in a culture that ignores death, even seeming to hide the fact of death or obfuscate it with various euphemisms. Or, it celebrates the death of the innocent with the so-called right of abortion, or entertaining the hope that euthanasia will be a pleasant way to end all suffering. It is no wonder that the people of the West are terrified by so many things. We are controlled at the root of it all by a fear of death. Yet, from God's people, the church, goes forth a message of light and life in the celebration of Christmas as we stand with the angels, the shepherds, and the magi in their joy of this greatest of gifts. Buried under the layers of greed and silly sentimentality, we find a word of powerful, unstoppable *hope*, for one has been born who was dogged by death and Satan from his beginning of life in this age, and who was finally caught and executed and buried. But he emerged from that grave full of new life, an immortal life, one that could never again be ended by death. Satan had lost the battle against life.

And Jesus offered that deliverance also to his followers, who can now lose their fear of death, fear of an event that is no more a threat, but is rather the hope of release to a new age. And that offer extended far beyond the people of the Jews, who first received his offer of immortality, but also to us, even to a people who have sat in a land of darkness and death, but now can have lives of joy, even in the midst of their dying: "Do not be afraid; for behold, I bring you good news of great joy, which will be for all the people, for today in the city of David there has been born for you a Savior, who is Christ the Lord" (Luke 2:10–11).

So, as in the first Christmas, so now we see the end of that which threatens us most, but which will no longer cause us to be afraid. For now we have a Savior who was born to bring us light and life, who beat death and the devil at his own game, taking the end of life and turning it into the beginning, weeping into laughter, tears of sorrow into tears of joy.

A Positive View of Death, Part 1

January 1, 2022

Thanks be unto Jesus
Thanks be unto God
He has won the battle
Through the power of the cross!

Where oh death (Where is your victory?)
Where oh death (Where is your sting?)
Where oh death (You are the enemy)
But Jesus is my King!
The saying that is written will be true!

Death is ended, yes!
Death is ended, yes!
Death is swallowed up in victory!"
— James Ward, "Death Is Ended"

A Positive View of Death

Unlikely as it sounds, there is actually one perspective described in the Bible that is a positive view of death. As it should, of course, my discussion of this view begins with Jesus in the gospels.

Going to Sleep

Jesus in his talk with his disciples about the death of their friend, Lazarus, describes Lazarus's demise not as death: "Our friend, Lazarus, has fallen asleep; but I go, so that I may awaken him out of sleep" (John 11:11). This description of Lazarus's death confuses the disciples. John continues on in his account to describe their confusion: "Now Jesus had spoken of his death, but they thought that he was speaking of literal sleep" (John 11:13). Jesus introduces a euphemistic phrase to describe death, but it is a euphemism with a point. Jesus is teaching them that death is only a temporary state and that he has the power to overcome it.

Jesus uses this phrase on occasion as reported in another instance where he raises the dead. In Mark 5:39, we read Jesus's words to mourners at a synagogue leader's house: "And after entering, he said to them, 'Why are you making a commotion and weeping? The child has not died, but is asleep.'" Here Jesus is distinguishing between the death of unbelievers who have no hope and the death of his disciples who believe in him for escape from the permanency of death, the death of Christians.

Once again, Jesus makes a very pointed statement to emphasize his power over death. Death is not death for those who call on him. Death, then, is like falling asleep for his disciples, for us as Christians, and should not be feared by them (or by us today).

The Death of the First Martyr

Take Stephen's martyrdom as an example of how this phrase continued to be used by the Christian community. In Acts 7, Luke describes Stephen's trial before the council of the Jewish leaders. At the end, the leaders could no longer bear Stephen's exposition of Old Testament history, nor his description of a vision he was having right then: seeing Jesus in heaven standing at God's right hand. Infuriated with Stephen's calm statements that convicted them of Jesus's murder, they summarily hauled him out of the building and stoned him to death (with the future apostle Paul holding their cloaks while they murdered Stephen). But Luke doesn't describe it as death; he instead uses Jesus's euphemism: "Then falling on his [Stephen's] knees, he cried out with a loud voice: 'Lord, do not hold this sin against them!' Having said this, he fell asleep" (v. 60).

Paul Continues Using the Euphemism

Paul, too, employs this same euphemism at times in describing death. For instance, in 1 Corinthians 15:17–18, he says, "and if Christ has not been raised, your faith is worthless; you are still in your sins. Then those also who have fallen asleep in Christ have perished." Once again we see the power of Jesus's phrase to describe death. Paul uses it to signal that he doesn't believe that Christ wasn't raised, as some were claiming. Instead, he indicates that he believes Jesus: we who believe in Christ don't have to fear death; we are only falling into a temporary sleep.

Another Positive Perspective of Death

There is a second strain of this view promoting a positive attitude toward death. Paul states in 2 Corinthians 5:1–4: "For we know that if the earthly tent which is our home is torn down, we have a building from God, a house not made with hands, eternal in the heavens. For indeed in this house we groan, longing to be clothed with our dwelling from heaven, inasmuch as we, having put it on, will not be found naked. For indeed while we are in this tent, we groan, being burdened, because we don't want to be unclothed, but to be clothed, so that what is mortal will be swallowed up by life." Paul here presents a view in which life in this age resembles living in a tent or temporary housing, as if our bodies now are only a disposable, paper-thin suit that makes us feel naked, and needs to be replaced. With death, then, we begin the process of receiving a permanent home, no longer living in a tent, but in our newly built final dwelling place.

Again, death is presented positively, for we have the hope that death will cause us to be released from what now Paul calls a burden, one that is filled with so much pain and sorrow and suffering that it causes us to "groan" (as Paul mentions twice). But death will be our relief as well as our release, something Paul expects us to look forward to with anticipation.

A Positive View of Death, Part 2

January 2, 2022

What consequences are there if we have a positive view of death? Let's consider some of those.

1. First and foremost, as Paul says in 2 Corinthians 5:6–8: "Therefore, being always of good courage, and knowing that while we are at home in the body we are absent from the Lord—for we walk by faith, not by sight—but we are of good courage and prefer rather to be absent from the body and to be at home with the Lord." Twice in this passage Paul says we are to be of courage, indeed of good courage, as we consider our death, for we "prefer to be absent from the body and to be at home with the Lord." Death is not to be feared, but embraced as we will only then be at home. And where is our home? *Where our heart is: with the Lord.* What a great hope! Our whole life can be summed up in that one statement: we prefer to be at home with the Lord. Our greatest hope and joy is to die, for then we will be with him for whom we have lived. What is there to fear then from death? There is nothing in this world to the unbeliever more frightening than death, but the Christian is not afraid of death. It is his entrance into the presence of him whom we love more than anything in this life. We have no greater desire or destination than our death.

2. Second, Paul gives another consequence of this positive view of death. In this same passage, earlier he says in 2 Corinthians 4:16–18: "Therefore we do not lose heart, but though our outer person is decaying, yet our inner [person] is being renewed day by day. For our momentary, light affliction is producing for us an eternal weight of glory far beyond all comparison, while we look not at the things which are seen, but at the things which are not seen; for the things which are seen are temporal, but the things which are not seen are eternal." Our troubles, sorrows, and sufferings in this age stand as nothing compared to the great weight of glory that they produce for us, if we bear them as God intended. Don't be distracted by all the siren calls of money, possessions, looks, accomplishments, or accolades of this age. Realize that from birth, your outer man is decaying, your years are numbered, and they are short, though they don't feel so at first. But inwardly, if you seek to be filled with the Spirit, you are realizing his fruit, and are being renewed not occasionally, but daily. Look at your sins honestly and see where you need to repent and change. Bear your afflictions with grace, with patience, kindness, and compassion for your brethren who are also suffering. Don't complain in your troubles and sufferings. Rather, rejoice that they will bring you a weight of glory that is very great compared to the light afflictions you bear now.

Let me close by saying that obviously a positive view of death doesn't mean that we will seek death. Quite the opposite! Hear Paul as he extols the joy of death in Philippians 1:21–25: "For to me, to live is Christ, and to die is gain. But if [I am] to live [on] in the flesh, this [will mean] fruitful labor for me; and I do not know which to choose. But I am hard-pressed from both [directions], having the desire to depart and be with Christ, for [that] is very much better; yet to remain on in the flesh is more necessary for your sakes. Convinced of this, I know that I will remain and continue with you all for your progress and joy in the faith."

Paul very much wants to die. Why? To be with Christ, which

is far better than to remain in this age. But as it is better for those in his care, he will not seek death, but life so as to care for those whom he loves.

This certainly has been my intention. When I was diagnosed with a terminal disease, I was stunned but elated as I was finally going to get what I had wanted for so many years: to die. When I was in high school, I had contemplated suicide (though not that seriously) from simple despair. What hope was there in this world of pain, suffering, and sorrow? There seemed no hope, no plan or purpose to life. But as a Christian, I learned that there was more hope, plan, and purpose than I had ever dreamed of. And in Philippians 1:21, I saw that in reality, as I had moved from a life lived in the illusion of hopelessness and chaos to one lived in the order and comfort of the kingdom of God, death was not to be feared. It was not an act to despair over, but an event of the greatest hope, because I would be with the one I loved most.

Yet, as Paul shows in Philippians 1:21–25, Jesus expects us to live *here*, to care for the ones that he cares for. So when I received that diagnosis that first day, my first thought was: how can I care for my wife, whom I love more than anyone in the world? I knew what it meant. It meant to seek to live and to fight against my death. So, now I endure chemo and immuno therapy and all their side effects in order to care for, as best as I am able, her and the ones I love—the ones whom Jesus loves—as Paul did for those whom he had in his care.

COMFORT FOR THOSE LEFT BEHIND

January 8, 2022

> And he will wipe away every tear from their eyes, and there will no longer be any death; there will no longer be any mourning, or crying, or pain...
>
> Revelation 21:4

Death Is Not Always Viewed Positively

Why would there be a need to wipe away tears if the experience of death is to be viewed positively, as I argued in the last chapter? Because death is to be seen as positive by the *dier* (the person dying) but certainly wouldn't be by the *diee* (the person left behind). The person dying has the joy and hope of being with the Lord before him, but the person left behind is now alone with no such immediate hope of departure. In fact, their mourning may involve more than just the loss of someone they love. It may be the loss of someone they need.

COMFORT FOR THE LOSS OF SOMEONE WE LOVE

But, as always, Scripture addresses our deepest concerns. Let's look first at how it helps to ease the suffering from the loss of someone we love. Paul, in writing to the Greek believers in Thessalonica, says these words: "But we do not want you to be uninformed, brothers [and sisters,] about those who are asleep, so that you will not grieve as indeed the rest [of mankind do] who have no hope. For if we believe that Jesus died and rose [from the dead] so also God will bring with him those who have fallen asleep through Jesus...the dead in Christ will rise first...Therefore, comfort one another with these words" (1 Thess. 4:13–14, 16, 18).

Paul obviously believes part of the reason for mourning is a feeling that death is final, that we'll never again see someone such as our spouse, since death has apparently won. But Paul reassures us that our fear is unfounded. First, he uses the expression I discussed in a previous chapter, that those who died in Christ are only "asleep," using Jesus's euphemism for death. Death is only temporary, and Jesus has the power to awaken us. There is no need to grieve as if we have no hope. We know that our loved one is in Jesus's care and that we will see them again the day Jesus returns.

HELP FOR THE LOSS OF SOMEONE WE NEED

But there may be other reasons for mourning and grief. One prominent one in the New Testament (NT) is the loss of someone we need. In the NT, there is a special concern for the plight of the widow. Throughout the Scriptures, God gives special attention to the needs of widows and orphans. For example, Deuteronomy 14:29 on the use of the tithe: "The Levite, because he has no portion or inheritance among you, and the alien, the orphan, and the widow who are in your town, shall come and eat and be satisfied in order that the Lord may bless you in all the work of your hand which you do." Or, in Job's discourse as he reports his submission and obedience to God's law: "But, if I have kept the poor from their desire, or have caused the eyes of the widow to fail..." (Job 31:16). Or, this report of God's care in the Psalms: "The Lord protects the strangers, he supports the fatherless and the widow, but he thwarts the way of the wicked" (Ps. 146:9). All these passages show that God expects his people to care for and support widows and orphans.

NEW TESTAMENT CONCERN FOR WIDOWS

We can see this same concern in the New Testament as was expressed by law and deed in the Old Testament (OT). First and foremost is Jesus's example: "...But standing by the cross of Jesus were his mother, and his mother's sister, Mary, the wife of Clopas, and Mary Magdalene. When Jesus then saw his mother, and the disciple whom he loved standing nearby, he said to his mother, 'Woman, behold, your son!' Then he said to the disciple, 'Behold, your mother!' From that hour, the disciple took her into his own household" (John 19:25–27). Jesus, while dying on the cross, once again fulfills his responsibility to obey perfectly the law of God, by ensuring that his mother's ongoing provision will be met when he turns her care over to his best friend and disciple, John. Jesus had brothers and sisters as we see elsewhere in the gospels, but evidently felt that they couldn't or wouldn't care for Mary adequately. Of course, this tradition of care for the widow continued on in the church as expressed by James: "Pure and undefiled religion in the sight of our God and Father is this: to visit orphans and widows in their distress..." (James 1:27). One of the hallmarks of our faith is our care for widows and orphans.

Concern Institutionalized

Further, we can deduce the importance of fulfilling this duty when we look at the book of Acts and see these words in chapter 6: "Now at this time while the disciples were increasing in number, a complaint arose on the part of Hellenistic Jews against the native Hebrews, because their widows were being overlooked in the daily serving food" (v. 1). The apostles provided a solution in v. 3: "...select from among you seven men of good reputation, full of the Spirit and of wisdom, whom we may put in charge of this task." We can see then that the primary impetus for what was likely the creation of the office of deacon was the need to insure the care of widows. The apostles saw the need to institutionalize the future fulfillment of this expectation of God.

I have discussed already Paul's further institutionalization of a way to meet the command for compassion for widows by directing that, first, the widow's children should support her, but, if not, then the church should do so. He lays down specific requirements for the widow to qualify for such care from the church such as being of a certain age, and also apparently requiring a vow of celibacy (1 Tim. 5:11–12). That vow was probably for service to the church, possibly modeled on Anna's role as described as a widow in the temple (Luke 2:36–37). Sadly, the Protestant church seems to have lost this focus on care for widows.

So, comfort for the *diee* comes first from knowing that the departed one, whom we love, is only asleep and will be awakened by Jesus; and, second, for widows and orphans who have lost someone they need, the assurance that God has a special concern for them, and that he expects his church to express that care and concern in a continuing way, which the apostles structured the church to do.

GRATITUDE IN DELIVERANCE

January 19, 2022

> Now one of them, when he saw that he had been healed, turned back, glorifying God with a loud voice, and he fell on his face at his feet, giving thanks to him. And he was a Samaritan. Then Jesus answered and said, "Were there not ten cleansed? But the nine where are they? Was no one found who returned to give glory to God, except this foreigner?" And he said to him, "Stand up and go; your faith has made you well."
>
> Luke 17:15–19

WE OUGHT TO TALK a little about those cases in which a person with a terminal diagnosis doesn't die in a short amount of time (like me, for instance, since I was given a terminal diagnosis in May 2021, and here it's January of 2022). As I told someone, I need to start one of these chapters this way: "This is embarrassing—I'm still alive!" Or, as a friend suggested, I could have changed the blog where I originally posted these entries: from dyingman.org to dyingslowlylikeeveryoneelse.org. How should we respond when we expect or prepare to die but don't? (My diagnosis hasn't changed. It's still just "treatable, not curable," so my life has been extended, but I'm not "cured.")

ALL WERE HEALED

Well, I think the passage above gives us some guidance. Here's an account of ten lepers who came to Jesus for healing. Leprosy was known to be a communicable disease, even thousands of years ago. They didn't know about the leprosy bacterium as we do, but they weren't stupid, just ignorant. God had required permanent quarantine for lepers to prevent its spread. And it was a terrible disease. But these lepers are given a reprieve by Jesus. He sends them to the priest as the Law commanded to be officially granted the seal of healing so they could re-enter society. They all were healed, but only one returns to Jesus to express his thanks.

GRATITUDE TO GOD FIRST

But notice that gratitude is, of course, first to God (v. 15), so it seems this Samaritan was a Jewish convert. And, of course, similarly, if we were healed of a terminal illness (I don't believe leprosy was normally terminal), who, if he were a Christian, wouldn't fall on his face and thank God? But the leper returns to the human (I'm not sure the leper knew Jesus was the God/man, but probably at least was a prophet) who was the instrument of God's healing. The leper's obedience to Jehovah not only resulted in thanking God for his healing in answer to the leper's request, but also in an act of thanksgiving to the man God had used to heal him.

BUT DON'T STOP THERE

I think some of us would be tempted to stop at the step of thanking

God. God answered our prayer for deliverance, and we certainly should glorify him, maybe with a loud voice! But I see a broader principle at work here. Gratitude should be first and foremost to God but should in no way excuse a failure to express that gratitude also to anyone that God has used to help answer our prayers for deliverance from death.

Who might that include? Well, it should certainly include those who have joined their prayers to ours in seeking our healing and release from the sentence of death (or its delay). Who knows if God was moved only by our individual prayers? Maybe, in his ordained providence, he was moved by the pleas of many to grant us his help. When the Israelites were in Egypt, and they suffered under the slavery imposed by the Egyptians, God was moved to deliver them by their groanings (prayers) as a people (Gen. 2:23–24). God had promised their release from bondage in Egypt, but it was the prayers of his people that moved him to send Moses to effect their deliverance.

But that's not all, of course. There were likely those in the medical community who were God's human instruments of healing. Certainly in my case I know that's true. I bought all of my wife's Mother's Day presents in April because I didn't think I would live to May 9th (Mother's Day in 2021). The treatments my oncologist and his Nurse Practioner (NP) administered were used by God to extend my life till now. I think God expects I should thank them for that service. And what of my wife, and my brothers and sisters in Christ, who supported and cared for and encouraged me in this time? I think God again looks for me to express my gratitude to them. So, I have indeed expressed thanksgiving to the medical community, but I also wrote a note of appreciation to the people of my church for their prayers and support, and I take every opportunity I get to say thank you to any who have cared for us in our time of need. And I cannot thank my wife enough for her care and love.

THE BOTTOM LINE

So then, don't neglect the opportunities you have to show gratitude. Don't let Jesus say to you: "Were there not ten cleansed? But the nine—where are they? Was no one found who returned to give glory to God except this foreigner?" Giving glory to God appears here to involve more than just praying with thanksgiving. It involves also showing gratitude to any human instrument he decides to use to answer our prayers.

PAUL'S ADVICE FOR FACING DEATH

February 1, 2022

> For I am already being poured out as a drink offering, and the time of my departure has come. I have fought the good fight, I have finished the course, I have kept the faith; in the future there is laid up for me the crown of righteousness, which the Lord, the righteous Judge, will award to me on that day; and not only to me, but also to all who have loved his appearing.
>
> 2 Timothy 4:6–8

Paul's Impending Death

Here Paul tells us of his impending death, likening it to the pouring of the drink offering in the Old Testament. He has completed the commission Jesus gave him when he was called in the Damascus experience. And so he is ready for his reward—a crown of righteousness.

I think there are lessons here for us as well. Paul makes clear that Jesus, as the righteous Judge, will award that crown not only to an apostle, but to us as well. So, whether we are shown our impending death, or are rather those who wait in love for his return, we should follow Paul's example. He offers a series of descriptions on how he has lived, summary statements of his life that provide us with his reflection on his approaching death. How did Paul, now at the end of his life, think of what he had achieved that had prepared him to receive this wonderful reward? Let's just very briefly look at each summary remark.

HIS LIFE IN THREE STATEMENTS

1. "I have fought the good fight": Paul's commission involved not just a scholarly life of prayer and study, but was a commission to an active engagement with the enemy, both within and without. The Christian life, then, for Paul, was to be seen as a battle, and a battle that would begin at the start of our new life and continue on to the end of our lives. That is Paul's warning and encouragement to us. The enemy is implacable, and we must never give up in continuing to take our stand against him in our resistance. It is, indeed, the fight of our life.

2. "I have finished the course": Here Paul emphasizes our need to persevere in our walk. Our journey and commission is not over at some artificial "retirement." There is no retirement from our course, no sitting down and taking our ease, watching television all day every day because we're done, finished our work. Our course, like Paul's, will end at death, and not before. The nature of our work may change as we age, but it will never be over. There will always be room for good works that our Savior has prepared for us, even in our old age.

3. "I have kept the faith": We can fall away just as easily in old age as in youth. We have only to look at Solomon, so wise and

zealous in his youth, but who was pulled away from that devotion by failing to follow the Lord's instructions for the conduct of kings, marrying many wives, often foreign ones, who weakened his resolve to obey his God. Up to death, we must be vigilant to guard our hearts and minds from weakening, and we must maintain our resolve to follow our Lord at the approach of our death as truly as we did at our new birth.

Our Goal

There is a death for each of us, and it should be our goal to reach that point as Paul did: prepared for it and glad of it, seeing it as the final offering to the Lord after a life of faithful service, knowing that our death opens the door to receive our reward as it did for Paul, a *crown* of righteousness following a *life* of righteousness. The view of life and death laid out by Paul here should give us purpose and hope, as well as the joy of anticipation when we find our death is impending, as his was when writing to Timothy.

Accepting Death

February 9, 2022

> As we were staying there for some days, a prophet named Agabus came down from Judea. And coming to us, he took Paul's belt and bound his own feet and hands, and said, "This is what the Holy Spirit says: 'In this way the Jews at Jerusalem will bind the man who owns this belt and deliver him into the hands of the Gentiles.'" When we had heard this, we as well as the local residents [began] begging him not to go up to Jerusalem. Then Paul answered, "What are you doing, weeping and breaking my heart? For I am ready not only to be bound, but even to die at Jerusalem for the name of the Lord Jesus." And since he would not be persuaded, we fell silent, remarking, "The will of the Lord be done!"
>
> Act 21:10–14

TO LIVE A FAITHFUL life, the acceptance of death is required, even if we're not apostles. As we see in the passage above, Paul is shown that he will encounter a very dangerous, likely deadly, situation if he continues on to Jerusalem. But Paul's response to this prophetic word is remarkable. Instead of taking the warning as a command to stop, Paul accepts it as only a word of warning, a foretelling of imminent danger to prepare him. And, despite the pleas of his friends, he refuses to be deterred from his course because of the fear of death, as so many have before him, because it is his commission from Jesus.

We can think of men like Moses or Gideon and others, who resisted God's call to go as he commanded them, and they resisted because their command, like Paul's, also entailed dangerous, possibly or even likely deadly, circumstances. But it is obvious why Paul's response was so different from others: he had already accepted death: "For I am ready ...even to die..." Suffering and dying for Jesus were a part of Paul's life. As Jesus told Ananias who brought word to Paul of his commission from Jesus: "But the Lord said to him [Ananias], 'Go, for he [Paul] is a chosen instrument of mine, to bear my name before the Gentiles and kings and the sons of Israel; for I will show him how much he must suffer for my name's sake'" (Acts 9:15–16).

However, this is a part of our commission also, for Jesus commands us to take up our cross and follow him: "Whoever does not carry his own cross and come after me cannot be my disciple" (Luke 14:27). We follow Jesus carrying our acceptance of death on our shoulder, so to speak. Our conversion involves not only new life, but a new attitude toward death, for now we accept death without fear, no matter what form death for us may take, whether spiritually in the power of sin or of guilt, or physically, as we have seen before in Hebrews 2:14–15: "Therefore, since the children share in flesh and blood, he himself likewise also partook of the same, that through death he might render powerless him who had the power of death, that is, the devil, and might free those who through fear of death were subject to slavery all their lives." We have been freed from the fear of death through him who accepted death without fear.

That acceptance of death, once begun, continues to permeate our lives so that we are no longer slaves to its fear but find that we would even be willing to die as Paul was, as Jesus was, for our families and friends, for our brothers and sisters, because we love them. And we believe that if somehow our life were not enough to aid them, then we would offer up our death as well.

To me, it is a failure to accept death that has driven the hysteria surrounding COVID-19, as shown in our willingness to accept the loss of any or all of our civil liberties not just for weeks or months, but for years, if only our government would keep us safe and alive.

For Christians, I believe that a failure to accept death is what is at the root of a belief that God has guaranteed healing to any and all believers in Jesus—saying rightly that God has the power and mercy to effect such a healing, but also exhibiting the misguided (in my opinion) failure to accept the fact of their own mortality. We are indeed all guaranteed as believers to be completely and finally healed of any sickness, even those unto death, but that absolute guarantee is not for this age. Only in the age to come will we not just hope, but actually see the fullness and perfection of life and health, fulfilling our desire also to see an end to death.

I have written an essay in the appendix on supernatural and natural healing and the two unbiblical extremes that people tend to fall into. If this is something you are curious about, please have a look at that.

THE VALUE OF COURAGE

February 15, 2022

Have I not commanded you? Be strong and courageous! Do not tremble or be dismayed, for the LORD your God is with you wherever you go.

Joshua 1:9

Even though I walk through the valley of the shadow of death, I will fear no evil, for you are with me; your rod and your staff, they comfort me.

Psalm 23:4

> Therefore, being always of good courage, and knowing that while we are at home in the body we are absent from the Lord—for we walk by faith, not by sight—we are of good courage, I say, and prefer rather to be absent from the body and to be at home with the Lord.
>
> 2 Corinthians 5:6–8

SURELY ONE OF THE most underrated virtues of our time is courage. We see cowardice in its most popular form in the cancel culture and in the craven responses of businesses, schools, government, and celebrities, and also in the surprising demand for "crying rooms" and the refusal to hear disagreeing opinions on university campuses, not only at the undergraduate level, but most recently, embarrassingly, in a law school (George Mason) when law students(!) wanted not only to cancel and fire a new professor, but also requested a crying room, as if they were not only victims, but also toddlers. Strange times we live in, with people openly asking for sympathy because they are cowards, which they openly demonstrate (people in past generations would have been embarrassed and ashamed to have been seen behaving in such a childish way).

And yet we see in the passages above the antidote to this problem. In the Joshua passage, we see one of many exhortations to Joshua from Moses and from God to have courage. For though God had promised Israel the land of Canaan, the people were still very afraid of the inhabitants. So it is with us in our fear of death. As we see in the saying of David in Psalm 23 and of Paul in 2 Corinthians 5, the key to conquering the fear of death is to have confidence that God is always with us. If we believe that, then even when walking in the valley of the shadow of death, we will have courage. If we have confidence that the Lord Jesus is with us, then we can say with

Paul that we will be of good courage and prefer death to being here because we will be with the Lord in a fuller way.

The presence of the Lord in our lives is our confidence that he is indeed Immanuel; he is the way we conquer our fear of death. Whether living or dying, when we believe that he is with us, then we will gain courage, and we will no longer be afraid. When Jesus approached his hour of death, he knew his disciples would desert him because of fear: "Behold, an hour is coming, and has *already* come, for you to be scattered, each to his own *home,* and to leave me alone..." But note his next words: "and *yet* I am not alone, because the Father is with me" (John 16:32).

Years ago several other guys and I went to visit a mutual friend who was dying in the hospital, and we lamented that we could not stay with him till his point of death. He did indeed die a short time later, not long after we had left, much to our sorrow. But I never forgot the passage he read to us from John 16, and I realized that Jesus (and our friend) was encouraging us to remember that even if we are humanly alone, we are never truly or completely alone, for though we face death and might be humanly alone, we can have courage, for we know that the Lord will always and everywhere be with us. Therefore, we can be of good courage as Paul says; death cannot make us afraid, for the one who conquered death is at our side.

DEATH AND THE DISCIPLINE OF GOD

February 21, 2022

Therefore whoever eats the bread or drinks the cup of the Lord in an unworthy manner, shall be guilty of the body and the blood of the Lord. But a man must examine himself, and in so doing he is to eat of the bread and drink of the cup. For he who eats and drinks, eats and drinks judgment to himself if he does not judge the body rightly. For this reason many among you are weak and sick, and a number sleep. But if we judged ourselves rightly, we would not be judged. But when we are judged, we are disciplined by the Lord so that we will not be condemned along with the world.

1 Corinthians 11:27–32

You have not yet resisted to the point of shedding blood in your striving against sin; and you have forgotten the exhortation which is addressed to you

> as sons, "My son, do not regard lightly the discipline of the LORD, nor faint when you are reproved by him; for those whom the LORD loves he disciplines, and he scourges every son whom he receives." It is for discipline that you endure; God deals with you as with sons; for what son is there whom [his] father does not discipline? But if you are without discipline, of which all have become partakers, then you are illegitimate children and not sons. Furthermore, we had earthly fathers to discipline us, and we respected them; shall we not much rather be subject to the Father of spirits, and live? For they disciplined us for a short time as seemed best to them, but he [disciplines us] for [our] good, so that we may share his holiness. All discipline for the moment seems not to be joyful, but sorrowful; yet to those who have been trained by it, afterwards it yields the peaceful fruit of righteousness. Therefore, strengthen the hands that are weak and the knees that are feeble...
>
> Hebrews 12:4–12

PAUL WARNS THE CORINTHIANS in his first letter that if they examine (I take that to be the meaning of "judge") themselves, they could avoid God's examination, since his examination of their sin would involve discipline. Discipline is no bad thing as it permits us to avoid something worse, such as being "condemned along with the world." The writer of Hebrews agrees with such an assessment of discipline. It is a fundamental prerogative of sonship. To be a son is to be disciplined so that we might grow in holiness, obedience to the Lord.

Death, as Paul makes clear in the Corinthian letter, may be a part of that discipline. That is how I have chosen to view my terminal diagnosis, as a sign of God's Fatherly love to help me to grow in godliness. Some may view that form of discipline as unnecessarily harsh, even cruel, but I would disagree. All discipline is to a greater or lesser degree sorrowful. But, as Paul makes clear elsewhere, nothing happens to us by accident: "And we know that God causes all things to work together for good to those who love God, to those who are called according to [his] purpose" (Rom. 8:28).

That verse is quite often mistakenly understood to mean that when bad things happen to us, God will always turn them around and make it all work out right. But I don't think that's Paul's meaning at all. That verse comes at the end of his discussion of the Spirit helping us in our weakness and praying for us "with groanings too deep for words" (v. 26). The following verse encourages us with the hope that tribulation, distress, persecution, famine, nakedness, danger, or sword, indeed even when we are slaughtered like sheep, we will be more than conquerors; in fact, not even death can separate us from the love of God in Christ (vv. 35–38).

So, once again, death is not to be dreaded or feared, even if God is visiting us in death with his hand of discipline. Death can be used in that discipline to protect us, to keep us from condemnation with the world. Or, it might be used to purify us: "But who can endure the day of his coming? And who can stand when he appears? For he is like a refiner's fire and like fullers' soap. He will sit as a smelter and purifier of silver, and he will purify the sons of Levi and refine them like gold and silver, so that they may present to the LORD offerings in righteousness" (Mal. 3:2–3). Or, as the writer of Hebrews says, "All discipline for the moment seems not to be joyful, but sorrowful; yet to those who have been trained by it, afterwards it yields the peaceful fruit of righteousness. Therefore, strengthen the hands that are weak and the knees that are feeble, and make straight paths for your feet, so that [the limb] which is lame may not be put out of joint, but rather be healed" (Heb. 12:11–13).

So, if you have been given a terminal diagnosis, rejoice! Now is the time for the painful discipline to train you and to yield righteousness in your life. Help others also under discipline to be strong and courageous. Walk the path God has laid before you, and do not falter or fail. You will be glad in the end that you did.

DEATH AND OUR PLANS FOR LIFE

February 25, 2022

> Come now, you who say, "Today or tomorrow we will go to such and such a city, and spend a year there and engage in business and make a profit." Yet you do not know what your life will be like tomorrow. You are [just] a vapor that appears for a little while and then vanishes away. Instead, [you ought] to say, "If the Lord wills, we will live and also do this or that."
>
> James 4:13–15

WHAT A MARVELOUS PASSAGE to give us back a true perspective on life. The biblical view of life is to try in one sense to focus us on today and to help us stop worrying about tomorrow. I'm an inveterate worrier and focus a lot on various scenarios of future disasters, the vast majority of which will never materialize (the ones that do only confirm my worrying; on the other hand, the ones that are the worst are always the ones I didn't foresee). Our lives are but a mist or fog, James says, so stop stating so absolutely your plans (or worries) for tomorrow.

"If the Lord wills…" The first petition in the Lord's Prayer is critical as it frames the rest of the petitions: "Your kingdom come, your will be done." Over all our petitions and plans and worries are God's plan and sovereignty. They supersede whatever we plan or hope or fear. It is pointless to act as if our plans or worries are so certain; they aren't. Only God's plan is, and that secret plan is not something we're privy to (except in a very general way: Guess what? Jesus returns and wins the war on evil and death. The end.)

Death as the final endpoint to our lives is just as certain and uncertain. It is certainly coming for us, but to believe that we know the day of our death is just as uncertain as to know what good or evil tomorrow will bring. Let me give an extended illustration. On February 11 (my 70th birthday this year), I had a CT scan to monitor my cancer. On February 18, my wife and I had an appointment with my oncologist for a scan review. What he said made me gobsmacked; I was so completely unprepared. I had seen the radiologists' interpretations: the gut radiologist said, in essence, "All clear: no new organ or bone metastases." The lung radiologist said, "Some nodules remaining in the lungs, but no changes in size; other nodules have disappeared or have shrunk significantly." My lungs are extensively scarred by the cancer, and will never recover.

But the oncologist had a very different view of the results. He drew a chart for me. It was an inverted hockey stick (I think it was a negative exponential curve), starting high on the Y axis, and as the line travelled along the x axis it curved quickly downward to the right near the bottom of the graph (the x axis). The left side of the graph (Y axis) was the number of patients and the bottom was time in months. He marked on the long handle of the line the ten month mark (I was diagnosed with a terminal diagnosis in April of 2021), and so February of 2022 is the ten month mark. The ten month mark was well past the curve of the elbow of the hockey stick going to the right. He said that to get on the graph, you had to meet two criteria: you had to have esophageal cancer, and you had to be on my treatment protocol. I pointed out that there wasn't much room at the bottom of the graph (as the line that was the hockey handle traveled to the right). He replied that that was because most of the patients at my time (ten months in) were already dead. Well, that will make you sit up and take notice. So, most people wouldn't have my terminal diagnosis that I received last April, but the vast majority who did would be dead by now.

So, what does this illustration show? Exactly what James is teaching: I was working full time—from January up to the beginning of April—in 2021 until I became so short of breath that I had to stop working at all. I bought all of my wife's Mother's Day presents in those first few weeks of April because I didn't think I would live to Mother's Day (May 9, 2021). And yet, ten months later, against the medical community's and my own expectations, here I am, still alive. Who knew, except God, that that timeline was going to occur?

My close friend intervened to get the best oncologist in town to set up my first oncology visit and PET scan to confirm the location of my primary tumor, and those events literally saved my life. The elders of my church anointed and prayed over me for healing. I think that was the beginning of God extending my life. I took a vow asking God to extend my life to my 70th birthday, which coincidentally (meaning I had no idea of the importance) covered the critical period of survival for my cancer and its treatment. And there were so many prayers from former classmates, coworkers, old friends, and especially members of my church family. Then, God granted my vow request (which my wife and I are preparing to repay shortly).

Take my word for it, and take God's word for it: James is right. Preface all that you plan or fear with: "If the Lord wills," whether verbally or in your heart and mind. Your life and death are in God's hands, and you need have no fear if you are a disciple of Christ. He is in control of all things, and you are safe in his sovereignty.

DEATH AND FORGIVENESS

March 7, 2022

But Jesus was saying, "Father, forgive them; for they do not know what they are doing." And they cast lots, dividing up his garments among themselves.

Luke 23:34

When they had driven him out of the city, they [began] stoning [him;] and the witnesses laid aside their robes at the feet of a young man named Saul. They went on stoning Stephen as he called on [the Lord] and said, "Lord Jesus, receive my spirit!" Then falling on his knees, he cried out with a loud voice, "Lord, do not hold this sin against them!" Having said this, he fell asleep.

Acts 7:58–60

IF LIFE IS OUR greatest gift and death our greatest fear, how could we ever forgive anyone who would cause our suffering, much less our death? We can see from the passages above that Jesus gave us the example we need to follow. If anyone was ever blameless, giving no cause to receive persecution, much less execution, it was the sinless Son of God. And from that example, we find Stephen paraphrasing Jesus at Stephen's own execution, asking the unthinkable as Jesus did: for God to forgive those who first persecuted and then killed him. And the crowd included Saul of Tarsus (likely one of the reasons Saul/Paul later called himself the chief of sinners). If Jesus was the sheep to be slaughtered (Isa. 53:7), who did not resist or cry out in bitterness or anger, how could we do any less? And, of course, as we see with Stephen, that is how the early Christians handled persecution and death. "You have condemned and put to death the righteous [man;] he does not resist you" (James 5:6). "For it is better, if God should will it so, that you suffer for doing what is right rather than for doing what is wrong. For Christ also died for sins once for all, [the] just for [the] unjust, so that he might bring us to God, having been put to death in the flesh, but made alive in the spirit" (1 Pet. 3:17–18).

How does this idea, this example, speak to us today—we in the U.S., who face no danger of physical persecution or unjust execution for doing right? There are several considerations we might reflect on.

First, we should be emboldened to be light that we do not hide under a basket. If we meditate on these passages, we should gain courage from our Savior's example and the examples of other righteous men and women who died without refusing to demonstrate their faith. If Jesus died for our sins, a just man, how can we not be brave enough to suffer unjust persecution for holding unpopular opinions? There are those today who have come to believe that all of life and morality can be viewed through the lens of homosexuality and skin color. But we should first see the hope of Christ as we have been delivered from death by his unjust suffering and execution, and draw strength from his example. Who knows? There may come a time when we will suffer more than just an angry word or gesture.

Second, we can give more thought and develop greater sympathy for our brethren in places where they suffer and die even today for their faith: places like China, India, Africa, Cuba, and predominantly Muslim countries. These are disciples who, much like first century Christians, are suffering not from COVID hysteria or woke attacks, but from peril for their very lives because they worship together, or study the Bible (perhaps using Third Millennium materials). These Christians can relate to these passages in ways we cannot imagine and can teach us much about choosing the narrow road that is full of obstacles and trouble, but with the certain hope of arriving safely at their destination of heaven.

Third, we can be encouraged to pray for our brothers and sisters suffering so much now in Ukraine. There are scores of Christians who fear for their lives because of the attack of Russia. Only by God's grace will they be able to put aside hatred, bitterness, and thoughts of revenge. Passages like those above might be used by God to help ease their suffering.

> Who will separate us from the love of Christ? Will tribulation, or distress, or persecution, or famine, or nakedness, or peril, or sword? Just as it is written, "For your sake we are being put to death all day long; we were considered as sheep to be slaughtered."
>
> Romans 8:35–36

We need not fear the attacks of the ungodly, for Jesus suffered them and yet triumphed. We know he suffered not only to gain forgiveness for our sins, but also to set us an example as Peter says and as John reports, of forgiveness of enemies, even when we must endure harm, perhaps even death, from those who are blinded by the god of this age. God is not asleep, nor will he forget us in our need (Ps. 44:23). He is here with us; Jesus endured worse than we can ever know, and his justice will triumph at last. We have no need for bitterness and revenge. All these wrongs and their reversal and redress are where they should be: in his hands.

DEATH AND THE RIGHT TO CAUSE IT

MARCH 19, 2022

> See now that I, I am he, and there is no god besides me; It is I who put to death and give life. I have wounded and it is I who heal, and there is no one who can deliver from my hand.
>
> Deuteronomy 32:39

> If a man takes the life of any human being, he shall surely be put to death.
>
> Leviticus 24:17

LIFE AND DEATH ARE in God's hands, but death may also be mediated through human hands. Death can be brought about by any human, even taking our own life. But God forbids taking of the life of another human being, even our own (covered as self-murder by the 6th commandment, "Thou shalt not murder"), unless he allows it. He permits a human to cause the death of another person only in certain circumstances, such as self-defense or in war or by execution. All this seems obvious, so why discuss it? Because it's not so clear anymore in our culture where the right to death comes from. The vast majority of Christians (now and historically) believe abortion to be the death of an unborn child, yet our government permits it (indeed, encourages it). It can do so legally (if you believe the Constitution somehow permits abortion), but ought it? That is, does it have not only the legal authority, but the moral right to do so?

The passage from Deuteronomy above supplies our answer. Only the Maker of us all, the ultimate giver of life, has the right to take our life. And in his word he delineates clearly the conditions that govern our right to cause death. It is his prerogative to decide how and under what conditions death should occur. In war, the bullet or bomb takes one and leaves another, according to his ultimate plan. We may engage in self-defense or in defense of our homes and so kill another, but not even then in all situations (see Exodus 22:2–3). Paul, in Romans 13:4, makes it clear that if we do wrong, we should remember that God has granted a civil ruler (even a Roman one) the sword, as the ruler is a servant of God, an avenger who carries out God's wrath on the wrong doer. That is both the ruler's right and duty.

So, God is the ultimate authority of death, the only one who can give life, and, therefore, the only one who has the right to take it. He links the two in the Deuteronomy passage above. If you can't create life (as none of us can *ex nihilo*, from nothing), we don't have the right to decide who can take it. Even women who give birth to another human being, though earning the right to be honored by their children, cannot claim to be the ultimate source of life, and so are denied the right to take the life of their unborn child. That child's life ultimately comes from God, and only he has the right to take it. The government may grant a so-called right to abortion legally, but they do not have the authority morally. It's God's authority alone.

Execution is another greatly debated right to death, but our culture seems bent on standing God's directives on their head: the right to take a baby's life it grants, but not the right to take a murderer's; the right to take an innocent life of a child, but not the right to take the life of someone who took an innocent life. Even imprisoning such a person for a lifetime takes years of life that can never be repaid, no matter how big the check written for reparation is made. A confused view to my mind, but not surprising in our very confused culture. Justice is thus confounded and overrun by social justice, the two being not, or only loosely, connected.

At our final judgment, though, the justice of God will prevail. A second death, more to be feared than the first one that we experience in this life, will be meted out, as the Lord of life and death will pronounce a sentence of death on those who refused to kneel to him in this life, a sentence that will never be reversed or mitigated. Death will then be truly final and irrevocable, in a way it is not now. The Lord will give out life eternal or death eternal. We need not fear that an unjust death in this life will go unaddressed. We do not need to seek revenge or hold back forgiveness. Final justice will be done, and there will be no reprieve, no loophole permitting escape from that final death sentence.

DEATH AND MODERN MEDICINE

MARCH 22, 2022

On the first day of the week, when we were gathered together to break bread, Paul [began] talking to them, intending to leave the next day, and he prolonged his message until midnight. There were many lamps in the upper room where we were gathered together. And there was a young man named Eutychus sitting on the window sill, sinking into a deep sleep; and as Paul kept on talking, he was overcome by sleep and fell down from the third floor and was picked up dead. But Paul went down and fell upon him, and after embracing him, he said, "Do not be troubled, for his life is in him." When he had gone [back] up and had broken the bread and eaten, he talked with them a long while until daybreak, and then left. They took away the boy alive, and were greatly comforted.

Acts 20:7–12

> Now in Joppa there was a disciple named Tabitha (which translated [in Greek] is called Dorcas); this woman was abounding with deeds of kindness and charity which she continually did. And it happened at that time that she fell sick and died; and when they had washed her body, they laid it in an upper room. Since Lydda was near Joppa, the disciples, having heard that Peter was there, sent two men to him, imploring him, "Do not delay in coming to us." So Peter arose and went with them. When he arrived, they brought him into the upper room; and all the widows stood beside him, weeping and showing all the tunics and garments that Dorcas used to make while she was with them. But Peter sent them all out and knelt down and prayed, and turning to the body, he said, "Tabitha, arise." And she opened her eyes, and when she saw Peter, she sat up. And he gave her his hand and raised her up; and calling the saints and widows, he presented her alive. It became known all over Joppa, and many believed in the Lord.
>
> Acts 9:36–43

THE TOPIC OF DEATH and modern medicine is obviously of great interest to me—someone with a terminal disease. Do MDs have the right to take a life (euthanasia)? Legally they might be granted that right, but morally, should they be extended that right? Do they have the moral right to help a person commit suicide? And when can they "pull the plug"? My opinion on these questions is derived to a large extent from a book called *Medical Ethics* by the theologian John Frame. What follows in this chapter is, however, my opinion, not necessarily his, so don't blame him for these thoughts. I strongly recommend, though, that anyone who has questions about this area should read his short book. Short as it is, it is an excellent and surprisingly comprehensive overview of questions in this area. So, let me give my very simplified view focused on the issues I raised at the beginning of this chapter.

From the way I framed the questions above, I'm sure you can surmise my answers: no, MDs should not (even if legally they can) have the right to euthanize patients. God alone, as we saw in the previous chapter, has the right of life and death. He has delegated the right in certain specific situations, but suicide is not one of them, as it violates the 6th commandment ("Thou shalt not kill"). In fact, a basic medical ethical principle is this one: first, do no harm. Further, the ancient Hippocratic Oath forbad euthanasia as well as abortion.

In modern life, of course, things are more complicated. There is the question of how we decide if someone is dead, which I won't get into (see Frame for his helpful discussion of making a pronouncement of death based on brain death, or the stopping of the heart or breathing). The passage I quoted at the beginning may give some the impression that Eutychus must have passed out if he was revived, but I think from both vv. 9 and 12, we can be certain that the fall killed him. Thus, what Paul did wasn't a revival, but a resurrection (like Lazarus). The Bible seems to indicate that people over thousands of years tended to see the time of death primarily as stopping breathing. But in this passage, there is no criterion of death mentioned. Eutychus's death must have been obvious to all, with no hope of revival. Thus, Paul's act was not just merciful, but miraculous.

For us, though, there may be decisions that Eutychus's family were spared. For instance, we may have to think about life support. To me, life support should be supplied with the expectation of recovery; otherwise it should probably be removed. Comfort care (also known as hospice) for pain, breathing, etc., should be provided, as should nutrition (food and water). But letting someone die from their disease or condition is not the same as killing them. Prolonging life may be good in one sense as life is a gift from God. But prolonging life is not an absolute good to be desired in all circumstances. A person may choose to avoid treatment to extend their life, even to avoid economic hardship for their family, but, again, that is not the same as suicide, which is self-murder, i.e., taking a life that otherwise would normally continue, being stopped only because we murder someone (or ourselves) to end it unnaturally (using means such as lethal injection or by denying them oxygen or nutrition). As we can see in the case of Tabitha (Dorcas), the loss of a life, as I discussed in a previous chapter, may impose a great burden on those who are left behind to mourn them. In light of that burden, I think Peter then agreed to raise Tabitha back to full health. In my case, my greatest motivation to live, as I've seen a number of times with other couples in my home health practice, is my wife's desire not to suffer my demise. But as for me, as I've discussed before, and for any believer, I believe that we should always be ready and willing to die, even gladly but for the pain it may cause those who remain, if God should so call us to do so. We shouldn't see a terminal diagnosis as an absolute evil, nor should our family and friends, though death itself is unnatural and an evil, as is the suffering and sorrow it causes us. Those who treat impending death as an absolute evil cause much trouble for the medical community and for those of the family and friends involved in that situation. I've seen it many times.

Other issues like comatose and terminal patients, as well as criteria of death (as I mentioned above), are discussed by Frame in more detail and far more clearly and better than I can do here.

Death and Hospitality

April 2, 2022

Surely goodness and lovingkindness will follow me all the days of my life, and I will dwell in the house of the LORD forever.

Psalm 23:6

In my Father's house are many dwelling places; if it were not so, I would have told you; for I go to prepare a place for you.

John 14:2

> Therefore, being always of good courage, and knowing that while we are at home in the body we are absent from the Lord—for we walk by faith, not by sight—we are of good courage, I say, and prefer rather to be absent from the body and to be at home with the Lord.
>
> 2 Corinthians 5:6–8

BELIEVE IT OR NOT, death in the Bible is even seen as a doorway to the hospitality of the Lord. For instance, in Psalm 23, we have the odd change of metaphors from the Lord being a caring shepherd to him being a gracious host, mentioning first him having us at a dinner party ("Thou prepare a table for me..."), then surrounding us in this life with goodness and mercy, followed by one of the few instances in the Old Testament of a mention of life after death, with David looking forward to living in the home of God forever. Though there is no time to discuss it, it seems clear to me (see *Who Shall Ascend the Mountain of the Lord: A Biblical Theological Study of the Book of Leviticus*, by L. Michael Morales) from the book of Leviticus that the "house of the Lord" (i.e., the tabernacle, which David would have been familiar with as the temple was built by his son, Solomon) is a metaphor for the garden of Eden, and, thus, as we see in the book of Revelation, a metaphor also for the new age, the new heavens and earth.

We see this theme picked up by Jesus, as John reports, when he is reassuring his disciples in a discussion on his imminent departure from them, saying that it is to their advantage for him to leave as he is going to finish what will be their new home. There will be room for all who believe, so our place is assured, obviously in a large home where we can breathe freely, not feeling cramped or crowded, but comfortable and open. And when it's ready, Jesus promises that he will return to take us there so that we can live with him.

And, of course, the apostle Paul, who has, as I have mentioned before, one of the most positive views of death of all the New Testament writers, would also discuss this theme. In 2 Corinthians 5, Paul develops the idea that our present courage in facing trials and troubles, comes from this basic truth: that while we are still alive, at home living here, we are absent from the Lord. I find this statement quite surprising. Where else in the New Testament are we ever described as being apart from the Lord? But Paul is making an important point, using this simple metaphor: that death permits us to go home, to finally, at last, be where our hearts have always wanted to be—in our ultimate, complete, spacious, wonderful home, being all those things because that is where the one we love most lives: the home of Jesus our Lord who has prepared it for us and is ready to welcome us there.

DEATH AND THE TRAJECTORY

April 6, 2022

Then to Adam he said, "Because you have listened to the voice of your wife, and have eaten from the tree about which I commanded you, saying, 'You shall not eat from it'; cursed is the ground because of you; in toil you will eat of it all the days of your life. Both thorns and thistles it shall grow for you; and you will eat the plants of the field; by the sweat of your face you will eat bread, till you return to the ground, because from it you were taken; for you are dust, and to dust you shall return."

Genesis 3:17–19

For I am already being poured out as a drink offering, and the time of my departure has come. I have fought the good fight, I have finished the course, I have kept the faith; in the future there is laid up for me the crown of righteousness, which the Lord, the

> righteous Judge, will award to me on that day; and not only to me, but also to all who have loved his appearing.
>
> 2 Timothy 4:6–8

THERE IS A TRAJECTORY to our lives that unbelievers seem to ignore, or at least pretend to. When our parents—Adam and Eve—disobeyed, their sin launched us like a shell that follows a trajectory as surely as a shell from a cannon. It can end only in the death of our world, our race, our own person. The central problem for us, as it has been since the Fall, is death. As God reminds us in Genesis 3, we are only dust and will return to the ground; as he said to our parents: "to dust you shall return." This curse is a fulfillment of the warning he gave our parents at their creation: "The LORD God commanded the man, saying, 'From any tree of the garden you may eat freely; but from the tree of the knowledge of good and evil you shall not eat, for in the day that you eat from it you will surely die'" (Gen. 2:16–17). Satan, of course, disputed that disobedience to God would result in death: "You surely will not die!" Believing that lie, Eve, then Adam, disobeyed, following Satan's assessment rather than God's warning. But when that disobedience occurred, God pronounced the sentence of death that he had warned them of.

So, now our lives, our whole world, lies under the curse of death, and we as well as all other creatures will, sooner or later, return to dust. Most of our race seek means to obviate it, and yet there is no way to do so. We will all die. "No one gets out of here alive," as I have reported that a friend of mine has said. We can rage against it, protest it, mourn it, deny it, or claim its unfairness, but we will face the end to our life nonetheless. The frequently pronounced "unfairness claim" reminds me of the old joke about the man hauled before a judge having been caught killing his parents. He pleaded for mercy. "On what grounds?" asked the astonished judge. "I'm an orphan," pled the murderer. Our parents disobeyed and we follow in their footsteps daily, increasing their disobedience with the whole of our lives. We are no different, no better than they, yet we expect mercy where they had none. We claim no fault, but in our hearts, we know better. We claim unfairness when our disobedience is no less than theirs, wanting to be our own god as they did.

Yet, as Paul points out, our death need not end in despair; we can find another trajectory. There is hope yet, even from the God who acted as judge in pronouncing the sentence he had warned our parents of. He has offered a different trajectory. If we will return to him, submit to his rule, receive his mercy in Christ, then we can receive life once again, as was promised by the presence of the tree of life in the garden, and we will be blessed beyond our understanding. God himself became human to take that curse of death upon himself, and will give us again a life full of joy and reward. But to do so, we must fight the good fight, we must finish the course, we must keep the faith. There is no other way. Life in this age is only temporary, a life that will inevitably lead to death forever, unless we seek that other trajectory.

DEATH AS A SHEPHERD

April 11, 2022

> This is the way of those who are foolish, and of those after them who approve their words. Selah. As sheep they are appointed for Sheol; death shall be their shepherd; and the upright shall rule over them in the morning, and their form shall be for Sheol to consume so that they have no habitation. But God will redeem my soul from the power of Sheol, for he will receive me. Selah.
>
> Psalm 49:13–15

As we have discussed previously, the view of death in the Bible is more complex than saying simply that it is evil. For a believer, it may be positive by being a door to join Jesus in a better place; or, for the believer that the dying one leaves behind, it may cause great sorrow and consternation at the loss of a loved one. But death for the unbeliever has a singular perspective in the Scriptures: uniformly, without exception, it is a cause for fear and sorrow.

And it is one particular subgroup of unbelievers that this psalm portrays: the wealthy. This psalm is one of a number called the wisdom psalms. It treats subjects, much like Proverbs, of everyday life that require mature understanding to deal with. The wealthy in this psalm are those who, because of their wealth, believe themselves to be untouchable, supreme in their power and control. They believe that their greatness will endure even for generations to come: "Their inner thought is [that] their houses are forever [and] their dwelling places to all generations; they have called their lands after their own names" (Ps. 49:11). The arrogance of the wealthy is that they think they will somehow escape the anonymity of death, for most people in a few years, wealthy or not, are forgotten by all but a few.

Wealth in our culture is now seen as an almost unmitigated good. Who doesn't in our world think that riches are to be desired above almost all else? We accord wealthy people the greatest respect, deference, and adulation, often just ignoring the repeated warnings in Scripture about the dangers of wealth, even the desire for wealth. The only negative emotion we experience concerning wealth is jealousy, or anger that we lack what others possess.

It was not always like this in our country. The greatest generation, many of whom were born during or lived through the Great Depression, were not obsessed with wealth and the status it brings. They did not take jobs only to make the maximum amount of money, or believe that the rich were somehow better than their contemporaries who had less.

And, as we see in this Psalm, the WWII generation, probably more informed by biblical teaching and practice than most in our culture, were correct. (Or maybe it was their experience of death in war and the lessons one learns from that.) The wealthy cannot control, much less buy off, the fact of death. The great divide in life is not between the rich and the not rich, as the wealthy suppose—as they should be able to deduce from seeing that their demise is little different from the death of an animal. Instead, as this psalm points out, the great divide is between the righteous in God's sight and the wicked. For the wicked, death is their shepherd, who tends his flock in the afterlife where there is no hope of escape, and where they will remain forever. Life in that place is so dreary that it says they have no habitation, no home forever.

But for the righteous, a different shepherd cares for them, as is discussed in an earlier psalm (Ps. 23). The righteous have hope, even in death, whereas the wicked have none as the psalmist says in v. 15: "But God will redeem my soul from the power of Sheol, for he will receive me. Selah" (Ps. 49:15). The righteous, as surprising as it is to find it in the OT, have the hope of a miraculous resurrection when God will deliver us out of the power of death. The wicked (here the wealthy), though, believe that somehow they can afford to ransom their souls and deliver themselves even from the power of death without God's help. And yet, "No man can by any means redeem [his] brother or give to God a ransom for him, for the redemption of his soul is costly, and he should cease [trying] forever, that he should live on eternally, that he should not undergo decay" (Ps. 49:7–9).

The wicked (wealthy) should see death for what it is—an implacable foe, one who cannot be bought off. There is no hope for them, and so the rich are not to be feared: they have chosen foolishly what to value in this age, as Jesus will later say: "For what does it profit a man to gain the whole world, and forfeit his soul? For what will a man give in exchange for his soul?" (Mark 8:36–38).

May we rather choose the Lord of eternal life as our Shepherd, and leave off striving for wealth, which may lead us to find that death shall be our shepherd. It's not worth the trade, as this psalm makes clear.

DEATH AND WISDOM

April 26, 2022

For he who finds me finds life and obtains favor from the LORD. But he who sins against me injures himself; all those who hate me love death.

Proverbs 8:35–36

But he does not know that the dead are there, [that] her guests are in the depths of Sheol.

Proverbs 9:18

As I've mentioned before, when I was still practicing as a PT in home health, there was a principle I noticed at work among many of my patients: the worst problems were the ones that were self-created. Certainly esophageal CA, or a severe injury from, say, a fall, are bad; but they don't hold a candle to the wrack and ruin of problems that people cause for themselves and those who care for them. From medical problems caused by obesity (e.g., hypertension, diabetes, COPD, heart issues, joint pain in the back, knees, and hips, etc.) to relationship problems caused by being angry, stubborn, selfish, or just thoughtless and lazy—these were all problems that the patient caused, not something that just happened to them and was outside of their control. To me, these were all instances of what this passage in Proverbs 8 is pointing to: acting without wisdom is death to our soul and bodies, indeed to every part of our life.

And, quite often, as Proverbs 9 points out, people cannot see the part that they played in their own (and others') suffering. That part was often obvious in the finger pointing and blame shifting that patients would engage in, believing that their pain or other medical issues were the fault of medical personnel who couldn't find a way to just cure their diabetes or hypertension or joint pain, any or all of which were caused by their lifestyle that usually resulted in morbid obesity, even though it was obvious to everyone around them where the problems originated and why the patient was suffering from them. They were often symptoms of a greater problem, mainly unwise behavior such as overeating, or drinking soft drinks nonstop while sitting and watching television all day, but these were problems that they would shy away from ever seeing. If that sounds incredible or unkind, then you should have just followed me around as I traveled from home to home and saw this pattern repeated over and over. I wouldn't say that obesity is the cause of all the health problems I saw, obviously, but it was a cause of many of them, and one that is a great problem in our culture generally.

As Proverbs 8 makes clear, wisdom and the life it brings don't just happen by accident or even easily. Wisdom in how to live must be sought after intentionally and will be found only when we truly want it. And it will produce a certain amount of discomfort and perhaps humility, even humiliation, as we must submit to correction and discipline not only from God, and so perhaps may avoid public notice, but often from human instruments to prod us or to help us make needed changes that will bring us a life we can be glad of instead of a life full of sorrows accompanying premature and unnatural death. Resisting those corrections cuts off the gift that is offered to us in them. To change in order to gain wisdom is always necessary because wisdom isn't just a philosophy but a lifestyle. Unfortunately, acquiring wisdom, as I've said, isn't always easy or pain free. Believe me, I know from my recent experience, acquiring more wisdom came first and foremost from an evil, a trouble that I never anticipated. Yet God has used it to help me seek more wisdom.

The path of one who lacks wisdom ends in a death accompanied by regrets and sorrow, both now and eternally. That lack of wisdom, that pride and stubbornness, only lead to suffering for us and for those bound to us, our spouse, our children, our friends. A life of folly may perversely have its appeal as we all know, and Proverbs 9 explains: "The woman Folly is loud; she is seductive…" (9:13). "Stolen water is sweet; and bread [eaten] in secret is pleasant" (9:17). But, in the end, the outcome is always the same—death in so many forms, sorrow without relief, for in Folly's house, the dead are there. Better to pursue wisdom and find life and joy.

LEARNING HOW TO DIE PROPERLY

May 3, 2022

Therefore I have sent him all the more eagerly so that when you see him again you may rejoice and I may be less concerned [about you.] Receive him then in the Lord with all joy, and hold men like him in high regard; because he came close to death for the work of Christ, risking his life to complete what was deficient in your service to me.

Philippians 2:28–30

For bodily discipline is only of little profit, but godliness is profitable for all things, since it holds promise for the present life and [also] for the [life] to come.

1 Timothy 4:8

IS THERE A WAY to prepare for dying? I guess my answer would have to be a wishy-washy "yes and no." Yes, in one sense, as the

Scriptures are full of talk about death and what our view of it should be. No, in another sense, as everyone's death, or cause of death, will be somewhat different. Even when dying of cancer, one person's cancer may be similar and yet very different from another person's type of cancer, not to mention the person who has even the same type may be of a different age or sex or race, etc. Dying of cancer is not like dying of ALS (Lou Gehrig's disease), a heart attack, a stroke, a car accident, a fall, etc.

Why, then, do I even raise the original question? Because we should realize that no one except God knows the how and when of your death. The manner of your death will likely be a surprise to you (as it was to me). You may have a family history of, say, heart disease, and have had several relatives, maybe even a father and uncle, who died from a heart attack. But that means you also had many relatives who didn't die of heart disease. Of course, as my dad used to say, "You have to die of something." As we all believe that simple truth, what we begin to focus on is the *manner* of our death, and not the *fact* of death. We begin to look for ways to compensate for or correct our genetic flaws, such as a predisposition to heart disease. But to think that we can thereby congratulate ourselves as we eat better and exercise more than the general population is to confuse our attempt to extend our life (which may or may not be successful) with the idea that we can avoid death, and that is obviously pure folly. Yet I think most of us believe deep down inside that death can be avoided, or at least managed or controlled like many other problems in our lives. The idea of preparing for death seems easier to accept when we think we will have time to prepare later, as we intend to die much later.

I'm here to tell you, however, that death is not so easy to manage or control. A runner may die of a heart attack, the healthiest eater die of cancer or a heart attack or a stroke. There is no way to cheat or manage our own death. Is there no point, then, in attempting to extend our lives? The simple answer is, of course, yes, there is a point to such an attempt. Life is a gift that should not be lightly treated or tossed aside. But it's not as simple as believing, therefore, that extending life is the highest good. As Christians, we serve someone who was born for the sole purpose of dying. The servant is not above the master, nor the pupil above the teacher. If our master and teacher spent a short life preparing to die, how can we do less? Our lives cannot be governed by a denial or avoidance of death as our greatest concern.

As we see in the initial two quotes, Paul had a different view. Healthy eating and exercise are good things, but their worth should be diminished in our estimation by the fact that their value is only counted in this life, as is money, or acquiring skills, or achieving career success. They are good, but not in the way our culture views them. They are only for this life, and our death will make a mockery of them. None of those things will be of any benefit after death when we face our Creator on Judgment Day.

When I worked for HP, I remember reading a company newsletter that reported an interview with some very senior VP who was retiring. One of his comments was especially jarring. Despite his obvious success in his job, he said: "I wish I had spent more time with my family." Retirement for many who have been successful in their work is a kind of death and often an occasion for reflection on what we have valued over the course of our lives. Even our own review of our lives at that point may be disappointing.

Does that mean that the fact of death can be interpreted as a license to be lazy, obese, or careless, with our health? Of course not; it should instead cause us to reflect on what we have come to value. Are our values those of our culture, things that will be worthless at death, important only in this life? Or, like Epaphroditus, are we willing to value things that are more important than our death? That, then, is one way to help us prepare to die: look at what we have come to value. Is it profitable only before death? Or, as Paul says and we should ask, Is it profitable for this life but also for the one to come? Chew on that a while and see what you think if you were to receive that terminal diagnosis today.

CREMATION OR BURIAL?

May 10, 2022

By the sweat of your face you will eat bread, till you return to the ground, because from it you were taken; for you are dust, and to dust you shall return.

Genesis 3:19

Now when the inhabitants of Jabesh-gilead heard what the Philistines had done to Saul, all the valiant men rose and walked all night, and took the body of Saul and the bodies of his sons from the wall of Beth-shan, and they came to Jabesh and burned them there. They took their bones and buried them under the tamarisk tree at Jabesh, and fasted seven days.

1 Samuel 31:11–13

I THOUGHT I WOULD do a brief discussion of a current topic: cremation vs. burial. In the past year or so (according to sources online), for the first time the number of cremations in the U.S. has surpassed the number of burials. Of course, the reason seems to me to be obvious: simply that the cost for a cremation is vastly less than a burial. Most people in the U.S. now have no funeral service as was conducted in the past (which was a type of church worship service with Scripture reading, a sermon, hymns, and prayers). Nowadays I think people have a celebration of life service, and often provide an extensive obituary online in the newspaper or on the funeral home's website. Obviously, there would be no viewing. Many people are not members of a church and so hold the celebration of life in various venues.

For a Christian, however, other considerations are important besides just the cost. Interment is the normal and historical mode of caring for someone's body after death (thus, burial has been the Christian practice for thousands of years). But is it required by God? Is cremation a sin? The vast majority of places in the Bible that record what is done with the person's remains after death describe a burial of the body, or what's left of the body (as with John the Baptist, who was decapitated for his execution and so only a headless corpse could be buried). Only in the passage I quote above do we have recorded a cremation and then burial of the bones (yes, there was also Achan, who sinned by stealing during a battle and whose family was stoned and then burned—I'm not sure why). So, do all the incidents of burial indicate a mandate for burial?

I think not for several reasons. First, the curse in Genesis 3 is that we will return to dust. Nowhere is there any indication that this process will be fast (as with burning) or slow (as with burial); it doesn't seem to matter. Either way, we return to dust. Second, in no place does Scripture seem even to imply a mandate to bury the dead. First Samuel 31 is the only place I have found with burning (cremation) and then the burying of the remaining bones. But, again, there's no indication (as we might assume with Achan) that the burning was a result of sin, a curse (especially as they were burning not only Saul but also Jonathan), or a violation of some burial mandate. Perhaps they burned the bodies as they were decomposing, but I somewhat doubt that as that situation may have occurred elsewhere in the cities or fields of the nation of Israel, and there's no mandate in the Mosaic Law to burn or to bury in that situation. Or, perhaps as my wife suggested, maybe it was because they feared that the enemy would dig up the bodies and further desecrate them. Third, though I'm no Near Eastern history expert, my guess is that Israel buried because that's what most nations did to deal with the body after death. There may have been also the problem that the nations who practiced burning did so for pagan religious reasons. But that's just my guess; I have no evidence in the Scriptures or elsewhere that that was Israel's motivation.

Yet Christians today are in no danger of making unbelievers think we are trying to satisfy Moloch, or enter Valhalla, or follow the Hindu practice of a funeral pyre (yes, in India that is the most common method of disposing of the body). In fact, the Roman Catholic Church has now approved cremation for its members as an alternative to burial, provided that it is not done for pagan reasons and that the ashes are not scattered. In the Roman Catholic Church's eyes, the ashes are the remains of a person and should still be buried out of respect for that individual's physical remains.

There's one place in the New Testament where burning is mentioned, a remark made by Paul in 1 Corinthians 13:3: "And if I give all my possessions to feed [the poor,] and if I surrender my body to be burned, but do not have love, it profits me nothing." I'm not sure what to make of his remark. I thought at first that maybe it was an analogy having to do with the burnt offerings in the OT. But a friend of mine has convinced me that it more likely refers to the practice of the Roman empire during Paul's time using immolation as a means of execution (gruesome to say the least). In either case, I can't see that his remark has any bearing on the question of cremation vs. burial. I think this issue is completely unrelated to Paul's remark.

I should mention something that may provide some further guidance. Joseph had his father, Jacob, embalmed by the Egyptian physicians according to Egyptian customs: "Joseph commanded his servants the physicians to embalm his father. So the physicians embalmed Israel." But, as with cremation and burial, I don't think there was any particular mandate associated with the act (i.e., we're not required to embalm our dead just because Joseph did). It seems more likely that Joseph was simply following a common Egyptian practice, Egypt being where Jacob's family then lived, but without attaching any Egyptian religious ideas to it. And that is how I see cremation vs. burial. It is now a common cultural practice of the country where I live, and I believe I'm free to practice it as my neighbors might do.

So, for me, the bottom line is the bottom line. If it's significantly cheaper to cremate than to bury, and if I'm free to follow this practice in this country with no particular scriptural mandate to bury, then I'll choose to be cremated (though we have decided to have the ashes placed in an urn and buried in a cemetery). I have read the arguments for burial, but was not persuaded. There are simply too many situations where people may be lost at sea or disappear, or whatever, to think that burial is a mandate for Christians to prepare for death and resurrection. To me there is little difference between burial and cremation. We still are planning on having a funeral (memorial) and possibly a graveside service with the presence of ashes rather than a body.

LIVING AS SOJOURNERS
May 12, 2022

Pharaoh said to Jacob, "How many years have you lived?" So Jacob said to Pharaoh, "The years of my sojourning are one hundred and thirty; few and unpleasant have been the years of my life, nor have they attained the years that my fathers lived during the days of their sojourning."

Genesis 47:8–9

For we are sojourners before you, and tenants, as all our fathers were; our days on the earth are like a shadow, and there is no hope.

1 Chronicles 29:15

Beloved, I urge you as aliens and strangers to abstain from fleshly lusts which wage war against the soul.

1 Peter 2:11

> All these died in faith, without receiving the promises, but having seen them and having welcomed them from a distance, and having confessed that they were strangers and exiles on the earth. For those who say such things make it clear that they are seeking a country of their own. And indeed if they had been thinking of that [country] from which they went out, they would have had opportunity to return. But as it is, they desire a better [country,] that is, a heavenly one. Therefore God is not ashamed to be called their God; for he has prepared a city for them.
>
> Hebrews 11:13–16

A SOJOURNER IS SOMEONE who lives in a place only temporarily; an exile or transient is someone who has had to leave the place of their home and go to an alien land, where they are not native. And that is what these Scriptures call us. As Solomon says also in 1 Chronicles 29, our days "are like a shadow, and there is no hope." I'm assuming Solomon's "no hope" refers to our lives having no hope of escaping that fate of sojourning, or being exiles, and more to the point that our days are like a shadow, fleeting and temporary. There is no escape, no hope of breaking free from the imminence of death; outside of Christ, there is indeed no hope.

Death shows us that we are indeed sojourners, for our lives are so brief compared to God: one day is like a thousand years and a thousand years like one day for him, says 2 Peter 3:8. Or to put it another way, our lives are a mist, a fog of the early morning, according to James 4:14. We are here for a short while, and then gone. These texts show us we are also exiles, tenants, renters so to speak. As God explains to us, we are living in a place that is not our true or final home. He has already prepared for us a city, a place where we will not be aliens, but rather natives, members of a people who are finally at rest because they have come home. And there our lives will not be a shadow, but eternal, full, complete, never-ending, full of joy and quite the opposite of "no hope."

It is this perspective that I believe leads Paul to say to those rich in the things of this world: "[Instruct them] to do good, to be rich in good works, to be generous and ready to share, storing up for themselves the treasure of a good foundation for the future, so that they may take hold of that which is life indeed" (1 Tim. 6:18–19).

"That which is life indeed." Paul points out to us an application of being a sojourner and exile. We in America are among the wealthiest people in the history of the world. And it is so easy not only to take that fact for granted, but also to never be satisfied, to always want more, to wish we could be among the wealthiest elite. We tell ourselves that we would be different, that we wouldn't be changed by that kind of wealth. But the Scriptures are full of warnings about money: You can't serve God and money (Matt. 6:24); it is hard for a rich man to enter the kingdom of heaven (Matt. 19:24); the love of money is a root of all sorts of evil (1 Tim. 6:10), and so on. *We* wouldn't forget those warnings—of course not. *We* would take hold of that which is life indeed. Sure, we would...

As I've mentioned in an earlier chapter, I took early retirement from HP, and we sold our home and moved to another city so I could get my doctorate in physical therapy. Eventually, however, even after receiving my degree and working in that city for five years, we decided that we needed to return to our hometown, since my wife's mom could no longer live alone and care for herself safely. When we were planning the return, a dear friend who sold real estate told us he knew a Christian brother who had bought a new home but left the old one with a minimum of furniture and was not yet ready to sell. The owner of the home graciously offered us his old home to live in while we waited to close on the home we had purchased and then waited for the floors to be refinished. We were then sojourners—living in what wasn't our home, using furniture and appliances that weren't our own.

And that is exactly our situation while living in this world. Even the wealthy are living in homes that are ultimately not theirs, and using things that don't finally belong to them. Should my wife and I have bought new furniture and appliances? Should we have settled in as if we would live in that house for decades? How foolish those acts would have been had we done them—a waste of time and money. We were preparing to move into the home that would be ours and working on plans for that next home so it would be ready for us.

Let me encourage you to remember that picture: your life here is short; don't let yourself be distracted by things that will be gone soon enough. Remember, you are only a sojourner. Live that way. I know it's hard to shift to that perspective. It's like someone trying to stop smoking cigarettes. It takes the power of the Holy Spirit to do it. Pray for that strength.

DEATH AND RESURRECTION

May 19, 2022

> Truly, truly, I say to you, that you will weep and lament, but the world will rejoice; you will grieve, but your grief will be turned into joy.
>
> John 16:20

DEATH USUALLY MEANS SORROW for those left behind. The world rejoices as it thinks that each death of a Christian is a victory. Death in their eyes has won, and there is no stopping it. Christians, then, are of all people most to be pitied. But because of the resurrection, our sorrow will be turned into joy. *Joy* is the emotion we know when we believe that death has been completely and finally defeated. *Rejoicing*, though falsely, is for the world because it believes we have been deceived, and that death has conquered us. The real issue is as Paul stated it in 1 Corinthians 15: has Jesus been raised or not? If not, then our faith is futile; we are doomed; we have no hope, no expectation that life will extend beyond the grave. If we have that belief, we will come to death with the greatest fear and sorrow. But if Jesus has been raised, then all our hopes have been realized, and we can believe that death has truly been defeated.

And that is the difference ultimately between the world and us. They rejoice in our sorrow; we find joy in our hope of the resurrection. So, when we are finally made aware of our terminal diagnosis, we may be initially surprised, caught off guard, but we are not fearful and sorrowful, even though we know that our end is near. Our joy is in knowing that Christ has been raised and us with him. We believe that we will be raised and will enter a life like his: no sorrow, no pain, no suffering. We will live forever in that joy of resurrection, knowing that we will be forever blessed.

So, as a Christian, what will your response be to your diagnosis of impending death? Will you be frightened, failing to believe in Christ's resurrection, or will you be full of joy because you believe in the resurrection of Christ, your hope, and the source of your joy? Even if you confront initial fear, Christ is with you, and his Spirit will bear you up. But be prepared even now, as sooner or later, you will hear that pronouncement: "You are going to die." Bless Christ and give him thanks that you have such joy and hope, for unbelievers have no such joy or hope. They rejoice in death for us, but not for themselves, as we rejoice in our resurrection. When they see your joy and patience and kindness as you face death, they will recognize the difference between your view of death and theirs.

Don't weep and lament as if you have no hope; have *joy* because you have the expectation that our Savior has been born again. He has been raised from the dead, as you will be. Your death doesn't mean all is lost. Instead, it means all is gained. You have gained the hope of a new life, a life of joy without sorrow, pain, or suffering. They have their false rejoicing; you have the true one, true joy and gladness. Many of your brethren have trod this same road. You will walk it as they have, sooner or later. Be prepared to imitate their faith and courage. Be prepared to imitate their joy.

A Long Dying Is a Blessing

May 20, 2022

> In this you greatly rejoice, even though now for a little while, if necessary, you have been distressed by various trials, so that the proof of your faith, [being] more precious than gold which is perishable, even though tested by fire, may be found to result in praise and glory and honor at the revelation of Jesus Christ.
>
> 1 Peter 1:6–7

I HAVE MENTIONED BEFORE that a delayed death can be a blessing. I know of some who died suddenly without any expectation, so their family and friends had no time to prepare for their departure. I think of the saying we had when I was a young man: "a long time of dating, and a short time of engagement," meaning we could control our desires while dating, but had a difficult time controlling them when we knew we were to be married soon. Having an extended death is having a "long dating time"—time to get to know death, and time to prepare ones who are closest to us. An extended time of death is a very different experience from being told to expect to die very shortly, as in hours or days. With an extended time of dying, we can prepare others—telling our spouse, our children, and our friends things we had always wished we had said but never had; to arrange our finances and make funeral arrangements to prevent those burdens being dumped on others. These are hardships that will try the genuineness of faith in a way that we may have never otherwise experienced. An immediate expectation of impending death, when it is truly imminent, means we can do little more than prepare ourselves for departure.

But when there is some time before we expect to die, what a great opportunity God has given us to demonstrate our faith in the resurrection of our Lord, and in the hope of our own resurrection! Don't lose this opportunity to show the *genuineness* of your faith. By your kindness, your joy, your patience, you can reveal the true nature of your faith. This trial is a proof of our faith, one that every single person will undergo at some point. You can help others by leading the way with your stalwart adherence to God's promise of eternal life.

Be strong and courageous. Show your cheerfulness even in the face of impending death. Set an example for others to emulate with your joy and cheerfulness and thoughtfulness and kindness even as you face your own physical demise. If you are certain in your future resurrection, then you can point the way by acting with certainty and joy in facing your final adversary, the defeated foe—death. Be glad you have been tested by fire; that by the power of the Holy Spirit you can overcome the fear of death that so grips the heart of the unbeliever. Instead, you can die with the hope that you are going *home* to receive your long awaited reward: reunion with our precious Lord and the great gathering of his people!

NO GRUMBLING ABOUT DEATH

May 21, 2022

> The sacrifices of God are a broken spirit; a broken
> and a contrite heart, O God, you will not despise.
> Psalm 51:17

DEATH IS NOT EASY to bear. It is surprising to us for some reason, as if we believed that we were going to live forever in this age. Operating under some strange delusion, we act as if—though we say otherwise—that we will never die. But the fact is, at some point, now or in the near future, we truly are going to die. But because we live in a culture that avoids the thought of our own personal death, we can avoid thinking of our end, as if it would never arrive, which is why it is such a shock when it finally does! We live as if each day would lead into the next, pretending that they are an endless stream that will continue until we are ready for them to stop. As Christians we have to know that is nothing but foolishness.

But what this passage in the Psalms warns us against is not deluding ourselves that death would never come, but against grumbling against anything, including our impending death. When we receive our terminal diagnosis (assuming we are granted that mercy), the worst thing we could do, as Christians, is to complain about our expected end. I saw it many times when I was working as a PT in home health care. Because people gave so little thought—if any!—to their or their spouse's or parent's personal death, when the time did finally arrive, they were completely unprepared. And their reaction at that point was usually one of not just shock, but anger, as if they had been betrayed by God or the universe, as if death was not a fact that had been staring them in the face since the day of their birth. It was never a question of *if*, only one of *when*.

But we as believers need not proud or angry hearts, but humble and contrite ones. God expects us to accept the fact of our impending death as we should receive every other event in this world, as a part of his plan, and not to complain that our death is messing up the plan. Our prayer should always be: "Your kingdom come, your will be done." Does that not mean that God is the Lord not only of our life, but also of our death? We live in a culture that avoids thoughts of personal death and so Christians have begun to adjust to it, to accommodate that viewpoint. Yet the Scriptures teach us that every day is a *gift* that we are to use for God's glory, without grumbling or complaining, no matter what comes to pass, even if it might be our last day, or the beginning of the end.

Accept your notice of death for what it is—a part of the plan of God for you, in its time, place, method, and fact. Don't grumble or complain against it. Rejoice that you now have the opportunity to display the glory of God as you've never had before. God has given you this time to test, to try, and to show your faith. Don't fail to do that! And lean heavily into God's Spirit as you strive to rejoice.

DO YOU BELIEVE HIM?

May 22, 2022

> Jesus said to her, "I am the resurrection and the life; he who believes in me will live even if he dies, and everyone who lives and believes in me will never die. Do you believe this?"
>
> John 11:25–26

WHEN YOU ARE GIVEN that terminal diagnosis, what will go through your mind? Will you think that this is the final and complete end? That there is no hope? These words of Jesus should fill and reassure your heart and mind.

The Lord of life in these words has given you the hope that a terminal diagnosis is not the end. Your death will not be terminal in the most important sense. Though you will die, yet shall you live. Don't be frightened, as if this pronouncement was the final conclusion of all you could ever expect. You have a new life awaiting. You don't have to be afraid. Jesus died and was raised for the primary purpose that you might then and there have hope. When you receive that pronouncement of death, that terminal diagnosis, that is when your faith will grow and expand to receive the hope that our Savior offers. You will die in this life to be sure, just as everyone will. But the difference is that your death is not eternal, as the death of the unbeliever.

You die that you might finally receive life immortal. That eternal life, that eternal hope is without question our greatest joy and comfort. You won't at that moment be reassured by your bank account, your looks, or your job success. You'll see at that moment what their true value is. Instead, hold onto that hope of eternal life; look to that joy that Jesus has promised. If he was raised, then you will be also; if he has eternal life, then so will you. If you truly believe the words that he spoke in John 11, then you should see that your life, and especially your death, will open up the greatest difference between you and your unbelieving neighbors and co-workers and acquaintances: you have every expectation of a having another life when this one ends. Your greatest time of happiness is about to *begin*. Embrace that hope and rejoice in it. Let all those around you see it in your face, in your speech, in your behavior. Let go of your concern for merely yourself, and make the needs of others your primary focus. You can finally afford to!

The most important question you will ever answer will be the one Jesus poses at the end of verse 26: "...everyone who lives and believes in me will never die. Do you believe this?" Well, do you?

DEATH AND JOY

May 28, 2022

> For the choir director; on the Gittith. A Psalm of the sons of Korah. How lovely [amiable, KJV] are your dwelling places, O LORD of hosts! My soul longed and even yearned for the courts of the LORD; my heart and my flesh sing for joy to the living God.
>
> Psalm 84:1–2

As I've discussed before, the Old Testament doesn't give much attention or detail with regard to our abode in heaven. And yet it is not as if it gives no attention to that place or state. In this passage, I believe that once again the Psalms look to our future for help and encouragement before God, not just our current situation.

There are two aspects mentioned here related to our heavenly dwelling. First is the psalmist's appraisal of that place: "How lovely [amiable, KJV] are thy dwelling places..." The psalmist calls God's abode an amiable, a lovely, living place. "Amiable" or lovely is a somewhat surprising description of where God lives and the home in which he resides, but to me it is a very comforting term. God's residence is lovely, friendly, inviting, open to us as his people.

My first thought about the dwelling of a great and mighty King, one who is King of Kings and Lord of Lords, would be to think of it like that of a Nebuchadnezzar, or that of a Caesar, or the President of the United States (POTUS), a residence great and impressive (but not amiable), terrible in its display of power and might. For most such sovereigns, it would not even be open to the average citizen. I'm reminded of King Ahasuerus, the king from India to Ethiopia, who is one of the central characters in the book of Esther. Entrance into his presence was by invitation only, and if uninvited, then entrance had to be immediately granted or the subject was summarily executed. That is more the picture of any Lord such as Caesar or the POTUS (try approaching him uninvited in the White House). Hardly the picture of an amiable dwelling, welcoming to the masses. And yet, God does not hesitate, through the psalmist, to describe his residence as "amiable" or "lovely." That doesn't mean, of course, that just anyone could walk in. Yet if our holiness is a prerequisite, it is still an open court for all who meet that requirement.

As we see in the second aspect described by the psalmist relating to God's heavenly home: "My soul longed and even yearned for the courts of the Lord; my heart and my flesh sing for joy to the living God." Though we know from elsewhere in the Scriptures that there is a great risk to entering into God's court, yet the psalmist's reaction isn't what Esther's was: fear of death. Instead, the psalmist describes his feelings as just the opposite: he longs for, yearns for, and is full of desire for entrance into the great King's court. This is a King that the psalmist obviously loves and whom he knows loves him. No summary execution awaits the psalmist, or us either, for that matter. On our death and entrance into the Lord's courts, we expect no second death as a result of a rejection of entrance. Rather, we look forward to an *amiable* reception, a prodigal son being feted as he comes into the courts of his heavenly Father. What longing is fulfilled, what yearning is met, what a song of joy at being united with the one who loves us even more than we love him! What a wonderful picture of what awaits us at our death—the God who resides in an amiable home.

DEATH AND LIFE IN THE WORLD

JUNE 10, 2022

> Do not love the world nor the things in the world. If anyone loves the world, the love of the Father is not in him. For all that is in the world, the lust of the flesh and the lust of the eyes and the boastful pride of life, is not from the Father, but is from the world. The world is passing away, and [also] its lusts; but the one who does the will of God lives forever.
>
> 1 John 2:15–17

JOHN HERE WARNS US about life in the world: a life with desires generated by the world of the flesh, of the eyes, and of pride. He gives an indictment that sounds much like our modern life. Once again, as Christians, we need the long view of life, a life that doesn't end with our death or the time of this world. The world—which is John's word for a system of thinking and living that is arrayed against God and, therefore, against his people—is battling for what God and his kingdom is also concerned about: the desires of our bodies, eyes, and heart. We must always be aware of the world's pressure points on us. To do otherwise is to yield to what Satan most yearns for: our desires as we live in this age. Only by the power of the Holy Spirit are we able to control and overrule those desires in those areas generated by the world. My wife and I pray daily that we would be filled with the Holy Spirit, and that his fruit would be seen growing in us: love, joy, peace, patience, kindness, goodness, faithfulness, gentleness, and self-control (and, yes, we name them all in our prayer). We pray for the Spirit's filling that by his power we might be able to put to death the old Brian and Karen, and see him raise up as a part of the new creation the new Brian and Karen.

The desires of the world are increasing in the West with the explosive growth of sinful desires, especially immorality: homosexuality and all manner of sexual perversions. There is also a desire to increase racial animosity and divisions. Greed is our national obsession. By despising and attacking sexual normality as biblically defined, rejecting the biblical call for racial harmony, and loving money above all else as our standard of success, the world promotes its hatred of God and its love of death. Yet we know that this hatred comes at a great cost to those who practice it: oftentimes misery here, and final and irrevocable death at the last Judgment. As John says, the world and its desires are passing away, fading, declining, disappearing. The world and its desires will come under God's condemnation and his final sentence: hell with eternal suffering.

But John offers us the hope of the gospel: if we will, by the power of the Spirit, do the will of God, we will live forever with him. As we have seen before, this is not an eternal life in some colorless, drab existence; it is a life with our Savior, in his world, even in his home that he has prepared for us. And as a further blessing, it will be a life with his people, the earth full of peace, growth in use of talents and abilities God has given us, a time of never ending prosperity, of joy, and gladness!

So resist the lures and traps of the world as it attempts to distract you from the long game; prepare to live in eternity. Stop worrying about the world and its passing desires that will be here only briefly, attempting to blind us with the tyranny of the immediate. Do the will of God by his grace so that you can abide forever as John exhorts us!

DEATH AND VACCINES
JUNE 20, 2022

Man, who is born of woman, is short-lived and full of turmoil. Like a flower he comes forth and withers. He also flees like a shadow and does not remain. You also open your eyes on him and bring him into judgment with yourself. Who can make the clean out of the unclean? No one! Since his days are determined, the number of his months is with you; and his limits you have set so that he cannot pass. Turn your gaze from him that he may rest, until he fulfills his day like a hired man. For there is hope for a tree, when it is cut down, that it will sprout again, and its shoots will not fail. Though its roots grow old in the ground and its stump dies in the dry soil, at the scent of water it will flourish and put forth sprigs like a plant. But man dies and lies prostrate. Man expires, and where is he? [As] water evaporates from the sea, and a river becomes parched and dried up, so man lies down and does not rise. Until the heavens are no longer, he will not awake nor be aroused out of his sleep. Job 14:1–12

Our culture has many serious problems. And as we live in this culture, even as Christians, we may share the central problem to a very great degree. The problem can be stated like this: *we live as if we have been vaccinated against death*. But the passage above from Job warns against such a view. Job discusses both the finality of death and its uncertain timing. It is with God that life's length is held; he knows our beginning and our end. We don't know it. Yet we, as a part of this hedonistic culture, often live as if we do. Along with our neighbors, we might in foolishness, or ignorance, or arrogance, act as if we can plan our future, including the time of our own death. The simple truth is: we cannot, and it is folly to pretend otherwise. Our life's extent and the time of our death are ultimately determined by God's plan.

As I've said before, that is certainly one reason behind the first petition of the Lord's Prayer: "Your kingdom come, your will be done." The number of months you will live has already been counted by God. He knows the date, time, and place of your death. Don't continue to live as if *you* know. There are actuarial tables that insurance companies use to give you a length of time you are likely to live, but for you and your time of death, that actuarial life span is merely a best guess. You may exercise and eat healthy foods, not be overweight or a smoker, but the limit God has set for your life cannot be passed. It is unbendable in his eternal plan. Humanly speaking, your life may be extended even with a terminal diagnosis. Mine certainly has been. As I've discussed before, the oncologist advised me that most people with my diagnosis and treatment protocol at this point in their cancer cycle are dead. Yet, I am alive. There are certainly secondary reasons that I hold are behind that extension: the love of a friend who helped get my oncology treatment initiated, an anointing, a vow taken, many, many prayers, and, of course, my medical treatment protocol.

But Job is not speaking of that earthly temporal process. He speaks of the eternal and immutable plan of God, which cannot be known or changed or thwarted by us. We have no control over that plan. It is fixed and certain, as well as perfectly just, wise, and loving. But the time of our own individual death is hidden from us in that plan. May God grant that each of us take no day for granted, never believe our plans will prevail, and live each day prepared to pray, as my wife and I do each day from *The Book of Common Prayer*: "And grant us grace always to live in such a state that we may never be afraid to die; so that, living and dying, we may be thine, through the merits and satisfaction of Thy Son Christ Jesus, in whose Name we offer up these our imperfect prayers. Amen."

Medical Update

I had my status CT scan last Friday and a scan review appointment with my oncologist yesterday (Monday). The scan shows that the cancer nodules in my lungs are active again: they are increasing in size and number. The oncologist discussed my options (remember my prognosis is treatable, not curable): first, I could go back on my immunotherapy drug (Opdivo) in addition to taking my oral cancer drug, Xeloda (which I have never stopped taking). Second, I could go on one of several second string cancer drugs. Third, he could try to get me into a clinical trial at some big university hospital setting (e.g., UVA or Duke).

I chose the Opdivo course—and I believe that was his first choice—reasoning that it had worked for more than a year; and further, I preferred the devil I know to the one I don't (as the saying goes).

He feels that the cancer is not in any rapid growth phase, and told me I could start treatment when my family returns from our beach vacation in several weeks. I'm not looking forward to this restart of the Opdivo, since last spring when I started it, my immune system went nuts, and he had to shut down my immune system with a large dose of prednisone and then restart the therapy, this time giving me a cocktail of steroids before the IV administration of the Opdivo. I hope it goes better this time. At least this time we know I should have the steroid IV cocktail before the Opdivo injection!

DEATH AND JUDGMENT
June 30, 2022

Man, who is born of woman, is short-lived and full of turmoil. Like a flower he comes forth and withers. He also flees like a shadow and does not remain. You also open your eyes on him and bring him into judgment with yourself. Who can make the clean out of the unclean? No one! Since his days are determined, the number of his months is with you; and his limits you have set so that he cannot pass. Turn your gaze from him that he may rest, until he fulfills his day like a hired man. For there is hope for a tree, when it is cut down, that it will sprout again, and its shoots will not fail. Though its roots grow old in the ground and its stump dies in the dry soil, at the scent of water it will flourish and put forth sprigs like a plant. But man dies and lies prostrate. Man expires, and where is he? [As] water evaporates from the sea, and a river becomes parched and dried up, so man lies down and does not rise. Until the heavens are no longer, he will not awake nor be aroused out of his sleep . . . For now you number my steps, you do not observe my sin.

> My transgression is sealed up in a bag, and you wrap up my iniquity.
>
> Job 14:1–12, 16–17

IN THE LAST CHAPTER, I discussed the certainty of the time of our death. It is fixed in God's eternal plan and cannot be changed. But Job raised another consideration about our death: our judgment. Here Job voices a dismaying thought: that no one can turn something unclean into something clean. The Mosaic Law made possible the cleansing of unclean things, having them return to being clean—but not in all situations. In the context, however, in which Job raises this problem, we probably should think that he's concerned about a more longterm solution. For as the writer of the letter to the Hebrews in the New Testament points out, there was no permanence to cleanness under the old covenant. What is clean today becomes unclean tomorrow in that system. Even the high priest, who can enter the most holy of places, has to be cleansed once every year to make an entrance into the Holy of Holies. The process of cleansing had no end in the OT. It might seem that Job is saying that there is fixity to our uncleanness just as there is to our death.

But Job reports he has a comforting hope: that God himself can and will make us clean. Our faults will be sealed up, put away and hidden as they are covered over by God himself. What a wonderful thought: that the infinite and perfect Judge will also be the infinitely merciful and gracious Redeemer, who brings forgiveness to us who are under a certain and fixed sentence of death, awaiting final condemnation at the day of final Judgment.

How can this be? Job has no clear vision of such reconciliation of the God of judgment to the God of salvation. The same God who condemns our sin is the God who accepts for us our condemnation that results in a fixed and certain death. He offers to take our penalty, our sentence of death. Despite our seemingly fixed uncleanness, he instead will change it into a reprieve of eternal cleanness with a reward, our death sentence being commuted into a stay of execution. And even better, a stay of execution is transmuted into a pronouncement of blessing, a gift of life that can never be rescinded or withdrawn. It is not temporary, needing constant renewal as cleanness was under the old system. It is finished, just as Jesus proclaimed as he died on the cross. We are finally and completely and permanently free of all the filth of our sins.

DEATH AND ITS POWER

July 5, 2022

> The king is not saved by a mighty army; a warrior is not delivered by great strength. A horse is a false hope for victory; nor does it deliver anyone by its great strength. Behold, the eye of the LORD is on those who fear him, on those who hope for his lovingkindness, to deliver their soul from death and to keep them alive in famine. Our soul waits for the LORD; he is our help and our shield. For our heart rejoices in him, because we trust in his holy name. Let your lovingkindness, O LORD, be upon us, according as we have hoped in you.
>
> Psalm 33:16–22

THE PSALMIST HERE LISTS a range of means to keep someone safe from harm—an army, great strength, the power of a horse, all means of war in the ancient world. But the psalmist goes on to relate what is the only hope we have ultimately: the protection of God. He mentions God's deliverance from death—in an age when such means of death as famine were a very real fear (and still are in parts of the world today). But death in our age is a very great concern for us, and in that sense, we are no different from people in the ancient world. Just ask me: I had a terminal diagnosis, which at that time (in the spring of 2021) was the last thing I expected to hear. I was still working full time and felt fine with no health issues except some shortness of breath.

But death in this age can come at any time for anyone, as I found out. And as I have related elsewhere (see the appendix on healing), it truly and obviously is only God's mercy that has thus far spared me from death. As much help as modern medicine can be, much like the psalmist's army or warrior, it could not deliver me from death.

So, where is your hope? In money, your skills or talent, your job or company position, your spouse or friends, your exercise and healthy eating habits? No one and no thing can ever guarantee your deliverance from death's powerful hold. In the end, it is only the power of God that can open that lion's jaws.

There is, however, a greater need that we have, a need for deliverance from another death beyond the first death of the psalmist's description. That second death is far more terrible than the first one, as terrible as the first one may be. The first death is only the conclusion of our brief stay in this present age. The second death has no end; there is no conclusion to it, no stay or reprieve. Once again, it is the psalmist's words that point us to the only hope we can have: the power and care of our God.

If the elements of the greatest power for war (in the ancient world) had no hope of deliverance from death in this age, what hope is there that there can be any human deliverance from a greater and more frightening fate, a permanent death?

There is no hope of escape made possible by anyone or anything—even the best medical treatment available—in this current age. We must turn to the One who created us, the Lord who would protect and deliver us from that final death. He is our guarantee, our certainty of eternal life. Once he is, then we can say with the psalmist: "Sing for joy in the Lord..."!

DEATH AND THE BREATH OF LIFE

July 15, 2022

> LORD, make me to know my end and what is the extent of my days; let me know how transient I am. Behold, you have made my days [as] handbreadths, and my lifetime as nothing in your sight; surely every man at his best is a mere breath. Selah. Surely every man walks about as a phantom; surely they make an uproar for nothing; he amasses [riches] and does not know who will gather them. And now, Lord, for what do I wait? My hope is in you.
>
> Psalm 39:4–7

Here is a wonderful prayer of the psalmist. He first asks God to help him realize the shortness of his life, how fleeting it is. This is a great request to meditate on, a request that would change our lives, or our lifestyle at least. It's a request for God to help us not to lose perspective on our situation, to remember that our days are short, no matter how long they may feel.

Second, in verses 5–6, the psalmist describes the state of all men: they are a breath, as insubstantial as a shadow. They are in uproar on the one hand, and on the other acquire wealth but are unable to take it with them. Further, they cannot even be sure who would inherit it. I take from that idea that their children will be arguing over their accumulated money, but cannot accept the dying man's directives or desires. Wealth is no guarantee of happiness; in fact, it may precipitate strife and hard feelings among the inheritors that would never have developed without its presence, indeed, even toward the benefactor who may have expected some gratitude.

Finally, in the third part, verse 7, we see where the psalmist lands in this account of brevity and trouble, and that is exactly where he should be: waiting on and hoping in the Lord. What other sure hope do we have? What other certain treasure—one that will last throughout the ages, throughout all eternity? There is nothing in this age that will make it into the age that is yet to come. Our only sure treasure is the one our Lord is preparing for us, even now, before we die to be with him.

So, be sure that you don't focus on what you own or achieve in this age from a life of such short tenure: money, possessions, status, position, relationships even. They will last only as long as a breath, and are as substantial as a shadow. Put your hope in the King who is over governments, the Lord who is master of all of life. He is the only one who will give you an eternal possession. Your turmoil over the things of this age, your 401k and stocks and accumulated things will not last, and will not be of any benefit at the final judgment that leads to your final state. Keep your perspective and your eye fixed on what is lasting and is eternal, and so is of greatest importance.

DEATH AND OUR FRAILTY

July 16, 2022

> But he, being compassionate, forgave [their] iniquity and did not destroy [them]; and often he restrained his anger and did not arouse all his wrath. Thus he remembered that they were but flesh, a wind that passes and does not return.
>
> Psalm 78:38–39

THE PSALMIST IS HERE relating the history of Israel, saying that God delivered them out of the furnace of Egyptian slavery. Yet even having experienced such a miraculous and powerful release by God, Israel was constantly complaining and rebelling against their covenant Lord. He would discipline them and even, at times, execute some of them for their obstinate disobedience. That punishment would cause them temporarily to relent from their sins, and yet they would almost immediately turn back to them. But, as the psalmist notes here, God is a compassionate God, one who was willing to forgive their rebellion and ingratitude. And he did this not just from his own trait of mercy, but also because of the nature of his people. He *knew* that he needed to corral his anger and should not release it fully against his covenant people, even when they deserved it. That restraint was because of their construction, for they were flesh, made like the wind, so insubstantial compared to their God that they could pass by and never be seen again.

This lesson from the psalmist is a warning to all humans, even to those of us who are among his covenant people. We should always remember the power of God's anger. Though we may feel solid, rooted, substantial, even safe, in reality, compared to God, we are frail, weak, as thin as the wind, and just as fleeting.

That perspective should temper our view of life every day, for we are passing by and are here only as briefly as a breeze that blows by us. What difference will our wealth, position, and accomplishments matter when we receive that diagnosis of death? It is at that moment, if not before, when heeding the psalmist's message, that we will finally realize how brief and fragile our lives truly are.

CLEMENCY FOR BREVITY

August 9, 2022

> How long, O LORD? Will you hide yourself forever? Will your wrath burn like fire? Remember what my span of life is; for what vanity you have created all the sons of men! What man can live and not see death? Can he deliver his soul from the power of Sheol? Selah.
>
> Psalm 89:46–48

THE PSALMIST HERE PLEADS with God about the rejection of his anointed because of his disobedience. But the nature of the psalmist's plea is most interesting and instructive. He asks for mercy and an end to God's absence in his anger for a simple reason: the brevity of his life. He reminds God that our lives are so short that we are inextricably tied to death. Our only hope is that God will be merciful, patient with our brevity and fragility.

I have prayed this type of prayer when approaching God about my cancer, using words like these: "Please remit my sentence of death from this cancer. Remember that I am made of dust and can bear only so much." We have seen these themes of brevity and fragility repeatedly in the Scriptures. They are echoes of the curse of God on Adam and his role in creation, and thus of all creation:

> Then to Adam he said, "Because you have listened to the voice of your wife, and have eaten from the tree about which I commanded you, saying, 'You shall not eat from it'; cursed is the ground because of you; in toil you will eat of it all the days of your life. Both thorns and thistles it shall grow for you; and you will eat the plants of the field; by the sweat of your face you will eat bread, till you return to the ground, because from it you were taken; for you are dust, and to dust you shall return."
>
> Genesis 3:17–19

The curse on Adam was not that he was taken from the dust, but rather that to dust he would return. His death was the final punishment in the string of curses pronounced by God over the serpent, Eve, and now Adam.

It is surprising that the psalmist uses our cursed condition, then, as an argument for mercy. And yet, this argument reveals to us an insight into the nature of our God: he is a compassionate God. He is aware of the pain and struggle of our lives under this curse. It is a burden hard to bear, and we should be unafraid not only to remember that it is to teach us wisdom, but also to use it in our prayers as an argument to gain God's patience and mercy according to his sovereign will. For we understand that he knows in a way that the psalmist had never imagined: the coming of God in the flesh of a doomed race to deliver them from that corruption, even from the hopelessness of the death of their flesh. For now we can not only present the brevity of our lives as a plea for mercy, but better still we can rejoice and give thanks that the immortal put on mortality, the incorruptible put on a flesh subject to corruption that our flesh of dust may one day regain the life it was created to live.

SHORTNESS OF LIFE AND THE LENGTH OF GOD'S YEARS

August 12, 2022

> You turn man back into dust and say, "Return, O children of men." For a thousand years in your sight are like yesterday when it passes by, Or [as] a watch in the night. You have swept them away like a flood, they fall asleep; in the morning they are like grass which sprouts anew. In the morning it flourishes and sprouts anew; toward evening it fades and withers away.
>
> Psalm 90:3–6

Part 1

I'd like to take the next chapters to discuss several passages related to death and dying in Psalm 90. I'll cover two parts in this chapter. The first set of verses are verses 3–6, which I have quoted above. I'm sure that at this point you can guess what the psalmist's theme is in this passage. It probably sounds repetitive to you. After all, I've highlighted this perspective in many of the previous chapters, but the fact that it continues to return should tell us something. It should indicate its importance in the first place; and second, it should tell us how hard it is for us to keep this perspective in our minds.

God reminds us of our fragility here by describing our final destination: dirt. We came from dirt, and as we said in the last chapter relating to the curse of Genesis 3, God's pronouncement there and here is the same: "Return." We came from dust, and to dust we shall indeed return. And that perspective is contrasted with the life of the One who made us from dust. The psalmist says that for our Creator, a millennium is no more than yesterday or last night. To him, it is a brief period of time. To us, trying to imagine a thousand years is like to trying to picture a billion dollars. It's so large; how can anyone comprehend it? Trying to imagine the world of 1022 AD is almost impossible. And yet for God, it's like us trying to remember yesterday or last night—not hard at all.

To demonstrate our brevity, the psalmist compares our lives to grass growing in the desert heat. It may sprout up in the morning but, because of the heat, it is dried up and dead by evening. We've all seen that phenomenon when we planted a sprout and came back the following day and found it desiccated, dead, from heat and lack of moisture during the previous day. That plant is our life—alive in the morning, and yet our whole life is gone by the end of the day. Once again, that gives us some idea of God's perspective on our time here.

It is so easy to lose that view. To us our life seems to go on and on. But to God, it is so brief; it's as if we were born, lived, and died all in a single day. We marvel when we hear of some insect that hatches, lays eggs, and then dies all in the course of only days. Its life seems unbelievably transitory, short to the point almost of being meaningless. Should it worry about the size of its home, the color of its carapace, its renown or fortune? Sounds faintly ridiculous, doesn't it? And yet we should remember the shortness of our lives and the length of God's. May the view that God gives here inform our view of each day of our life.

PART 2

> As for the days of our life, they contain seventy years, or if due to strength, eighty years, yet their pride is [but] labor and sorrow; for soon it is gone and we fly away. Who understands the power of your anger and your fury, according to the fear that is due you? So teach us to number our days, that we may present to you a heart of wisdom.
>
> Psalm 90:10–12

Psalm 90 is a psalm full of regret, suffering, and pleas for mercy. Here the psalmist pens what is now a famous passage: the expected length of our lives—sometimes seventy years, maybe by good health eighty. Yet, shorter or longer, those years will be full of hard work and sorrow followed by our death. Not exactly a happy-clappy view of life, but one I believe it is important to contemplate.

I worked in home health care as a physical therapist for six years and went into literally hundreds of homes in my area. Of course, you might point out that I had a biased sample as I was seeing only the sick and dying and not the healthy aged; nonetheless, unless you drop dead in perfect health at say, age sixty, you will find that at some point you will be in that weakened state, and will likely say with the psalmist that life is never easy and often full of sorrows, the worst being the ones we create. That is us living in likely the most peaceful and affluent culture in the history of the world.

Instead of believing that God is the happy-clappy sort, we are enjoined by the psalmist to remember that our Creator is also our Judge. He brooks no sin in his presence and warns us of the price of its stain—his anger. And so we reach verse 12: a warning and instruction that is just as germane to us now as it was in the psalmist's day: a request that God help us to number our days so that we might somehow gain a heart of wisdom.

Perhaps the idea of numbering our days seems somewhat abstract. Here are my thoughts on that elusive task: every morning I get up and drink three or four (or more) mugs of tea. But only in the first one do I put one teaspoonful of sugar. In the rest, I use in each one a packet of sweetener. Here's the surprising thing, though: I'm amazed when I lift the lid of the sugar bowl and see that it needs to be refilled. When that happens, I often blink at the bowl and think to myself, "Where did all the sugar go? I use only one teaspoonful each day." And that to me is the story of our lives: God gives us a bowl full of days, not telling us how many are in the bowl, but it seems to have so many. Each day is a spoonful of life from our bowl of days, and sooner than most of us are prepared to believe, our bowl is empty. The days run out and we are finished.

Yet, as I've tried to emphasize, a heart of wisdom can come from watching that bowl of days being emptied and realizing that we must be ready for when the time of that final spoonful comes because at that point, we fly away. "Be ready," God here is telling us.

Medical Update

I was asked to say a few words about my current health. As I mentioned previously, my last status CT scan (July 8) showed that my cancer (the metastases in my lungs) has begun growing again. So, on August 1 I restarted my Opdivo (the immunotherapy drug). I have never stopped taking Xeloda, the old school oral drug—on for two weeks and off for one. I was apprehensive because the first time I took Opdivo (spring of 2021) was pretty rocky with lots of very bad side effects. But this time my oncologist had me take a pretreatment mixture of lots of drugs, primarily steroids and anti-nausea medicine, which helped me accept the drug with virtually no side effects. Last Thursday and Friday (August 25 and 26), I felt better than I have felt in a long time. As I told my wife, that's just the steroids talking. And it was true. By Monday morning (August 29), I was crashing and burning with severe shortness of breath, making lifting weights a real chore (while I usually enjoy it and feel better when I'm done). Tuesday and Wednesday were better, but Thursday was even worse than Monday, a real barn burner of a bad day. But today is Friday (September 2), and I'm feeling significantly better.

My real concern is what will happen in two and a half weeks. At that point, my wife and I are supposed to fly to California (San Jose) to see our oldest son (this time will be the fourth attempt). I have one more Opdivo treatment before then (September 13), since my oncologist wants me to not miss any treatments because of the change in my cancer status. I will have two questions for him in our next meeting (on the treatment day): (1) should I take the next COVID (and I guess the influenza B) vaccine; and (2) how should I prepare for and handle the flights and the rest of the trip (we'll be there a week). My thought is that I should bump my prednisone up significantly on the flight days, and then when necessary while I'm there. Of course, I'm limited in how many medications I can haul cross country as airlines are very concerned about weight (which translates into fuel), but I'll just have to guess what would be most helpful if I have a severe attack while there. The life of a cancer/chemo patient is always exciting—what meds do I get to take next? I'll provide another medical update once I meet with the oncologist and get his perspective.

MERCY FOR FRAILTY AND FAITHFULNESS

August 26, 2022

> For as high as the heavens are above the earth, so great is his lovingkindness toward those who fear him. As far as the east is from the west, so far has he removed our transgressions from us. Just as a father has compassion on [his] children, so the LORD has compassion on those who fear him. For he himself knows our frame; he is mindful that we are [but] dust. As for man, his days are like grass; as a flower of the field, so he flourishes. When the wind has passed over it, it is no more, and its place acknowledges it no longer. But the lovingkindness of the LORD is from everlasting to everlasting on those who fear him, and his righteousness to children's children, to those who keep his covenant and remember his precepts to do them.
>
> Psalm 103:11–18

A favorite passage—wonderful for meditation! It begins with the vastness of God's grace and mercy. It is so large

it is scarcely conceivable, which gives us, too, an idea of the greatness of our sins and the need we have for his mercy. This is a passage of great comfort for us as believers, as children of this wonderful Father.

The psalmist moves from there into a perspective we have seen before: the surprising idea (surprising to me, at least) that one of the reasons God is so munificent to his children is that he knows we are so frail, being made only of dust. Of course, he is aware of that delicacy because he constructed us that way at the beginning. But we know, in a way that the psalmist could not, that God is aware of our frailty because he decided to lower himself to come in the flesh and live among us. He too became a man, made only of dust (like the rest of humanity), feeling our weakness as much as we do.

From there the psalmist moves onto a description of our mortality, and especially the brevity of our lives, which seem so long to us. But from God's perspective, they are so short, comparable elsewhere in the Bible to plants in an arid and hot environment. They grow at first, but because of the heat and dryness, the wind blows over them and they are gone. Our lives are like those of some desert flower, blooming in the morning, and yet dead and gone by evening. To us, our lives seem full of days, but to God we hardly are born before we are ready to die. What a difference in perspective! A sobering thought that should teach us humility and wisdom.

And yet, there is joy at the end of this somber passage. God's mercy is not short-lived like our lives, but eternal, forever, without end. From generation to generation until the end of history, God's righteousness will be found always good—for generations long after our place in our generation is gone. Yet, such grace and mercy requires an appropriate response. For some reason, "cheap grace" always finds its way into the view of many in every generation, and in ours in particular it seems to have gained a large foothold in Protestant circles. The notion that there is nothing we can do to alter God's mercy toward us is one repeated often from pulpits everywhere. This idea is a perversion of mercy. We are saved by grace through faith alone but, as the doctrine of perseverance espoused by the Protestant Reformers taught, faith is never alone. Faith without works is a corpse (as James 2 teaches). It is stillborn, lifeless, and useless. But if we keep covenant and remember his precepts, as taught here, we show the life and health of our faith.

Keep your eyes, then, focused on what is important. Little time you have been given. Use it to prepare for the everlasting time in the new heavens and earth when God will show us the true fullness of his vast mercy.

THE BLESSING OF LIFE EVERLASTING

September 8, 2022

> A Song of Ascents, of David. Behold, how good and how pleasant it is for brothers to dwell together in unity! It is like the precious oil upon the head, coming down upon the beard, [even] Aaron's beard, coming down upon the edge of his robes. It is like the dew of Hermon coming down upon the mountains of Zion; for there the LORD commanded the blessing—life forever.
>
> Psalm 133:1–3

ONCE AGAIN WE SEE that there are clear statements in the Old Testament that show that there was an understanding that life does not end with death. Each of these allusions to eternal life has a facet that gives us another perspective on eternal life's meaning and character.

This is a very short psalm, with verses clearly interconnected, so I'll make a few remarks on the relations in it as it reaches its denouement.

The psalmist begins with what he sees is a huge blessing—the love of God's people for one another. That unity he says is both good and pleasant, a joy and a comfort. Whether in the Old Testament community or in the New Testament community, the love of God's people for one another is wonderful. It is something that Jesus prays for specifically in John 17:21: "...that they may all be one." And then in v. 22: "...that they may be one even as we are one." (What an audacious, seemingly impossible request!). Then v. 23: "...I in them and You in me, that they may become one, so that the world may know that you sent me and loved them even as you loved me."

The psalmist shows a glimpse of this source of our unity, our love for one another in a comparison: the oil poured on Aaron in anointing him a high priest. As the term *Christ* means anointed one, we know this anointing can be referring likely to the pouring out of the Holy Spirit on us. How else than being indwelt by God is there any hope of achieving the unity the psalmist commends or the unity of our Savior's request? Only by the sanctifying work of the Spirit, finding its ultimate fulfillment in the age to come, when there will be no divisions or strife, no factions or separations, but only one whole and harmonious people.

He then moves to the dew of Hermon falling on the mountains of Zion. I'm afraid I don't understand the geography of this comparison, but I can get the sense: a great refreshment on the land that was given by God to his people—another image of joy and gladness, as we see God care for and bless the inheritance of his own. Surely we can expect an even greater blessing on the whole earth as we look forward to the expansion of the inheritance of God's people as it comes to encompass the entire planet! (Matt. 5:5, "Blessed are the meek, for they shall inherit the earth.")

Finally, the psalmist tells us why this dew is so wonderful for our inheritance. It was on the mountains of Zion, I think particularly in the temple located there, that we see the fulfillment of our ultimate desire, indeed what is also our ultimate need: a banishment of death and a promise of eternal life. Though we cannot be sure what the psalmist refers to, possibly he has in mind the courts of God in the temple.

Life eternal is found there as we see the holy presence of the life and light of God displayed there: the bread, which is food shared with God; the light, dispelling darkness and evil and giving us wisdom and understanding; the oil of his Spirit; the sacrifices relieving our guilt and judgment. Our life everlasting is the culmination of our hope, not just for us as individuals, our solitary existence, but a life lived with a world full of those who love our Lord and who will love us. It is to be a place of contentment, of satisfaction, of peace, with so many saints to share meals with, to learn from, to laugh with, to rejoice and sing with, to work with, to help one another to build a world of beauty and wonder, but one without strife, without tension, without any animosity or anger, much less bitterness or resentment, fear or distrust, hatred or worry. This will be a world full of the unity of us all as believers, for these people will all be our brethren—forever.

THE FRAGILITY OF OUR LIVES

September 10, 2022

> O LORD, what is man, that you take knowledge of him? Or the son of man, that you think of him? Man is like a mere breath; his days are like a passing shadow.
>
> Psalm 144:3–4

THE PSALMIST REITERATES a theme mentioned often in the psalms. He never seems to tire of it: the fragility of the life of man. He describes man with a comparison we have seen a number of times, as a mere breath. As I've mentioned before, I think this comparison may be due to the Genesis account of the creation of our father, Adam. There God took dirt, molded it into human shape, and breathed life into it, making a living, breathing man. That breath gave us life from God, but also marked our frailty and dependence, a dependence we have had ever since. It has always amazed me how quickly we can die without a breath. For instance, we can drown in a matter of a few minutes. Truly, we live merely a few breaths away from our death.

Next he compares our lives to a shadow. Could there be anything more insubstantial? I will never forget one of my first plane rides on a large commercial jet. I looked down thousands of feet and saw the shadows of clouds slowly moving over the fields and mountains. Though the shadows were enormous, they had even less substance than the clouds that caused them. They were completely transparent and left no trace of themselves behind as they moved up and down and over and under, following the clouds that generated them. Yet another picture of our lives: so wispy, so thin.

But what words does the psalmist use to describe our Creator? He is a rock (v. 1), a stronghold and a shield (v. 2). All these are words about the One who is truly substantial, whom we can stand on as he is solid, the One who can give us refuge and shelter, since he can't be breached, one who can protect us as he can absorb any blow directed at him.

A life of fragility is no bad thing; it is a human thing. It is how we were constructed from the beginning before there was any sin. It is not the result of the Fall. Yet death was not part of that fragile dependency in the beginning. It only came in as a result of our forefather's (and our) desire to become god without needing the true God—a denial of our frailty and a rejection of our dependence on the One who made us, who shelters and now defends us, if we will but ask him to. Never forget that your life is only a breath away from its end, and your time here is as insubstantial as any shadow.

Our Lives Are Written

September 15, 2022

> Your eyes have seen my unformed substance; and in your book were all written the days that were ordained [for me,] when as yet there was not one of them.
>
> Psalm 139:16

THE PSALMIST EMPHASIZES A message that we have seen a number of times: before we were born, the literal number of our days was ordained. There is a fixed day and time when death will come for you. That can cause you consternation or comfort. It can cause consternation because you see that you do not have the control you thought you did. Your life is not an open-ended arrangement of days that you use until you finally just wear out and are ready to pass away. There is no guarantee for that. Just ask me—working full time as a physical therapist, planning on working one more year till I was seventy and then retiring with lots of ideas as to what I was going to do at that point. Instead, two months after my sixty-ninth birthday, I was forced to go on short term disability because of severe shortness of breath, and at the end of the disability, in August 2021, I was forced to retire. None of that was in my plan for my future; I could no longer work and most plans for my retirement went out the window. Don't permit yourself to believe that tomorrow is a certainty, that your life then will be just like today. That is a very foolish mindset.

The thought of a fixed day and time for death may not cause you consternation. It may instead be a comfort. How can that be, you wonder? Because if you are a true child of God, it assures you that the covenant Lord whom you serve *is* in control. Nothing happens by accident. My terminal diagnosis was under God's direction and was intended for my good. I firmly believe that. It was an act of discipline, as discussed in Hebrews 12, for my correction, to increase my obedience and lessen my sin. There was no need for me to be frightened or worried. And even now, with my life extended beyond what I or the medical community expected (I guess I must need extra correction or am a slow learner!), I am still comforted by the psalmist's words: "...in your book were all written the days you ordained, when as yet there was not one of them."

Why Hope in Mortal Man?

September 30, 2022

> Do not trust in princes, in mortal man, in whom there is no salvation. His spirit departs, he returns to the earth; in that very day his thoughts perish. How blessed is he whose help is the God of Jacob, whose hope is in the LORD his God, who made heaven and earth, the sea and all that is in them; who keeps faith forever.
>
> Psalm 146:3–6

WHAT A WONDERFUL PSALM of hope. You should get a Bible and read it in its entirety. It's only ten verses long, but full of comfort and joy, though its warning in the verses above are not so. Here the psalmist cautions about viewing people, especially the powerful, and particularly those in government, as our hope. I believe that's as much a temptation in our era as it was in the psalmist's. Being overly concerned about politics invites a constant state of flux between fear and anger, and a hope in a "good prince." But the psalmist here steers us away from such a focus. And for one simple reason: our mortality. People die, so there can be no hope of true salvation, or even great help in this age from them. Even those we love as family and friends will leave us sooner or later, whether parents, spouse, brothers and sisters, or close friends. As we grow older, we feel more and more the weight of those deaths.

But the psalmist moves on to point us to One who will never leave us, not even because of death, and offers us the greatest hope, the greatest dependability of our lives: the Lord our God. Somehow I think we see God as an old man because he is indeed the ancient of days, from everlasting, and has lived many millennia and more. And yet, another way to see him is to view him as eternally young, for he never ages, as we do. He never grows old. When we are young, we go from strength to strength, but in our later years we begin a process that's hard to accept, of going from weakness to weakness. But God never grows weak, much less tired, and so as the psalmist lists in the verses I didn't quote above what ways God can be counted on—unlike the government—to help us in our weakness: when we are oppressed (which probably comes from the government or the rich), hungry, imprisoned (again, likely by the government), blind, strangers, orphaned, or widowed. God is our sure hope in this life and in the one to come. The government, says the psalmist, is our hope in neither.

THE BLEAKNESS OF HELL

October 13, 2022

> The people who walk in darkness will see a great light; those who live in a dark land, the light will shine on them.
>
> Isaiah 9:2

PROBABLY MY FAVORITE BOOK by C.S. Lewis is *The Great Divorce*. I've read it a number of times and never fail to enjoy it. I won't spoil the surprise if you haven't read it (and you really should; it's very short), but I was reminded of it the other morning as I stepped out the front door around 6:15am and began walking down our front sidewalk to collect the newspaper. We're very early risers (often I'm up between 4 and 4:30am; between 5:00am and 6:00am is my sleeping in!). But the paper isn't delivered till somewhere around 6:00am. So, at that time it was still pitch black outside, and the main light on our sidewalk and driveway was from the pole lamp beside them, which I had left on (I used to tell my patients in my PT days—"Never walk in the dark when you're older, inside your home or outside. Your vision gets bad as you age, and your balance gets worse." I can't count the number of people I saw who were injured because they had violated that simple rule). There weren't many other lights on yet, and I was struck by how dark it was outside of my little circle of light.

We've been thinking about getting a whole house generator (they are very expensive now). I'm not sure because of my illness and the side effects of my treatment drugs how well my body would respond to, say, three days without power. Our lives pretty much depend on electricity to our home. We'd have water and almost nothing else. It's stressful going without power for an extended time, and I'm concerned how my body would handle it, especially as I'm on a daily dose of prednisone (which prevents my adrenal glands from producing the main hormone cortisol, which looks like prednisone to my brain). My body needs this to cope with stress or even good stimulation such as having a dinner party.

Anyway, I'm walking down the sidewalk and thinking about Lewis's book and home generators and how if we got one, we'd probably be the only little circle of light in the neighborhood, and how that was similar to the beginning of his book. It struck me that that scenario is really a good picture of our lives in this world. God has given us light and comfort even in this world, and yet so many of our neighbors live in darkness now, and possibly will for the rest of eternity, experiencing a dim and sad existence. We should never forget their current situation or their future fate, and pray regularly for those we know. Be a lamp and salt, sharing the joy and light of that One who came to be the great Light, and will return one day to be the sunrise of the world, dispelling all that darkness we now see around us.

THE CURE FOR ANXIETY
OCTOBER 20, 2022

> Search me, O God, and know my heart; try me and know my anxious thoughts; and see if there be any hurtful way in me, and lead me in the everlasting way.
>
> Psalm 139:23–24

THIS PSALM REPEATEDLY SPEAKS of God's omniscience. Asking God to search us is a brave and bold request. The Father (and the Son and the Spirit) always knows our innermost thoughts and desires. So, why ask? I believe the psalmist asks for such scrutiny to communicate his sincerity and openness to God's judgment of him. He is letting his heavenly Father know that he has nothing to hide, but is coming before his King in sincerity and humility.

The psalmist then points us to a problem we cannot solve—one that even today as modern disciples we need help with: worry. There seems to me to be no one on earth more afraid than our culture, our entire country. I recently saw that there are calls to screen everyone for anxiety when they come for medical problems. But how will the anxiety disclosed by the screening be helped? Most likely by medication. Yet our worries may have actual roots, serious problems that need attention; or they may be an overreaction to the stresses and strains of everyday life. How can any MD or any medical professional know which it is, or fix either one? The MD is not omnipotent and is unable to change our circumstances, which we may have good reason to worry about. Nor can any medical professional calm our hearts, reassuring us that the problem is only minor. They could do so only briefly, at most.

Further, the psalmist asks for God's gaze to find any hurtful or wicked way in him. Again, I believe that though the psalmist may be asking for help, it is more likely that he is assuring God of his confidence before him, his obedience in following God's laws, having no fear of the Lord's omniscience.

But where does this humble second request for scrutiny lead? To a desire for the Lord's help to increase his obedience. Note the psalmist's phrase for characterizing the path of keeping God's laws. He requests that God lead him "in the everlasting way." I don't believe he is making out his innocence or obedience to be the cause of finding an everlasting path. Rather, as elsewhere in the OT, and obviously in the New Testament as well, everlasting life and the path that leads to it is at the end of the road of submission and obedience to God's law. The gospel is not just a proclamation to believe. Rather, Jesus defined the gospel differently in Mark 1:15: "The time is fulfilled, and the kingdom of God is at hand; repent and believe in the gospel." Our hope for heaven lies along a way ending in everlasting life, and that path is characterized by taking up our cross daily and following Jesus in his way. Eternal life, then, comes at a great cost, but it is worth every bit of that cost, isn't it? Like the merchant in the parable of the great pearl, we must sell everything to make that purchase, and it is cheap even at that price. You are following Christ; you are walking in an everlasting path, a path of hardship and discipline, but ending in eternal peace and joy.

COME, SWEET DEATH

October 28, 2022

Come, sweet death, come, blessed rest! Come lead me to peace for I am weary of the world, O come! I wait for you, come soon and lead me, close my eyes. Come, blessed rest!

Come, sweet death, come blessed rest! It is better in heaven, for there is all pleasure greater, therefore I am at all times prepared to say "Farewell." I close my eyes. Come, blessed rest!

Come, sweet death, come blessed rest! O world, you torture chamber, oh! Stay with your lamentations in this world of sorrow, it is heaven that I desire, death shall bring me there. Come, blessed rest!

Come, sweet death, come blessed rest! Oh, that I were but already there among the hosts of angels, out of this black world into the blue, starry firmament, up to heaven. O blessed rest!

Come, sweet death, come blessed rest! I will now see

> Jesus and stand among the angels. It is henceforth completed, so, world, good night, my eyes are already closed. Come, blessed rest.
>
> Anonymous, set to music by J.S. Bach

J.S. Bach is one of my favorite composers for a number of reasons. I have the complete works of Bach that my wife kindly purchased for me (142 CDs! I'm slowly working my way through them). I feel as if I may detract from this poem by commenting on it (unlike Bach, whose music enhances it).

Nonetheless, I would like to make a few brief remarks. I had never heard this song or lyrics before last week. They are so wonderful to me for two simple reasons, one negative and one positive. The negative is his view of the brokenness of this world: "I am weary of the world"; "O world, you torture chamber, oh! Stay with your lamentations in this world of sorrow..."; "...out of this black world..." There's more than brokenness to this world, but as we prepare to die, it is appropriate to meditate on the curse from God on this age, with our death being the greatest curse of all!

The positive reason he relates is such a refreshment to me as I prepare to die: "...lead me to peace..."; "...it is better in heaven, for there is all pleasure greater..."; "...it is heaven I desire..."; "Oh, that I were already there among the hosts of angels...into the blue, starry firmament..."; "...I will now see Jesus stand among the angels..." Death can provide a release, a help to us.

It is for these two reasons that this unknown poet can say (and I say with him) repeatedly: "Come, sweet death, come blessed rest!"

Medical Update

As I have mentioned before, the oncologist stopped one of the two medications I was on back in March (Opdivo, an immunotherapy drug), and for the last two status CT scans, my cancer was found to be growing again. So, he stopped also the other chemo drug (Xeloda, an oral med), and started me on two new medications. These are the second string, I mean, second tier medications, both IV infusions using my porta cath. The first is Taxol, an old school med first used in the 1970s. It's a hammer that hits fast growing nails, I mean, cells. The second is a monoclonal antibody, targeting more specifically the type of cancer I have (GE cancer, i.e., gastroesophageal cancer). This drug is call Ramucirumab (the *ab* at the end tells you it's an antibody).

To try to prevent a reaction while receiving the drug, I have to take a steroid twelve hours before administration, and then six hours before. Of course, for me, if I receive the drugs at 9:30am, it means I'm being woken up twice as I go to bed quite early. It also means I'm pretty juiced the next day as steroids tend to have that effect.

There are several side effects they're watching for: one is significant blood pressure changes. Ramucirumab tends to raise your blood pressure; Taxol tends to lower it. The other side effect is an increase in my neuropathy (numbness and tingling, sometimes pain, in my hands and feet). So far, the neuropathy increased on day one, but returned to its normal state after that (mild neuropathy). The blood pressure has been odd. My blood pressure has been normal my whole life: 120/80. During my illness, it's been drifting upwards and has been around 150/80 in the past several months. Now, every morning it's 140/80, and every evening 120/80, for the past six days. The one exception was Monday evening when it dropped to 100/80, and I was very dizzy and unsteady—no fall, but I had to sit not long after I stood up. Then I drank a large glass of water, and it went up to 108/78, and I felt a little better. That's why I used to tell people on blood pressure medication to wait a second when they first stand to be sure their blood pressure wasn't going to bottom out (a hypotensive episode) and cause them to pass out. I also encouraged people to take their blood pressure *before* they took their blood pressure medication to be sure their blood pressure wasn't already normal or even low before they took their med. I had numerous patients referred to me because of that problem, with the result that they fall and hit their heads, sometimes acquiring a subdural hematoma (SDH), i.e., a brain bleed. Don't be one of those people, as the saying goes.

I go in today for my second treatment. The pattern is 2-1-2-0. In other words, I take the two drugs on one Friday, then one drug (Taxol) the next Friday, then the two drugs again the following Friday, then am off a week with no treatment. So, today being the second treatment session, I take only the Taxol. Last time, when I started chemotherapy (in April of 2021), the first session was a breeze; the second one and the ones following, not so much. So, I'll put a note in my entry next week as I see how this session goes.

THE WHOLE COMMUNITY

October 31, 2022

> Therefore, since we have so great a cloud of witnesses surrounding us, let us also lay aside every encumbrance and the sin which so easily entangles us, and let us run with endurance the race that is set before us.
>
> Hebrews 12:1

I write this entry on Monday, October 31, the day of Halloween, a day in some circles celebrated as the day of the dead. And I read an article in the *Wall Street Journal* over the weekend on cemeteries, expressing the idea that the community we live in comprises the living and the dead. Those thoughts prompted me to think about the verse above. It seems obvious to me that the writer of Hebrews had in mind a similar idea to the article's, namely that our faith community consists of more than just those alive in this world, but should also include those dead whose faith places them in what the writer calls "so great a cloud of witnesses…" And these dead, though they may be gone from this world, nonetheless surround us, and should be respected as ones who lived and finished their lives in this age with a great testimony of lives lived full of faith for us to emulate.

What comes next in Hebrews 12 is an exhortation to focus on Jesus, who, again, like the others of the cloud of witnesses, may be absent physically from this world, but nonetheless left us that example to emulate, one displaying endurance and perseverance. And next comes the reminder that the hardships suffered by the previous witnesses (now departed), including even Jesus, were used to discipline in order to teach obedience. It is suffering that will teach us to obey even as it taught Jesus: "Although he was a Son, he learned obedience from the things which he suffered" (Heb. 5:8).

The dead are not to be forgotten but revered for their faithfulness, their steadfastness. If you've ever heard stories from a child or grandchild about the faithfulness and love and example demonstrated by a parent or grandparent, you will see the kind of force for good that the dead can be. May you strive to leave that kind of legacy when you are gone!

Medical Update

I had my second treatment last Friday (today will be my third). It went okay, but I noticed over the weekend that I developed a sore throat and found a small ulcer on my right tonsil. It disappeared when I used my oncologist's mouth rinse (one quart of water with one teaspoon of salt and one teaspoon of baking soda—works amazingly well!). So, no major issue. The steroid juiced me Saturday so I washed my old Tacoma pickup truck, our CRV, and Odyssey van with the help of my wife and granddaughters. But I was very tired as I crashed when the steroid (dexamethasone) wore off for the next several days, though I was able to lift weights three times this week. My neuropathy hasn't kicked up a lot, so that's a blessing. But my blood pressure is still unpredictable. On Tuesday night, it was around 92/62, and I felt terrible, not just a little unsteady (though

I was); I felt really, really bad. Not sure why it has that effect, but it sure does in me. I went to bed early (okay, earlier than usual) that night and woke up feeling much better the next morning, though my blood pressure is now ranging from around 150 to 90 systolic (top number) to 60 to 90 diastolic (bottom number). Sheesh—new (chemo) drugs, new side effects. We'll see what today brings. But God will be faithful regardless.

THE GREATER TREASURE

November 3, 2022

Ill-gotten gains do not profit, but righteousness delivers from death.

Proverbs 10:2

Here we have another warning—one among many—about the problem of wealth. It's amazing with so many warnings about wealth in the Bible that we still yearn for it! Even when legally and morally obtained, the Scriptures warn often about the dangerous nature of money—or rather, the dangers that sinners face when handling it. The warning here is somewhat different from others about the trouble of wealth. Here we have a caution about obtaining wealth by wicked means, probably such as stealing, cheating, lying, murder, and so on. Though the possessors of such wealth may believe it to have been worth the means to gain the treasure, the writer of Proverbs states that (generally) wealth gained by those means eventually does not profit, even though it may in the immediate. Wicked men may certainly prosper, as the psalmist laments, but to echo the more important concern Jesus raises: "What will it profit a man if he gains the whole world but loses his soul?" In this passage, we see what may have been the germ of Jesus's remark.

This leads us to the second part of the verse: "but righteousness delivers from death." While the treasure gained wickedly is profitable literally, spiritually it is unprofitable. A life lived in submission and obedience to God's law, a life of righteousness, delivers a greater treasure, one that is truly and lastingly profitable: a deliverance from death. The message of the Scriptures as a whole is that we can no more escape death on our own than we can escape our sins and guilt. Only Jesus's death and resurrection, his righteousness, can deliver us. Nonetheless, as I've mentioned before, the gospel of the kingdom in the New Testament isn't simply to believe. In fact, in Luke 24:46–47, when the risen Jesus commissions his disciples for their mission, he says: "...Thus, it is written, that the Christ would suffer and rise again from the dead on the third day, and that repentance for forgiveness of sins would be proclaimed in his name to all the nations..." Here Jesus describes the gospel in a way more in line with this verse in Proverbs and less like the "easy believism" we often hear today. Righteousness of obedience is an absolutely necessary result of our faith. Faith without works is a corpse, as I've said before (from James 2). Professed faith without works may be described in other ways: hypocrisy, or self-delusion. Walk in humble obedience that you may receive the greater treasure: deliverance from eternal death.

OUR REFUGE

November 16, 2022

The wicked is thrust down by his wrongdoing, but
the righteous has a refuge when he dies.

Proverbs 14:32

WE FIND A FAMILIAR theme here, the contrast between the wicked and the righteous. The writer says the wicked is overthrown by his wrongdoing. At times, it seems the wicked do flourish as the psalms remind us. The wicked burns bright, but not long, like dry grass that flairs when lit, but leaves only ashes behind when it's gone. They have no hope when they die and so might naturally despair at the approach of death. In fact, they may even hasten its arrival if they see how pointless and hopeless their plight truly is.

But for those of us who follow the true King and submit ourselves to him, this passage offers us great hope. For the writer tells us the terminus of both the wicked and righteous. The wicked ends in defeat, in the ashes of their deeds, but the righteous ends with a place of sanctuary, a place of protection. What joy the righteous person may possess as his death approaches. For the Lord provides shelter to us in the time of our greatest need.

When death is near us, and we are tempted to be afraid, we can rely on our great Savior to draw nearer than death is able. Our Lord has faced death and walked out of his tomb. He promises that we will do likewise. He is our refuge in the time of our final trial. He will provide the safety that the writer speaks of. Unlike the defeat of the wicked, which I have likened to ashes, good only for the ash heap and nothing else ever again, the righteous' hope is eternal and abiding. We will live forevermore and flourish in the house of our Lord where he has gone to make ready our rooms of refuge, our place of safety.

I just finished a book called *The Emperor of All Maladies*, by Siddhartha Mukherjee, an oncologist in Ivy League territory. It's a history of cancer's diagnosis and treatments. The author opens the book with an arresting note on the cancer statistics in America: one in three women and one in two men will acquire cancer in their lifetime. The book was written in 2010. But I checked the National Cancer Institute website for 2022, and the statistics are unchanged. So, when you face that terminal diagnosis, which could very well be, as mine was, from cancer, fight the pressure to be afraid. *Rejoice*, for you of all people have a refuge even in death!

EMILY DICKINSON AND FLIES BUZZING

December 3, 2022

I heard a Fly buzz - when I died -
The Stillness in the Room
Was like the Stillness in the Air -
Between the Heaves of Storm -

The Eyes around - had wrung them dry -
And Breaths were gathering firm
For that last Onset - when the King
Be witnessed - in the Room -

I willed my Keepsakes - Signed away
What portion of me be
Assignable - and then it was
There interposed a Fly -

> With Blue - uncertain - stumbling Buzz -
> Between the light - and me -
> And then the Windows failed - and then
> I could not see to see -
>
> Emily Dickinson

I THOUGHT I'D HAVE some fun this time by taking an entry to look at this poem by Emily Dickinson. Though you may very well disagree, I think her poem is an illustration of a point I've mentioned repeatedly: the uncertainty of death, especially the lack of control and authority we have over our own death. For the first part of the poem, we see the calm, the solemnity of the dying speaker: the stillness, the silent weeping, the bated breath awaiting the final end. The dying person has arranged her affairs and is preparing to depart in peace when there comes the sound of a stumbling, bumbling flight of a fly. The controlled, restrained atmosphere is interrupted in surprising manner by this ordinary fly. The buzz of the fly interposes between the dying person and the window, interrupting the light coming in from outdoors. And, now at the end, the fly interjects this discord, this disharmony as the speaker's eyes are failing her even as the window's light is doing.

To me it's a picture of the inability we all have to control the circumstances of our death. As I've mentioned many times before, we seem to think that we will be able to predict and manage our dying, that we will orchestrate a stillness, a calm in the process of dying that we control. But we find instead that a fly buzzes in the middle of our plan of death—a buzzing that, if not mocking, then at least announcing the uncertainty, the slipperiness of our grasp of how and when and where we will die, probably none of which will be what we expected or planned.

Only the true King has that power. Though the dying speaker

seems to place the power of the uncertain, stumbling fly over even the power of the king, we as believers know that our King will be witnessed in his power, and all will end not in the unexpectedness of the intrusion of a bumbling fly, but with the certainty of how he intended it to end.

WHICH IS BETTER?

NOVEMBER 17, 2022

> A good name is better than a good ointment, and the day of [one's] death is better than the day of one's birth. It is better to go to a house of mourning than to go to a house of feasting, because that is the end of every man, and the living takes [it] to heart. Sorrow is better than laughter, for when a face is sad a heart may be happy. The mind of the wise is in the house of mourning, while the mind of fools is in the house of pleasure.
>
> Ecclesiastes 7:1–4

WE FACE HERE A saying that is hard to accept: the day of our death is better than the day of our birth. How can that be? Isn't it better to begin life than to end it? As I've mentioned before, death is seen from several perspectives in the Bible. On the one hand, death is the ultimate curse on our race, the most terrible result of our fall with Adam. It is a horrible and unnatural event; there was no death before Adam's sin, only following and as a punishment for that rebellion. Further, for those of us left behind when someone we love dies, it causes great pain and sorrow. On the other hand, death is seen positively in other places in the Scriptures (as we have seen previously). It is indeed not the end, but for a Christian a new beginning, a wonderful hope that we can hold onto when we are tempted to despair of life in this vale of tears. It's the door to another, better life than the one we were born into here.

It is no wonder, then, that the writer encourages us to contemplate the day of our death, to meditate on that end when we enter a house of mourning. As he says in verse 2: "It is better to go to the house of mourning than to go to the house of feasting, for this is the end of all mankind, and the living will lay it to heart." There is no escape from death. It is the final event that we all must face. It is better to be prepared for that end than assume that our lives will go on as they may falsely appear to do, as in a house of feasting, as if all our days will be only enjoyable and that our demise will never arrive, or be many years hence.

A meditation on death affords us a sober and clear view of who we are and where we will finally be. But such a view of death is not one of gloom and doom, of sorrow and sadness, for us who depart. It gives us a view of a feast that we are traveling to that will never end, the one that will be forever full of joy and gladness. Get ready, then. Don't be surprised at your terminal diagnosis. It is your ticket to your final destiny and God's final gift to you in this age!

Authority Over Our Day

November 22, 2022

> No man has authority to restrain the wind with the wind, or authority over the day of death; and there is no discharge in the time of war, and evil will not deliver those who practice it.
>
> Ecclesiastes 8:8

WE HEAR NOW ANOTHER familiar message—the limitation of human capabilities. Man may be the crown of creation, but his abilities are nonetheless very restricted. There are four limits listed here: the last two refer to our capability strictly speaking. The first of those two ("...there is no discharge in the time of war...") speaks of the inevitability of the evil that is war. When war surrounds us, there is no wishing we could escape. We cannot (as I write, the war in Ukraine rages on); war is too powerful a force to just walk away. Likewise, the second one ("...evil will not deliver those who practice it...") addresses the limitations of the force of evil. Unlike God's arm, the arm of evil is short; it cannot protect us, no matter how much we give ourselves to serve it or how afraid we are of it. Evil will not save us, for instance, from the force of war even if it was the cause, nor will it save us from God's just judgment. That day will come to finish the evil all around us that seems so powerful.

The first two limitations on our human abilities focus more on our authority. The first one mentioned is more a trope than a literal lack of authority. It reminded me of God's response to Job: what control of creation do you have? Here it's phrased more in terms of a right: what right have we to stop the wind with wind? God created all things, so he has not only the power but the authority to control any and all of creation. To create is to have authority over something or someone. This is one reason why parents have authority over their children. What authority we have over creation, however, is delegated, a gift that God has imparted to us as we did not make creation. We stand not as regents, but as vicegerents in this created order.

This brings us to a fact we have heard before: that the day of our death is not ours to choose. Here the writer states we have no authority over it—not just no power, but no authority, a different sort of wrinkle. We find now, much as with the first limitation, that we live and die in a created order not under our authority or our control. God created us and so has both the power and the authority over our lives, but also over our deaths. Remember that when your terminal diagnosis comes, it is no accident when it arrives from the One who is not only omnipotent, and so can control all things, but who is also the King of Kings, and the Lord of Lords, and so has the authority to give and to take life. It is in *his* hand to decide when and how our day of death is to come. He has both the ability and the right. Blessed be the name of the Lord!

THE REMOVAL OF ALL DEATH

JANUARY 11, 2023

> The LORD of hosts will prepare a lavish banquet for all peoples on this mountain; a banquet of aged wine, choice pieces with marrow, [and] refined, aged wine. And on this mountain he will swallow up the covering which is over all peoples, even the veil which is stretched over all nations. He will swallow up death for all time, and the Lord GOD will wipe tears away from all faces, and he will remove the reproach of his people from all the earth; for the LORD has spoken.
>
> Isaiah 25:6–8

Though I tend to personalize and individualize passages with promises and pronouncements on death—as many of us do—and find it worthwhile to meditate on our individual approach to the event of death, it still behooves us to remember also our great future hope of the fate of death in general. Here in this passage we are given a vision of what that fate will be. First, what God intends to happen is a celebration, a feast of rejoicing and gladness, of eating the best food and drinking the best wine. That is only the first positive. The second is a wiping away tears of sorrow from all peoples, not just for the ethnic believing Israelites, but also the Gentile believers from all countries, indicating the great comfort that God will bring to us all. Further, he will remove our reproach—our rejection and accusations and insults—from those outside the covenant community. We may have an individual celebration of our personal deliverance, but there will also be a global demonstration of joy that we will share throughout the earth (and history) in the work of God for us. We will rejoice not just privately, for our individual deliverance, but as with worship, we will celebrate as a part of God's people.

But, what is this work that causes such universal acclamation for the kindness and comfort of God? A swallowing of two things the passage tells us: first the swallowing of a *covering*. It isn't entirely clear to me what that might be. Perhaps a curse, the reproach that the writer is going to mention next. Or perhaps the ignorance that the apostle Paul refers to (in 2 Cor. 3), replaced by the true understanding found ultimately in Christ. A third possibility is that the covering and the second item to be swallowed are one and the same.

In any case, let's continue on to the second item, which seems to be much clearer in its referent: that which has been the enemy, the bête noir of the human race for the vast majority of its existence, that which causes so much worry and consternation, so much pain and sorrow (including tears to be wiped away), is the terrible item of *death*. And God promises that he will swallow it not for just a time, but for *all* time. Never again will any of the believing human race ever have to fear the affliction of death. It will be completely eliminated—not just stopped, but removed, made to disappear for all time. No wonder there is a great banquet to celebrate, to rejoice! How can we be told of such an occurrence and not want to stop whatever we're doing and attend such a feast for such a reason! Our race's greatest enemy will have been eliminated. And we are assured of this hope because the Lord has spoken it, and we in turn will speak great gladness and joy with him in that wonderful feast!

THE EARTH GIVES BIRTH

January 17, 2023

> The dead will not live, the departed spirits will not rise; therefore you have punished and destroyed them, and you have wiped out all remembrance of them.... Your dead will live; their corpses will rise. You who lie in the dust, awake and shout for joy, for your dew [is as] the dew of the dawn, and the earth will give birth to the departed spirits.
>
> Isaiah 26:14, 19

Here we see once again a contrast we have seen often before: the difference between the wicked and the righteous. And the difference is stated in terms of the fate of the dead. When death occurs, the wicked will find that it is the end of hope: "The dead will not live; the departed spirits will not rise..." When the wicked die, their lives—though not their existence—is at an end. They will not rise to a better existence, nor will they acquire a new and immortal life. In fact, Isaiah makes God's plan clear: to punish and destroy them, a destination we know (from elsewhere in Scripture) is unrelenting, eternal. It is no wonder, then, that the wicked fear when their death approaches. Who would not with such a vision pronounced upon them? God proclaimed their curse in the Garden of Eden: "You shall die." And here we see it repeated again by the mouth of the prophet receiving it from the mouth of God.

Yet how different is the fate of the righteous! First, we notice that these people are not designated "the dead," as the wicked were in verse 14. Foremost, they are claimed as "Your dead..." These dead belong to someone who cares about them. Here the Creator also speaks as the Redeemer, and his dead are not without hope; they "will live"! New and glorious life is given to them. Their corpses may decay for a time, but at the end, those bodies will rise again, with eternal health and strength. These dead are called from the grave to stand and shout for joy as they experience this new and unabated life. Their dew portends the beginning of the dawn, the initiation of a new and unending day. The earth now plays a new role in their existence. Far from just a grave holding them in, it becomes a womb giving birth to a new race of men and women with only joy and hope and life spread out before them. No wonder they are called to stand at this birth and shout for joy!

THE COVENANT WITH DEATH

January 21, 2023

> Because you have said, "We have made a covenant with death, and with Sheol we have made a pact. The overwhelming scourge will not reach us when it passes by, for we have made falsehood our refuge and we have concealed ourselves with deception." Your covenant with death will be canceled, and your pact with Sheol will not stand; when the overwhelming scourge passes through, then you become its trampling [place.] As often as it passes through, it will seize you; for morning after morning it will pass through, [anytime] during the day or night, and it will be sheer terror to understand what it means.
>
> Isaiah 28:15, 18–19

Here Isaiah makes an astounding statement: there are those who claim to have a covenant with death, to have an agreement of impunity from the effects of death. Those of this pact call themselves *deceivers*, liars in effect. From the fall, we see that lying, death, and Satan are bound together, for Satan is the father of lies, and to follow him is to court the sentence of death. Yet these liars claim to have broken these links so they will escape the condemnation of God with his pronouncement of death. Though Isaiah does not reveal the identity of these deceivers, it might remind us of remarks we have seen elsewhere by the most conspicuous and brash of the wicked: the rich, the influential, the powerful, who often pronounce the strength and invincibility to avoid God's judgment. They live as if the final verdict has been rendered in this age, and have or will escape it, refusing to see what even their own eyes tell them—that each generation lives and dies and then goes to prepare for that ultimate rendering of condemnation that will be irreversible.

Yet I fear we as believers often live as if we accept the statements of the wicked—that our possessions and positions are somehow a reflection of the final situation we will find at the end, that what we own and occupy (or a lack thereof) during this life will follow us into the age that is to come.

But if you are tempted to accept that deception, then listen to God's response to those who lie about their covenant for death. The so-called covenant with death for safety and exemption has been cancelled for the arrogant wicked. They have no more pact with Sheol. They are no more, if they ever were! There is no escape from death; the wicked will be trampled, crushed by its power and might. They should fear its reach and its certainty.

Yet in verse 16, the Lord God pronounces, "...I am laying in Zion a stone...a costly cornerstone for the foundation...he who believes in it will not be disturbed."

Believe, then, in Jesus, the cornerstone and foundation as named in the New Testament, and you will find that you need not fear the power of death ever again. He is our great hope and refuge!

WHAT ABIDES FOREVER

JANUARY 28, 2023

> A voice says, "Call out." Then he answered, "What shall I call out?" All flesh is grass, and all its loveliness is like the flower of the field. The grass withers, the flower fades, when the breath of the LORD blows upon it; surely the people are grass. The grass withers, the flower fades, but the word of our God stands forever.
>
> Isaiah 40:6–8

FLOWERS ARE A PARTICULAR love of my wife's. She never grows tired of their beauty, their colors, their shape, their smell. But the amount of work to reduce their impermanence is astonishing: the constant weeding, fertilizing, pruning (in blooming bushes), spraying to kill pests, and the seemingly never ending watering. Even with all that, it seems such a short time before they grow, bud, bloom, and then fade.

My focus is the lawn: I pay a lawn service to weed and feed for controlling dandelions, wild violets, as well as grubs, and careful mowing (when and how high). This doesn't even count wiregrass, a virtually indestructible weed. Then there are varmints to get rid of—moles, voles, and skunks. Even with all that effort, it still depends on the right temperature and watering for the grass to look healthy.

Isaiah picked a most apt picture of our lives. Humans can look lovely and healthy, but our lives, like the grass and the flowers, are much work to maintain and to protect. Just yesterday, at the oncologist's office, I was having my blood drawn. While doing so, I talked to the techs. Of course, they knew I had cancer and told me they had heard a story like mine many times. Patients would tell them that they had had no health issues and suddenly, out of nowhere, they were diagnosed with a terminal illness—cancer.

Isaiah in this passage reminds us of the insubstantial nature of our lives—a time perhaps of beauty like a flower or greenness and growth like grass, but that time of life is soon over. Our lives will end, and like the grass and flowers, the place where we lived will not remember us. One day the breath of the Lord will blow on you as it does on the grass and flower, and your time in this age will be ended. But Isaiah offers us hope, for he goes on to say that there is a permanence if we have eyes to see, ears to hear, and minds to understand. For God's *word* will never "be over"; it will never end. In the NT, we find that it is the breath of God that creates the Scriptures, which can never be broken, never abrogated, never wither or fade. Unlike our current lives, God has spoken his word to teach us that death does not have to be the end for us, that there can be life for us to look forward to when we fade and our loveliness in finished.

The surest word of all is Jesus, the Creator and Redeemer, the hope of eternity. He's the joy of all the fallen creation and our hope and joy too, when we bow the knee to him and serve him without being distracted by the heat, diseases, and pests that plague our lives while we live in this current age, this "yard" we now struggle in.

Medical Update

I thought I'd just give a quick update on my medical situation since my last treatment (last Wednesday, February 1). It's not been an easy transition to the three-drug routine. My neuropathy has gotten worse, though the oncology nurse practitioner said that none of the three drugs has neuropathy as a side effect, so it has to be the one drug that was dropped (Taxol). Maybe it will improve, I hope. It makes walking painful at times, and picking up things more difficult. And I continue to have "attacks" at times during which my neuropathy gets much worse, my eyes get sensitive to light, my brain is in a fog, and my legs feel really weak, making my balance less sure. The attack usually lasts thirty minutes or so, but the other symptoms I listed never really go away. My eyes are much more irritated this time as well. I don't have another treatment for a week (Friday, February 17), so maybe by then things will have calmed down. The Lord sustains in all these things, as he has in the past. And my wife and friends are always there for me. A great comfort indeed!

THE MIGHTY STUBBLE

February 6, 2023

> It is he who sits above the circle of the earth, and its inhabitants are like grasshoppers, who stretches out the heavens like a curtain and spreads them out like a tent to dwell in. He [it is] who reduces rulers to nothing, who makes the judges of the earth meaningless. Scarcely have they been planted, scarcely have they been sown, scarcely has their stock taken root in the earth, but he merely blows on them, and they wither, and the storm carries them away like stubble. "To whom then will you liken me that I would be [his] equal?" says the Holy One.
>
> Isaiah 40:22–25

An amazing passage that always fills me with wonder and awe, ever since I first became a Christian. Here Isaiah describes the transcendence of God: his might and sovereignty over all the earth. We saw in the last chapter that all people are small and insignificant beside him. And now Isaiah makes that point again but from another angle. We who are a part of the "hoi polloi" (the common people) were compared by Isaiah earlier to grass that withers and flowers that fade. Here our stature is pictured as a grasshopper, an insect that is small and frail next to the boot of a man. In fact, in Numbers 13:33, it is how the Israelites saw themselves in comparison to the inhabitants of the land of Canaan after Joshua and Caleb had spied out the land in preparation for invading it: "There also we saw the Nephilim (the sons of Anak are part of the Nephilim); and we became like grasshoppers in our own sight, and so we were in their sight."

And yet that is how Isaiah sees us when we are next to God: small and insignificant. Further, Isaiah says that the immensity of the sky when God is next to it is like a curtain we have in our homes, a sky whose enormity overwhelms us when we stare up at it.

But Isaiah also wants us to look at the force of God compared to that of our most powerful human leaders. Like us, the "hoi polloi" who live under their rule, they have only brief lives that are under God's complete control just as much as ours are. God merely has to blow on these mighty rulers and they, like us, will wither as the grass does and then will be carried away by God's breath.

It reminds me of using the leaf blower after I have trimmed the grass and the stems off some bushes. When I turn on the leaf blower even at a low setting, the blades of grass and small leaves from the trimmed bushes scatter and tumble away; they are light—they have no weight. That is how God sees our greatest and most powerful leaders, insignificant debris easily scattered by his breath. No wonder God then asks: who is indeed equal to such a great God, the God who has the life and death of all our mighty ones grasped securely in his hands?

WHY BE AFRAID?

FEBRUARY 9, 2023

> I, even I, am he who comforts you. Who are you that you are afraid of man who dies and of the son of man who is made like grass, that you have forgotten the LORD your Maker, who stretched out the heavens and laid the foundations of the earth, that you fear continually all day long because of the fury of the oppressor, as he makes ready to destroy? But where is the fury of the oppressor?
>
> Isaiah 51:12–13

ISAIAH CONTINUES IN HIS rebuke of those of us who lose sight of the big picture at times—and death is a key part of that rebuke. A friend of mine years ago introduced me to the phrase "The tyranny of the immediate," to help me see the difference between short term and long term thinking, with goals, plans, etc. We see something similar here in Isaiah. We may face someone who has the power to harm us, angry and powerful, and there is no escape that we can see. In Isaiah's case, the man is likely a king or a general capable of using political or military means to attack the Jewish nation. They physically saw no escape, no more powerful political or military leader to protect them. But this same principle applies to us: it could be a supervisor or manager at work, a large customer threatening to get us dismissed from their account, a professor, a coach, a government bureaucrat, a policeman, a neighbor, a family member, and so on. There's no end to those who threaten.

Yet God, through Isaiah, tells us we are seeing with "lying eyes." He enjoins us to look from a different perspective. We see all around us the work of our Creator, he who made the heavens that tower so far above us that we cannot see their end, and laid the foundations of the earth that support the mountains, plains, and vast oceans. Yet we are overwhelmed by the immediate tyrant, one who is only mortal, who will die just like us. He, like us, is only grass that will wither and be blown away (as we saw in the last chapter) by his Maker, just like us.

May death grant that you take heart facing whatever person immediately confronts you bringing trouble and fear. Fear no more, as you take refuge and remember the mighty and eternal Lord. He has the power to deliver you whenever he deems it right, as the One who cares for you.

Medical Update

I had my second infusion with two drugs last Friday (February 17), and it went fairly well, though I still felt somewhat shaky and weak afterwards. The treatment room nurse also started the pump with the 5FU drug, and I carried the pump home with me. Unfortunately, I would have to miss worship as the pump would end around the beginning of worship, and when it ends, it makes a lot of beeping noise that I wasn't sure how or even if you could shut off. So, come Sunday morning, around 7:30am, I was walking in our bedroom to go brush my teeth, and the pump began to beep. Very odd. It should have finished after 10:00am.

I looked at the LCD screen, and it reported something like,

"Occlusion in non-disposable tubing," whatever that meant. We checked all the tubing and the plastic clamps to see if anything was pinched—nothing. Finally, my wife (I think I've mentioned she used to be a surgical RN) told me to take my shirt off, and she noticed that under the tegaderm (the plastic patch covering the right angle IV needle where it entered the portacath), there was a big bubble. So then we were concerned the portacath may be occluded. My wife was leaving to teach the two-year-old Sunday School class, and so my daughter (who is also a surgical RN) came over to remove the pump with its needle. But, to our great surprise, the bubble wasn't 5-fluorouracil (5FU), but just air! We were very confused. The oncologist on call had told us to remove the pump and needle, and she scheduled a visit at the office for Monday (February 20).

On Monday, I dutifully went, and the treatment room RN checked my portacath, and it was fine (thank the Lord!). So, the conclusion was that the problem was likely in the pump itself, which was not an uncommon problem. I was fortunate to have received over 95% of the treatment drug, so all was good. Of course, the side effects continued this week with severe lethargy at times, somewhat painful skin breakdown, photo phobia (my eyes can get very sensitive to light), and all the usual suspects. The neuropathy is somewhat worse, but it waxes and wanes. My next treatment is on Wednesday, March 1 (so I can go to worship, I hope!).

COURAGE IN DYING

February 15, 2023

> Shadrach, Meshach, and Abed-nego replied to the king, "Nebuchadnezzar, we are not in need of an answer to give you concerning this matter. If it be [so], our God whom we serve is able to rescue us from the furnace of blazing fire; and he will rescue us from your hand, O king. But [even] if [he does] not, let it be known to you, O king, that we are not going to serve your gods nor worship the golden statue that you have set up."
>
> Daniel 3:16–18

WE ENCOUNTER HERE A passage that is part of a story that is familiar to many, even to those who have never read the Bible. My favorite part of the story when I was young was their adventure in the furnace and their miraculous deliverance. But now, as an old man, I find that their statement in verse 18 to Nebuchadnezzar interests me, as it displays a courage rarely encountered. Though threatened with death, they refused to compromise. It is obvious from their statement that they have received no assurance from a prophet, much less directly that God will deliver them from a terrible death (and being burned alive surely has to be one of the worst). And though they acknowledge that God has the power to deliver them, they go on to say, "But, even if he does not..."

These three men make it clear that for them, there are things worse than death. This is a statement and a belief that would be said and believed by few of us today. There are not many who would so order their priorities that avoiding death would not be their number one concern. Even among Christians, it is likely that many would fear death more than anything else, whether they admit it to themselves or not.

But I chose this passage to help us realize that unless we expire suddenly or are threatened with imminent destruction (which is not likely for most of us), nonetheless we will all one day hear the word that we are facing the end, finally confronting death. What will your reaction be? Will it be like mine was initially, of shock and initial fear? Will it be a cause of great distress and fear, or anger and bitterness? Or will you have the courage of these three men? Will you use it as an opportunity (as they did), to share your confidence that God can deliver you and give you more time (I call it a stay of execution)? But, with more or less time, will you testify to your confidence in him and continue to live out your life as one who is grateful for his mercy to you thus far? That moment will be an important one for you. It could be an occasion for worry and anxiety that might paralyze you and defeat you, or it could be the time when you can help your family and friends to prepare for your departure (and so with theirs also). No matter what your initial response, find your courage even as you face your death. May God prepare you even now.

Medical Update

I had my third infusion with the new drugs this past Wednesday (March 1). I have had it several times and so expected about the same effect this time: a little rubbery afterwards, but otherwise okay. Ha! I couldn't have been more wrong.

First, the good news: the oncologist was very pleased with my progress. He had planned to have me on this regimen for four sessions. But he has decided to increase it to six in light of my body's ability to handle the drugs. That assessment was something we were glad to hear.

Now the not so good experience: As I probably mentioned before, I receive a pretreatment cocktail of drugs to ward off the worst side effects of the chemo drugs. These pretreatment drugs included drugs to fight gastrointestinal issues and prevent allergic reactions (antihistamines and steroids). So, the treatment room RN asked me if I had received the Benadryl by syringe (they could give it by pill), and I said yes. Any side effects? No. Now, I've received this drug every time I've been for treatments for a long time with the same effect—nothing. This time when she pushed that drug into me, I experience what I guess crack cocaine users get, except mine was without any euphoria. Immediate effect. Ha!

I got a *whoosh!* in my brain, which then practically shut down, and everything got dampened and toned down for me. I couldn't think straight. She went back to the nursing station, and I was left with trying to figure out what had just happened. In a short while, I began to experience restless leg syndrome pretty severely, which is weird as I've only had that problem at night. It was driving me crazy, and when the nurse came back, I told her about it. She told me that was one of the side effects of the Benadryl and said that next time we might have to go the pill route. I didn't know what else to do to help, so I got up and, using the IV pole as an assistive device, wobbled to the bathroom. I found that just the walking made the symptoms almost disappear.

I was very lethargic, falling asleep a number of times and almost dropping my reading materials, which I always bring with me. At the end, I was able to make it to the first floor and wait for my wife to pick me up. But not only was I very tired, I still couldn't think clearly. That finally had mostly cleared up by the time I was ready to go to bed (which wasn't that long after getting home).

I have several thoughts about what may have happened. First, any medical facility may change drug suppliers, so maybe this drug came from another manufacturer. Second, maybe the nurse gave me a higher dose. Third, I've never had a nurse that I can remember just give the drug in a few seconds and leave. Instead of giving me a bolus (in this case, a single dose all at once), I think they usually inject some every minute or two and then inject some more to give the medicine time to be diluted. Fourth, maybe my body has just changed in its ability to handle the dose of Benadryl, and I will have to get the pills next time.

Of course, one of Brian's dictums is illustrated again. Remember the saying I taught patients all the time in home health: What does the referee tell two boxers entering the ring? "Defend yourself at all times." The medical establishment isn't your opponent or adversary, but they are human beings who are often rushed and have many things to attend to. You can help by watching, asking informed questions, and helping protect yourself against mistakes. Don't be aggressive or rude; but be politely unintimidated.

WHAT HAPPENS WHEN WE DIE?

FEBRUARY 19, 2023

And he was saying, "Jesus, remember me when You come in Your kingdom!" And he said to him, "Truly I say to you, today you shall be with me in Paradise."

Luke 23:42–43

But they were startled and frightened and thought that they were seeing a spirit.... "See my hands and my feet, that it is I myself; touch me and see, for a spirit does not have flesh and bones as you see that I have."... They gave him a piece of a broiled fish; and he took it and ate [it] before them.

Luke 24:37, 39, 42–43

WHAT IS THE NATURE of our life as we pass through the portal of death? We'll have more to say about heaven later, but here we gain a clearer picture than was possible in the OT.

We hear the words of the first man of the new age describing our new life. In the initial passage (Luke 23), Jesus comforts the thief who confesses Jesus as the Christ, as Savior, by telling him not that the man would just fall asleep, as would seem to happen from our perspective as ones who remain behind. That is a perspective on death in the New Testament that we have seen before. Rather, Jesus is looking at death from the *other* side, the side of our eternity. And from that perspective, the thief will be awake with Jesus in "Paradise."

How we can understand that when it seems we will not yet be residing in resurrected bodies, I don't really know, but the hope it should engender in us ought to be profound. For wherever and whatever paradise may be, it is a place of great joy, for there we will be with our Savior.

In the next passage, we gain another step towards understanding the nature of our life in the new age. For here Jesus reassures the disciples that they will not—as *he* is not—become disembodied spirits, transparent, translucent ghosts. Instead, we will be a re-embodied people, made of flesh and bone, able even to eat. Our life in eternity will be a full and rich one. As John writes: "Beloved, now we are children of God, and it has not appeared as yet what we will be. We know that when he appears, we will be like him, because we will see him just as he is" (1 John 3:2).

We shall be like *him*; that is our promise and our hope. We will be people as complete and incorporated as he was when he appeared to the disciples—human beings able to completely fulfill the creation mandate: to subdue the earth and learn, work, and explore the new creation for all eternity, making new music, architecture, books, crafts, food, all for our enjoyment in righteousness, peace, and joy with him and with those whom he loves. What better hope could there be?

DEATH COULD NOT HOLD HIM

February 24, 2023

> This [Man,] delivered over by the predetermined plan and foreknowledge of God, you nailed to a cross by the hands of godless men and put [him] to death. But God raised him up again, putting an end to the agony of death, since it was impossible for him to be held in its power.
>
> Acts 2:23–24

THIS IS A PASSAGE that we ought to read regularly. In a country that seems to be terrified of everything—an attitude of fear that many Christians seem to share—we have a passage that provides an antidote. For here Peter, preaching at Pentecost when the Holy Spirit descended, warns the unbelievers who are listening and comforts the believers who are present. Here he compares the power of God and the power of death.

If you are afraid of facing death, here's a message for you. Peter reminds the crowd of what they had done: nailing Jesus to a cross and putting him to death, thus ensuring their own inescapable guilt. But Peter reveals to them that even such a wicked act was not outside

God's control; it was a part of his secret plan. The greatest evil act in history was not only known to God beforehand, but planned by him! No lesser wickedness, even those acts against us, who are only his disciples, can be outside of that same plan.

"But" says Peter, making them pause for what follows. He goes on to inform those who had conspired to murder Jesus that this act of wickedness had been a forlorn hope in another way also. It never had a chance of succeeding because God was ready for the attack of death. God raised Jesus by his greater power, destroying the agony of death. My translation footnotes that the word "agony" is actually a translation of the word for "birth pains." As we saw in an earlier chapter, this means that the grave then became for Jesus not a final resting place, one of worms that eat and decay that consumes the corpse, but a *womb*—a place that would give birth to new life, in fact, a new kind of life, one immortal and invincible, never ending and never able to be defeated.

As Peter proclaims, death has now lost its power to hold him. It is "impossible" for it to do so. Jesus's new life is full of a power that creation has never known before. There is no more possibility of death for Jesus. Nor, we find out later, is there for us either. For if we are in him, we share in that death and also in that being raised from the dead, and in the end of the pain of death. A new day has come, the most important in history, because on that day a new life arrived. Death's power was broken. You can now rest easy when death comes for you. For in Jesus, you too will be raised to the same new life he has. When you hear that terminal verdict sure to be delivered to you one day, remember also the impossibility of death holding you. It is "impossible" because it is not the end. It is instead the birth into a new and better life, one far better than you have ever had here. So I ask you to remember that when you hear that diagnosis. Remember.

THE PRINCE OF LIFE

February 28, 2023

> But you disowned the Holy and Righteous One and asked for a murderer to be granted to you, but put to death the Prince of life, [the one] whom God raised from the dead, [a fact] to which we are witnesses.
>
> Acts 3:14–15

WE CONTINUE TO LOOK at Peter's sermons in the book of Acts as he points the finger at his countrymen, holding them responsible for the death of Jesus. Peter uses a number of titles for Jesus in this sermon: the Christ, (God's) servant, the Holy One, the Righteous One. The title that seems most important to Peter in his accusation (the one he uses in the passage I quote above) is in verse 15: "[you] put to death the Prince of Life…" Another possible translation for "Prince" is "Author," so we would read: "the Author of life." How can one who is in charge of, or the one who created life itself, be put to death? It would seem impossible. Yet Jesus, who brought about life in the universe at the beginning of creation and begins again with new life in the new creation, still died on a cross. Though he was God, Jesus was also a man and so subject to death, and could be executed by his own people, as Peter says.

But God the Father raised him from the dead. Death could not hold Jesus because of the power of the Spirit. This escape from death was not imaginary, fictional, or a wishful and hopeful dream. It was "a fact to which we are witnesses." Peter declares that just as a flesh and blood Jesus died and was put in the ground, so a flesh and blood Jesus woke up and became the Author of life yet again, this time of a new life of immortality, one no longer subject to death or decay.

Once more, we who are still subject to death and may have already received (or definitely will receive) a terminal diagnosis, now have the certainty, hope, and even joy of knowing that we have not just a great example or teacher, but the author of life who cannot be held by death. That hope has been attested to as *fact*, his new life proclaimed by his earliest and closest disciples. Those who found new courage to speak of this work of life had that courage *because of* this new life. They proclaim it to others who are also in great need of hope to escape their fear as well as their certainty of death.

Peter pronounces not just an accusation of guilt and condemnation, but offers the blessing of a springtime of never ending life. We must reflect on that message when we receive our terminal diagnosis, or whenever we have the opportunity to share this fact with those who live still under the shadow of death, a sad place of despair and darkness.

LORD OF THE DEAD AND THE LIVING

MARCH 3, 2023

> For not one of us lives for himself, and not one dies for himself; for if we live, we live for the Lord, or if we die, we die for the Lord; therefore whether we live or die, we are the Lord's. For to this end Christ died and lived again, that he might be Lord both of the dead and of the living.
>
> Romans 14:7–9

ONCE AGAIN WE HAVE a passage expounding on Christ's lordship over death. What a great hope that brings to us who are believers. Paul's formulation is very interesting: we don't live or die to ourselves—we are the Lord Jesus's in either case. Even if we die, we die *to* Jesus. Whatever our circumstances as Christians, living or dying, it is *for* Jesus. The surprise is that Paul uses that fact in a passage about doctrinal disputes.

In this passage, Paul examines the question of doubtful things, or as a friend of mine termed it "doubted things." There seems to be no question of who is right or wrong in these issues about celebrating days or eating meat. Paul's focus is not on who is right or wrong, though he makes it clear who he thinks is correct in these issues. The issue for Paul in this passage is who ultimately makes that determination. Who is the judge of the living and of the dead? He clarifies that by naming who is the Lord of both. Because Jesus is Lord of both, he is the final judge of both, and so he has the final say in these disputes. Outside of conflicts that involve heresy—which are for me doctrinal statements that would make the church declare someone a non-Christian—we are not to consider ourselves judges of others, especially on nonessentials. We may discuss and dispute, but not condemn and treat with contempt. Jesus is Lord of the living and of the dead, and so we in our capacity are not to judge now of the sincerity and the correctness of such differences with our brothers and sisters.

Our worries about orthodoxy—in eschatology for instance, and many other issues that Protestants split over—should be looked at with great care because Jesus is Lord of when we live and when we die. We should remember our place in the hierarchy of his church, and remember too that Jesus will perfectly adjudicate the rightness and wrongness of conflicting views. He is the Lord of your death, and so Paul says is Lord of your doctrine and of your brother's. You can rest in the confidence that he will set all these disagreements to rights. May we take comfort and peace in that knowledge as we contemplate our own death.

PAUL'S POIGNANT STATEMENT

March 3, 2023

> For if the dead are not raised, not even Christ has been raised; and if Christ has not been raised, your faith is worthless; you are still in your sins. Then those also who have fallen asleep in Christ have perished. If we have hoped in Christ in this life only, we are of all men most to be pitied. But now Christ has been raised from the dead, the first fruits of those who are asleep.
>
> 1 Corinthians 15:16–20

Here I find one of the most poignant statements of Paul. He makes the strongest contrast possible in this statement between Christians and non-Christians. If Christ was never raised, then what hope is there at all? If he wasn't raised, we have never been forgiven our sins. I must pause here to note that most Christians focus on the death of Christ, almost to the exclusion of the importance of the resurrection (with the exception of Easter, of course). But here Paul shows the centrality of Christ's resurrection from the dead. Anyone can be crucified and die (though Christ's death was unique as our sacrifice). But to come back from the dead is a great and unique act of power altogether. I'm not dismissing the significance of Christ's death as the Lamb of God. But I think we have vastly underrated Christ's resurrection in our faith (and statements of faith), and even in our evangelism. (Notice that Paul's evangelism includes only the resurrection, with no mention of Christ's death, and the Greeks were highly offended by the concept of a resurrection of the dead, vv. 30–32).

The centrality of his return from the dead cannot be overstated. Christ's resurrection was paid for, certified by, and approved by God our Father as a testament to Jesus's life and death. Otherwise, as Paul says in v. 18, "those also who have fallen asleep in Christ have perished." Our hope in Christ must be grounded not only in his death, but in his resurrection. Unless we have that as certainty, "we have hope in this life only, [and] we are of all people most to be pitied." What a dire statement! It's a state worse than hopelessness, but one of foolishness as well, since we will waste our lives as they are pervaded by an empty belief—a people to be pitied for being so completely duped by the Christian faith.

But as Christ has been raised, he is the first fruits of those of us who have died. Paul uses a phrase that he got from Jesus in the gospel narratives. "Fallen asleep" is a Christian phrase that describes how we see dead believers. Their death is not the end. They have only "fallen asleep" as viewed in this life. From the perspective of Christ's resurrection, we who die as believers will be a part of the harvest to life because our Savior was the first fruits of that same harvest.

And so, we who are believers and have received the verdict of a terminal diagnosis need not be afraid, for we know that Christ was raised from the dead. The tomb that held Jesus's body is empty. He came back to life as a living and breathing man, the start of a new life. When you receive that diagnosis of death, remember that Christ has been raised, so you will be too!

THE LAST ENEMY

April 3, 2023

> But each in his own order: Christ the first fruits, after that those who are Christ's at his coming, then [comes] the end, when he hands over the kingdom to the God and Father, when he has abolished all rule and all authority and power. For he must reign until he has put all his enemies under his feet. The last enemy that will be abolished is death.
>
> 1 Corinthians 15:23–26

WHAT A JOYFUL AND hopeful passage! Jesus our Lord was the first fruit of the harvest from the dead. He came to life as he was the beginning, the first portion from the harvest to life as he began it all. He was a portion from the harvest time as we see prefigured in the festival of harvest in the OT. We are the remaining harvest that Jesus has begun to bring in and that he will fully gather in when he returns. We are his portion that he will offer up to God as his sacrifice. For at that time, all will be completed. All will be finished, unlike now when the harvest has only begun. For now, there are enemies that are still alive and actively sowing weeds in that growing and incomplete harvest crop. Jesus's kingdom has begun: he was born and died, but with his resurrection, the harvest has commenced and the completion of that harvest is certain.

He will destroy all those enemies that we now face among and around us, and yet, unfortunately, in our country we often fail to acknowledge the devil, the demons, and the spiritual forces of darkness that ceaselessly battle against us. We must put on the full armor of God in this spiritual warfare. We must not lose heart or feel that the battle is hopeless. The Kingdom of God is here, the battle goes on, but we know that Jesus will one day crush all these enemies of ours beneath his—and our—feet.

The wonderful end of this passage is what Paul names is both Jesus's and our final enemy: death. We may receive the terminal diagnosis in this age, but we need not be afraid. That terminal diagnosis, that pronouncement of death, is not the final pronouncement. Jesus will return and reverse what appears to be your final defeat, just as the Holy Spirit did for Jesus when he died. But, as with Jesus in his return from the dead, you too will one day be raised, to be gathered to him in his great harvest of life. So, when you receive that diagnosis of death, recall that the harvest of life is on its way. Do not be full of fear or doubt. He *is* risen indeed! Rejoice then in hope!

TOMORROW WE DIE

April 1, 2023

If from human motives I fought with wild beasts at Ephesus, what does it profit me? If the dead are not raised, let us eat and drink, for tomorrow we die.
1 Corinthians 15:32

PAUL HERE DESCRIBES SOMETHING that is not done often in the Scriptures: the non-Christian advocacy of the idea that death is final, that there is nothing else beyond it. "Humanly speaking": I think for Paul this phrase indicates a viewpoint or statement not according to God's perspective, but our attempt to see things apart from him, involving the idea that death is natural and normal and always has been. The lifestyle that view may engender—and one that we see increasingly in our country—is hedonism, living for today as there may be no tomorrow. It produces a pessimism about life in general that belies the happiness it seems to promise. Why have children if there's no real hope for the future? We see so many young couples consciously avoid bearing children. They'd rather not burden themselves with responsibilities that have benefit only in the long run when there is no long run. And I see in our culture especially in those approaching or barely in early adulthood a lack of long term thinking. Why save money? Why not incur debt? In other words, why make sacrifices for later when there is likely no later?

This short term planning has led to a fixation on two means for immediate gratification. In Paul's day, it was partying, and for Western countries, it is similar: *sex* and *wealth*. The sex here is not in a marriage relationship, but only outside of that covenant bond, which would normally produce children. This sex of hooking up (or one-night stands, as they used to be called), has for some people developed into a sort of commitment to living together, sort of an imitation of marriage. But, worse, it has deteriorated into more and more perverse variants on sexuality. I cannot imagine a more short term lifestyle, incapable of producing progeny.

Earning money now is not a building of an inheritance for a future generation, but an opportunity to gratify immediate desires—"for tomorrow we die." Why save for a future when there's no hope of such a future? Not only is our individual death being predicted, but the supposed death by natural means of our entire world. Wealth in that scenario can be only short term. Now we are told that not only our individual lives are short term, but our planet is also short term. Get all you can as quickly as you can for death—the end of all—is coming soon. No wonder the children and young people of our culture are riddled with anxieties and fear and doubts. What a hopeless view; there is no certainty of a tomorrow. Why prepare for it? There is only darkness, decay, and death. That is what a Western non-Christian view of death produces: a pursuit of two things they hope will bring some modicum of pleasure before the end comes but offer nothing but false hope.

But in the midst of this despair, Paul announces another perspective—a true hope, which I will discuss more in the pages ahead.

The Hope of Handel

April 17, 2023

> Now I say this, brethren, that flesh and blood cannot inherit the kingdom of God; nor does the perishable inherit the imperishable. Behold, I tell you a mystery; we will not all sleep, but we will all be changed, in a moment, in the twinkling of an eye, at the last trumpet; for the trumpet will sound, and the dead will be raised imperishable, and we will be changed. For this perishable must put on the imperishable, and this mortal must put on immortality.
>
> 1 Corinthians 15:50–53

WE COME TO A passage made unforgettable by the music of Handel in "The Messiah": "We shall not all sleep, but we shall all be changed…" Paul does not use the word "mystery" very often, but here is one of those instances. The libretto used by Handel highlights this passage with good reason. Here is a wonderful description of our great hope, one that is mentioned by us too little in our modern faith.

What Paul focuses on is not this present life, this vale of tears.

To study our plight in this fallen world is necessary, but cannot offer the consolation we receive from Paul as he discusses our fate when Jesus returns. The mystery he tells us here is not just something previously unknown but now revealed, but also the manner of this revealing, the mechanism as it were. The kingdom of God has already been revealed and established with the first coming of Jesus, but we cannot fully take it on if we stay as we are now. We are only flesh and blood that will perish, corpses walking and waiting to complete our decay in the grave. We cannot possibly inherit and completely participate in a kingdom that will never end, never decline or decay, if we are not made fit to be part of such a kingdom.

That change is, of course, the mystery. How will such a change occur? There is no process, as it were, says Paul. It will not be like waiting for flowers to grow, bud, and bloom over time in the spring. Instead, the surprise we learn and the mystery that will one day occur, what will be "revealed," will be instantaneous, in the blink of an eye. Instead of being people who live a life of constant decay, or perhaps joining the multitude who have died and completed that cycle, we will be transformed into a race that is whole and who can never experience that decay, who will never perish again. That transformation will be immediate when Jesus returns a second time. No wonder Paul says elsewhere in this letter: "Our Lord, come!" (16:22)

And so Paul encourages us to see that this change is the culmination of all we hope for, a change so complete and dramatic that our joy will be full, no longer one of hoping and waiting, but one of completion, a stunning healing of all that is wrong with us now. This is a blessing that we should meditate on in this present life to keep from being overwhelmed or discouraged, or worse, despairing, as we see not only our own lives, but the life of the entire planet share in the ultimate decay: death. For Jesus will come back to transform us and give us life not just as he did Lazarus, as part of the old and still dying creation, but an eternal life, a life with no more growing old, no more suffering or pain, because our new bodies and our new planet will no longer be capable of corruption, no longer doomed to perish as they are now. As Paul says, our mortal bodies will put on immortality. Let that thought, that hope, give us joy as well as courage. It is no wonder that one of the fruits of the Spirit is joy!

DEATH IS SWALLOWED UP

April 29, 2023

> Death is swallowed up in victory. "O death, where is your victory? O death, where is your sting?" The sting of death is sin, and the power of sin is the law; but thanks be to God, who gives us the victory through our Lord Jesus Christ. Therefore, my beloved brethren, be steadfast, immovable, always abounding in the work of the Lord, knowing that your toil is not [in] vain in the Lord.
>
> 1 Corinthians 15:54–58

WE CONTINUE IN PAUL'S discussion of death in one of his most famous passages. Here he brings together several Old Testament (OT) passages and extrapolates to reach a somewhat surprising conclusion from the fact of death.

Paul writes from not only his experience of near-death events on a number of occasions as he traveled to bring the gospel to the Gentile world, but also writes from his deep knowledge of what God promises concerning death in the Old Testament (especially in Isaiah and Hosea). And expounding on that knowledge, he addresses Death; in fact, I would go so far as to say that he taunts Death: "O Death, where is your victory? O Death, where is your sting?" This address reminds me of King Ahab's reply (1 Kings 19:20) to an attacking king who insisted that there was no hope in resisting: "Tell him, 'Let not him who girds on his armor boast like him who takes it off.'" In other words, no king should boast of certain victory before the battle has been fought as if he had won, until he is removing his armor after victory.

Death fought the battle of the grave with Jesus—and lost. The tomb is empty. Jesus removed his armor—his grave clothes—and has now emerged as the first man of a whole new creation, victorious in his battle against Death.

We should look also at Paul's conclusion, his extrapolation from this miraculous victory. In v. 58 he begins with the word, "Therefore..." He is saying that in light of this victory through Jesus over death, not only as we might expect—i.e., don't fear death, look with hope and joy to the age that is to come—but instead, death's defeat and Christ's victory changes not only how we look at the future, but also how we live in the present: "Be steadfast, immovable." We should be a rock in a world that is confused, frightened, unsure, changing directions and convictions as the wind blows. We, on the other hand, know that the battle has been won, and so have courage for the present life.

Further, we should abound "...in the work of the Lord, knowing [that our] toil is not in vain in the Lord." Though we may often fear our work here might be in vain—family and friends unconvinced of their sin and of Christ's resurrection, our personal failure to change and grow in grace as we ought, wondering if the church of God will survive—Paul says, "Therefore..." Death has lost. There is no hope of victory for it, and so Paul mocks it. It seemed so sure in the BC era but in AD, history changed.

He concludes that instead of being defeated, Jesus has been raised, and so we have every expectation of success. Paul did not have perfect success on every missionary journey or in every sermon. Even then he was absolutely certain that because Jesus had won, the Spirit has the power to reverse every defeat that Death was sure of in the past: to soften any heart hardened by sin, open any eye blinded, unstop any ear deafened, for the gospel has now been freed, and it can never be stopped. We are, therefore, immovable, steadfast, and all our works in the Lord will be fruitful, never done in vain. Jesus the King has arrived and established his Kingdom, and we are part of that Kingdom, where there is no fear of death, only a joy of life with him and one another—to which we should say, "Hallelujah!"

Medical Update

I'm late getting this entry out today because of health issues. My blood pressure this morning dropped to 88/58, with a heart rate of 110 bpm, giving me a slightly out of body experience! At least I knew the feeling well enough to sit down immediately and then check my blood pressure (BP). I began drinking fluids to help raise the BP to 139/79, heart rate of 91 bpm, making me feel better, though still very weak. I have done only some small chores this morning, since I would have to sit down occasionally to have the strength to finish the jobs. I truly live day by day as I have no other choice; my health dictates everything I want to do. But God is merciful in giving me a wonderful wife, but one who also happens to be a surgical nurse and so is a great help in managing my health. And wonderful friends who are such a great help and encouragement.

My oncologist wants me to continue with the current chemo drug regimen, so I intend to try to do that, but the side effects are sometimes difficult to manage, so we'll have to see what the Lord enables me to do.

CARRYING ABOUT DEATH

May 6, 2023

> But we have this treasure in earthen vessels, so that the surpassing greatness of the power will be of God and not from ourselves; [we are] afflicted in every way, but not crushed; perplexed, but not despairing; persecuted, but not forsaken; struck down, but not destroyed; always carrying about in the body the dying of Jesus, so that the life of Jesus also may be manifested in our body. For we who live are constantly being delivered over to death for Jesus's sake, so that the life of Jesus also may be manifested in our mortal flesh. So death works in us, but life in you.
>
> 2 Corinthians 4:7–12

Here's one of those remarkable passages that gives us some glimpse into why, humanly speaking, Paul's ministry was so successful. For though he and the other apostles have suffered cruel and harsh circumstances, Paul is still able to rejoice and see the good that God has brought out of those sufferings. By suffering as they did, they showed that they carried about the dying of Jesus, his pain and affliction, and yet because of his death, they never suffered defeat, never despaired, never gave up but continued to work to complete both the sufferings of Jesus and to finish their commission, so that they may show the new resurrection life and power at work in them. And the Corinthians were a part of that manifestation of the new creation life.

It is difficult to remember here who Paul is writing to: a church that is rife with problems of the most serious and diverse kind. Problems involving warring factions, misunderstandings of marriage, the Lord's Supper, spiritual gifts, as well as the report of incest. How could Paul see the life of Jesus being displayed in these professing disciples with these terrible sins roiling the entire Corinthian congregation? Only because the apostles carried with them the dying of Jesus. Jesus suffered so greatly for the Corinthians' sins that Paul and the other apostles were willing to endure that same suffering and dying of their Savior to bring new life to the Corinthians. He knew that Jesus's dying would move the apostles to continue in that mission and could bring repentance to this congregation.

But he knew also these afflictions of death the apostles suffered could be suffered by any believer. So his examples of carrying both the death and life of Jesus, and even rejoicing in these afflictions, were not some abstract theological points and a practice limited to a few, but the reality of the power of God. This power was not only in Jesus and then Paul, but in the Corinthians as well. And, of course, it means it is in us also. We will suffer afflictions and troubles without end in this age because of the curse and afflictions of Satan. We, too, must carry about the dying of Jesus that the world may see our union with him. Yet as with Paul and the Corinthians, life still works in us. The dying of Jesus may cause us to suffer for his name and for the good of others, but it is also so that we may have an unshakable joy and hope in the new life we have received.

So, don't let the trials and worries that you suffer in this present evil age, not even when you receive that terminal diagnosis, move you to despair. You carry about not only the death, but also the power of the new life of Jesus. Rejoice in suffering as well as in hope!

DEATH HAS BEEN ABOLISHED

May 13, 2023

> Therefore do not be ashamed of the testimony of our Lord or of me his prisoner, but join with [me] in suffering for the gospel according to the power of God, who has saved us and called us with a holy calling, not according to our works, but according to his own purpose and grace which was granted us in Christ Jesus from all eternity, but now has been revealed by the appearing of our Savior Christ Jesus, who abolished death and brought life and immortality to light through the gospel.
>
> 2 Timothy 1:8–10

H ERE PAUL MAKES ANOTHER one of his surprising remarks. For us Protestants, what is most importantly revealed in the gospel is forgiveness of sins. Hands down, that is our greatest concern, and deservedly so. But Paul reminds us that this needed and wonderful gift should never become our sole conception of what's pronounced in the good news.

Paul is reminding us that the gospel needs to be broad enough to include not only a message of repentance and faith but also of a different need and gift: the total destruction of death and the start of a life that never ends. I think we tend to get distracted by all the immediate and personal problems and so focus on problem solving. We neglect the linked evils of decay and demise that are of monumental concern not only for us individually, but also for the rest of mankind, and even our planet.

Perhaps to our amazement, the gospel is not just a message to individuals as we so often think. It also is a message to the human race, to all people everywhere, that in Jesus's death all death has been abolished. Its power has been broken for us and for creation. There is no more need for any person to be afraid of death. We have seen before that the abolition of death, and its concomitant fear, was one of the reasons Jesus became a man (Heb. 2:14–15). This end of death is indeed a vital part of our good news. It is the announcement of the end of the bad news that every single person, indeed the entire human race for most of its history, has heard: *you are going to die*. Maybe not today or tomorrow, but one day. There is no bargaining or negotiation. It is fixed and certain, and you must face that momentous fact. Don't be distracted by all the noise you hear around you every day. Focus—you are going to die. Be ready.

The good news of the gospel includes the fact that Jesus came to deliver us from the certainty that the present end is the final end: from the delusion that it is a natural end. Rather, he shows us that it is an eternal death and punishment. But Jesus also offers hope to escape from eternal death and find the assurance of eternal life, of joyful immortality. If we will only meditate on that message daily, our lives will be much less stressful and, at times when we truly believe, much more hopeful. Our greatest problem and fear has ended. May we regularly thank God for that hope!

THE HOPE OF REVELATION

May 25, 2023

Then another angel, a third one, followed them, saying with a loud voice, "If anyone worships the beast and his image, and receives a mark on his forehead or on his hand, he also will drink of the wine of the wrath of God, which is mixed in full strength in the cup of his anger; and he will be tormented with fire and brimstone in the presence of the holy angels and in the presence of the Lamb. And the smoke of their torment goes up forever and ever; they have no rest day and night, those who worship the beast and his image, and whoever receives the mark of his name." Here is the perseverance of the saints who keep the commandments of God and their faith in Jesus. And I heard a voice from heaven, saying, "Write, 'Blessed are the dead who die in the Lord from now on!'" "Yes," says the Spirit, "so that they may rest from their labors, for their deeds follow with them."

Revelation 14:9–13

I HAVE OFTEN WRITTEN about Paul and his letters containing his pronouncements on death as seen from the perspective of his perception of the need of his readers and the answer that his gospel offers them. But here is another apostle, John, the author of a gospel and a number of letters including what is quoted above, though a different sort of letter, written to seven churches.

There are lots of controversial things in this letter of Revelation, but these two matters are not: first, in the end Jesus wins and Satan does not. The second is that everyone dies, is judged, and sent to their fate. This is an aspect of the gospel that is rarely discussed in the church today. We want unbelievers to hear about the mercy of God, most especially brought by Jesus at his first coming. But what we don't want unbelievers to hear about is that when he returns that he will bring final judgment including God's wrath, as we clearly see in this passage. So, here we learn about both: the love and anger of God.

The wrath of God is something we shy away from so let's start there. Here we learn that those who follow the enemy of God (Satan) are punished as the enemy is: they drink his cup—the cup of the wrath of God—and consequently will be tormented forever as he will be.

There was a time in the church in the Western world when all knew that the gospel offered choices that had eternal consequences, accepted or rejected in this age, which determined the fate of those who made them as revealed at the time of the final judgment. It is a fate that comes from drinking from the cup of the full anger of God, then suffering under that wrath for an eternity. The gospel isn't just preparing us for suffering in this age, but also for the final separation in the age to come. It is hard to read of these things, but they are a pending reality. So the death of the wicked is to be dreaded, for in it there is no more hope, no escape from the eternal punishment. That should be a powerful motivation for missions and for proclaiming the gospel whenever we can.

But what of the fate of believers in Jesus? As we read in vv. 12 and 13: for the saints who persevere, who keep God's commandments and their faith in Jesus, we find that their death is a blessing. For they (we) die in union with the Lord Jesus. The Spirit says in this passage that we receive not the torment of the wicked and unbelieving from our labors in this age, but true rest at last. We retire not just from the sweat of our brow and the thorns that prick—whether we work digging ditches or suffering in an air-conditioned office—but also from labors and suffering for the Kingdom's sake. Our rest will come from knowing that King Jesus has fully and completely established his reign and will produce a rest as eternal as the torments of the unbeliever.

The Spirit also says we shall rest as our deeds follow with us. Our labor and suffering for King Jesus are a necessary part of our faith and will be rewarded by him. For the believers' rest will be a life full of joy, peace, and fruitfulness, of gladness and harmony with others and even with creation, all under the Kingship of our Savior, Jesus. What a wonderful hope and vision by John of the age to come. Rejoice!

MARRIAGE AND DEATH
June 2, 2023

> The Form of solemnization of Matrimony: N[ame], Wilt thou have this Woman to be thy wedded wife, to live together after God's ordinance in the holy estate of Matrimony? Wilt thou love her, comfort her, honour, and keep her in sickness and in health; and forsaking all others, keep thee only unto her, so long as ye both shall live?
>
> I N[ame] take thee N[ame] to be my wedded Husband, to have and to hold from this day forward, for better for worse, for richer for poorer, in sickness and in health, to love and to cherish, till death us do part, according to God's holy ordinance; and thereto I give thee my troth."
>
> The Book of Common Prayer (1928 ed.)

You may not have been aware that your marriage began with a pledge involving death. I quoted from the Anglican Book of Common Prayer from their ceremony of marriage vows, and you may not have used those particular vows, but my guess is that it was probably something similar. Marriages are usually thought of as covenants, which in the Bible may be between God and people, or they may be between two (or more) people. Here we have an example of the latter: two people, man and woman, take covenant vows—to promise to complete certain responsibilities, no matter what the circumstance. (In fact, in my opinion, especially in this culture, we should have one Sunday worship service annually in which all the married couples should stand and renew these vows. In biblical terms, that would be a covenant renewal event, something that happens a number of times, especially in the Old Testament).

But those situations, those vows, are concluded when either partner dies. And Paul uses this situation (i.e., death ending our responsibilities under our vows) to explain our relationship to the Law (see Rom. 7:1–3).

So, those marriage vows are a very serious obligation. Nonetheless, the finality of death ends those obligations completely and absolutely, even freeing us to marry again and to take vows just as solemn and binding as they were with the first spouse. There is no shame or penalty for such an act.

My point is a simple one: death is absolute and final. Our obligations, responsibilities (and even opportunities) to anyone in this age, even to the one we cherish most, to whom we have promised exclusive loyalty ("forsaking all others...") is ended by death. Death is the bookend to our entire life. After that, there are no more pages to turn, no other dates in our journals of experiences to fill; there is only judgment coming to assess that life that has been written. Was it a life lived out in faith, bearing fruit consistent with that faith, or was it a life of disbelief as shown by the lack of fruit? (Again, I point you to Matthew 25 and Jesus's parable of the sheep and goats in which he acts as Judge to separate professing Christians, true believer vs. hypocritical believer, based not on their profession, but on the fruit of that profession.)

My conclusion is this: the bookend of your life approaches,

and God will then read the books of your life, those journals you have filled every year, and yet you don't know when he stops those journals and begins to open them for judgement. Jesus (and Paul) warns us to be ready for the close of our last book as we approach God's revelation of the book of life. In Scripture (Matt. 25 and elsewhere), we are given the test questions (i.e., the judgment day assessment). May God in his grace and mercy help us to be prepared for that Great Day!

THE END
June 5, 2023

Despite the ominous title, all I mean is that I am coming to the end of this project as a regular entry every Friday for several reasons. First, my medical entries normally occur every other week after my treatment with the three current drugs. I'll continue those updates as things change in my condition or as the treatment regimen occurs. My oncologist will do another status CT scan sometime in the next month.

Second, this project was originally begun at the urging of a number of friends to document what it is like to have a terminal diagnosis, as well as chemo treatments. My treatments are specific to the type of cancer I have, and so I report on the drugs and their side effects for my own cancer. There are many other cancer drugs because there are many other cancers as well as other treatments, such as radiation and surgery, which I am not undergoing. I've documented about all I can for my treatments and feel that I'm probably just repeating what I've already said about them, though they are still a daily battle for me.

Third, and probably most important: this project had to do a great deal with my thoughts on death. As God has granted me an extension of life of more than two years—way beyond what the medical establishment expected—I've had ample opportunity to give my thoughts on death, especially as I've read through the entire

Bible interacting with its comments and teachings on dying. I kept going through the Bible because I knew of no other place where the subject of death was discussed in detail. It bothers me that this topic is not addressed in the pulpits of evangelical Protestant circles. Most, if not all, of the focus there is on the cares and worries of this age. Now that I've received a terminal diagnosis and have treatments to extend my life as God grants, I've begun to see how important our view of death is for providing a boundary, a limit to our lives. And just as important, it leads us to reflect on what follows death: our judgment.

The New Testament speaks often on that topic, and yet it's rarely mentioned in sermons I've heard. This life is not only temporary, as death teaches us, but is also preparatory. The temporary nature of this life should teach us great humility, that we should hold all things loosely: wealth, possession, jobs, achievements, even relationships. But one thing that dying has taught me is that God cares more about people than anything else in our lives. As important as other matters may be, our relationships are what he is most interested in. And the first relationship he most cares about is our one with him. And, second, those with our brothers and sisters as formed and nurtured in his body, the church. Our relationship with Jesus isn't just a line directly to him. Jesus identifies so closely with his people that what we do is done both *to* as well as *for* him.

Which brings me back to the other concern: that this life is preparatory. One day we will be judged by Jesus for loving or failing to love God's people as we are governed by God's law in directing that love. We should always be mindful of that.

I know you're probably tired of hearing about Jesus's parable of the sheep and the goats in Matthew 25, but it seems to me to be such an applicable passage for our age. There he separates professing Christians from one another, not by doctrine or creeds, as important as those certainly are in guiding our lives and faith, but by the *fruit* of those professions of love for Jesus. He focuses on the sick, the widows and orphans, the poor, and believers who are incarcerated for their faith. But Jesus's questions seem to me to be directed primarily to the professing Christians about their care for other believers in those situations. Jesus identifies so tightly with his people that we cannot have a relationship with him if we're not caring for his body. There is a test, an evaluation, coming on Judgment Day (hence the name), and Jesus gives us the test questions. The problem is that we evangelicals just ignore the questions or preparing for them!

The difficulty to some degree is that we live in the richest country, possibly in the history of the world, and so may have let the social programs of our government crowd out our responsibilities to our people. As I've said elsewhere in this book, we tend to see what we're looking for. If we're not looking in our churches for the believers that Jesus tells us to see, we are likely to look right past them. We won't be aware of believers with chronic illnesses, of widows in our midst, much less those in nursing homes, or of single moms who are often functionally like widows. Or, we'll miss those who struggle financially or those who are or have become believers in jail. As we meditate more on death and judgment, I believe it will change the way we think of living, of the stewardship of our money, cars, homes, even the use of our time. Though my thoughts on death have been primarily to help us lose our fear of death, I hope the thoughts I have provided here will help us also to see how the need to face of death shifts our priorities. If we were to live forever in this age, it would lead to a very different view of life. But the temporary nature of our lives that will one day be judged should change our view of how we should live. I am trying to take these things to heart, even at this late stage in my life. May God grant you that same desire.

God is good, even in these trials, and never gives us more than we can bear. This discipline is unpleasant for me, but he means it for good, to humble me, and I hope that I might see an increase in the fruit of the Spirit. My wife Karen and I pray for that increase daily. May we always, in all circumstances, show grace to those around us, that we might strengthen and encourage one another in this age of trials and sorrows. Then we can give thanks to God for his patience and mercy, displaying that fruit of joy, which we have only because the Spirit of Jesus is always there with us.

TREATMENT CONTINUES

July–October 2023

July 27, 2023

I had my status CT scan on July 19. I read the report, and the two radiologists (one read the pelvis scan, the other thoracic) said that there no metastases and no change in number or size of cancer nodules in my lungs. So, a good report!

Yesterday (Wednesday, July 26) I received another chemo treatment, consisting of two drugs infused through my portacath. My appointment with the oncologist before the treatment and the chemo infusion lasted about four hours. My dear wife ferried me to and fro, as she usually does. The oncologist met with me before the treatment and told me several things.

First, he was surprised with the results of my status CT scan. He viewed it with his nurse practitioner, and I believe his exact words to her were: "Damn, he did it again!" (I've been going to that clinic for over two years and have never heard him curse). The fact that the cancer was not growing (and no metastases) and his surprise at that told me that he's amazed that I'm still around! Plus, he commented on my CBC (complete blood count), which includes hemoglobin, white cell level, and platelets (for clotting), which he said showed how resilient my bone marrow has been.

Second, another surprising comment (to me) was that he is stopping the chemo drug administered through my home pump over the course of two days. He explained that I've received a lot of chemo drugs over (more than) two years, and he thought I might regain some energy if he halted this drug. So, I'm to see if I detect any more energy over the next two treatment cycles (that's four weeks as I'm treated every other week). If I do sense increased energy, the he'll leave it off my treatment for the next three months (to the next status CT scan). Of course, he doesn't really know how my cancer will react to this change. Are the two drugs enough to hold the cancer in check, or like last time we stopped a drug, will it began to grow? But it grew at a very slow rate. Anyway, if I do not detect any increase in energy, then he will just restart the drug (it's the 5-FU drug).

The last minutes of my treatment time were bad, as if someone had thrown a switch, and all of a sudden I was very dizzy, and my stomach began to act up. I was like that all evening (oh, I forgot to include nauseated), but I figured it would be helped a lot by sleep. Unfortunately, on the night of treatment I lose about half a night's sleep because of all the steroids they give me before treatment to help reduce side effects. The good news is that this morning (Thursday), I was significantly better: my dizziness gone, neuropathy improved, but still some queasiness (I took some Zofran and .25ml of my sublingual cannabis). God once again has shown me great mercy. Now I'm praying for increased energy. We'll see what answer God may give to this request!

AUGUST 14, 2023

Well, we just got back from the beach (Saturday, August 12). It was quite surprising: for four days I basically had no "attacks" (as I've described before—side effects appearing that had disappeared, or side effects that intensify in severity). In fact, it's the best I've felt for days at a time in months. Obviously, it's a wonderful answer to many prayers for our trip, but it might also have been secondarily because I didn't take the 5-FU (the two-day home pump drug) during the last treatment session. Who knows? I have also noticed that several of my side effects have lessened or disappeared. I was able to drive about five and a half hours, not including several stops, though I got weary at the end. And I had very few problems coming back and felt good arriving home. While at the beach, I did have several attacks beginning on Tuesday. Fortunately, my wife—always with so much wisdom—had hired Beach Bell Hops (a couple of high school guys) to unload and load our van, which turned out to be a great idea.

I couldn't stay at the beach long each day, usually only between one and two hours, and only under a canopy. After that I would get in the ocean water and then go back to the vacation house. The first day I went out into the surf up to my knees, and the movement of the water knocked me sideways, and I fell. My legs were weaker than I had thought. I was able to dive under a small wave and struggled to get up.

The second day was steadier walking in the water, and I came up easier from the wave. The third day was the problem. I was somewhat unsteady walking in the surf, but when I dove under the small wave (up to my chest), I was knocked back on my haunches, but then the next wave pushed me down into a sitting position facing the ocean. I couldn't get up from that position with each successive wave pushing me back and down. I was constantly having to take a breath and then try to stand. I couldn't. After three or four of those waves, I thought, "I can't keep this up; I don't have enough lung capacity." Fortunately, my wife was standing nearby and came over and helped me up. Okay, lesson learned. My legs are not ocean certified any more. I can enter the ocean only when guarded.

But, in general, God was very good to us. We were able to have my sister-in-law drive down to visit for several days, and then my daughter and her family came for more than half the week. And I'm home now, and have suffered no ill effects from the drive back. In fact, my wife and I lifted weights today (Monday), and I'm feeling pretty well. My next treatment is Wednesday (August 16), and we'll see how that goes. But I'm so thankful to God that our trip went so well.

BOOK REVIEW: REMEMBER DEATH BY MATTHEW MCCULLOUGH

First, this is not a real book review. It's not that well organized, and the book is not critically analyzed. So, let's just call this a "book report." This book was recommended to me by a friend, since he said that McCullough touches on some of the same themes I have covered in this book (though McCullough does it much better). McCullough says that there is a branch of church tradition known as the *ars morendi* ("the art of dying"). It sounds as if there was a common practice in the ancient church to help people who were terminally ill to die well. This book, however, is not written for that purpose (though it certainly should help), nor for those grieving someone who has died (again, it would be helpful). This book is about another branch of tradition that deals with *memento mori* (roughly, remember death). It is concerned more with the topic of Psalm 90:12: "Teach us to number our days that we may get a heart of wisdom." As McCullough says (and I have said), it is a problem that receives almost no attention in our general culture (here and elsewhere in the Western world). It is only rarely touched on in evangelical churches. But he argues that if we contemplate our own death, we will gain an understanding that we desperately need.

It certainly has helped me by fostering humility, a deeper effort at repentance, and an increased joy because of the hope Jesus gave us in his resurrection. McCullough meditates on several aspects of death, such as why death has disappeared from our culture and vocabulary. Also, he gives a reflection on the fact that death teaches us that none of us are too important to die. He has chapters on death and futility, death and loss (the idea that absolutely nothing lasts), all of which he avers should help us correctly order our priorities.

I would highly recommend this short book. The author is a young pastor with a young congregation. If I remember correctly, he relates that he had never preached at a funeral, and I believe had never seen anyone die. He was drawn to this topic as he was preaching his way verse by verse through the Bible and was struck by how many times the Bible addresses the problem of physical death. Though his congregation was comprised mainly of young people, he decided to preach on this topic. I'm sure his congregation was more than a little surprised. But my guess is that they, like us older folks, needed this perspective—maybe even more than us elderly need it. Death should remake any Christian's values, from the beginning to the end of our lives. This book is worth reading not only once, but annually to remind us of the importance we have to "Remember Death."

SEPTEMBER 29, 2023

I finished another treatment on Wednesday (September 27), and effects were very similar to the last treatment: nausea, dizziness, hoarseness, and some bowel issues. I forgot to take the Zyprexa (the new anti-nausea med they started me on last time). So, of course, Thursday I had moderate nausea (which in my book is pretty miserable) and dizziness. I took half a tablet on Thursday night and slept better and am less nauseated today (Friday, September 29). The Zofran really did little, if anything, though eating crystallized or candied ginger cubes (which are actual cubes of ginger soaked in sugar) seemed to help slightly. The gummy I took might also have helped somewhat. My labs looked good for the most part: platelets and WBC (white blood cells that fight infections) are normal. My hemoglobin (the red stuff in red blood cells that carries oxygen) is a concern. It was 11.6 g/dl this time, whereas the time before it was 13.2. On August 30th, it was 12.1, and on August 16th it was 12.6. He's thinking my bone marrow is starting to give up so that I eventually will become anemic (with accompanying shortness of breath and chronic fatigue, worse than now). I'm not sure he's correct. My historical review of my hemoglobin shows that I've had test results that were similar in the past. For instance, on January 6th, it was 11.7, and on January 13th, it was 11.6. So, maybe it's just the normal bouncing around. It's hard to say without more results. So, things are okay, though I still am weaker and have less stamina than I did several months ago.

Just a note speculating on the future: The oncologist has said a number of times recently that they've "given me a ton of chemo drugs in the past two years." And he mentioned maybe cutting me back to once every three weeks. I think what's going to happen is that I'll get one more treatment on October 18th (taking a week off for our fiftieth anniversary!). Then he'll order another status CT scan, and if it shows my cancer is pretty stable, we'll go to the once every three weeks schedule with the hope that I feel better and the cancer remains dormant. There's nothing much we can do differently. What we can and will do is what we've done since the beginning: pray for God's mercy. Where would any of us be without that?

OCTOBER 19, 2023

I received another treatment on Wednesday (October 18). Usual suspects accompanied the treatment: nausea, dizziness and weakness, hoarseness. I took half a Zyprexa that evening, and it helped some with nausea during the night, but I was still nauseated Thursday morning. I took a Zofran (8 mg), and that helped some with the nausea, but it's still there, so I'll try the cannabinoid route to see if that will help. I have also eaten some candied ginger that usually helps for a short period.

The last time I had a treatment was three weeks ago, and my labs this time looked very good: almost all my CBC (complete blood count) tests were normal. So, that was all great news.

Next on the agenda is my status CT scan on Monday, November 6, to check mainly the cancer in my lungs to see if it's grown since dropping the 5-FU chemo drug and going three weeks without any treatment. It is also meant to check for any metastases. Then I have my review appointment on Wednesday, November 8, with the oncologist to go over the scan results and to plan for the future. My guess, as I said in the last chapter, is that he will recommend going to every three weeks to give my body a rest of sorts. I have been on chemo for two and a half years. My body is starting to droop from the effects. I have even developed generalized itching, which was helped by an antihistamine (Zyrtec), but the itching has gone away (mostly), and I'm hoping it doesn't come back after this treatment session.

I'm so grateful we were able to celebrate our fiftieth wedding anniversary, and I was able yet again to see my two sons and the older one's wife, who flew in to celebrate with us. Praise God for that great kindness! I'm so thankful for many peoples' prayers and kind and encouraging words.

WHAT SEASON IS IT?

OCTOBER 23, 2023

> Now learn the parable from the fig tree: when its branch has already become tender and puts forth its leaves, you know that summer is near.
>
> Mark 13:28

THIS VERSE IS PART of a discourse by Jesus in response to the disciples' question about the timing of the second coming. Their query is really one only of a date: "when will these things be..."? (v. 4), to which Jesus ultimately replies: "No one knows, not even me; only the Father knows." But I would like us to focus on a different part of his answer.

Regardless of whether the second coming is soon or many years from now, Jesus includes a word telling us what should be more important than being given a date—which we do not and cannot know—but rather the nature of the coming. Jesus says that whatever signs may indicate that the second coming is near, what we should focus on is what is near: "you know that summer is near."

What we should be looking for is not just a specific day or hour, but rather the arrival of a season. We live now in a fallen world, broken in so many ways: full of sickness, sorrow, pain, suffering, but especially death. If what we are awaiting is the season of summer, then what we are living in is a different season altogether. I would describe it as winter. And especially for someone like me, the current season, even on a summer day, may feel as if I'm living in winter: bleak, gray, sad. I believe I'm in good company, as that was the season chosen by C.S. Lewis for his book, *The Lion, the Witch, and the Wardrobe*, in which the land where the children traveled was always in winter (and never Christmas).

The end for each of us in this age is a winter ending, an inescapable end of the coldness of death. It is indeed a stark conclusion, departing from loved ones as well as brothers and sisters in the Lord. It leaves behind a sad and depressing feeling as we judge the end of our lives and even the popular belief about the end of the world. It is no wonder that there are many in Western culture now who decline to bring children into such a hopeless closing.

And yet, Jesus here lifts our hearts, for what we as believers await is not a seemingly endless winter season, but the anticipation of something wonderful—the arrival of summer. The cold and barren wind gives way to a warm and encouraging breeze that carries with it the scent of new life. It reminds me of stories I've read of sailors who have survived harsh, bitterly cold storms in rounding the horn and then finally enter warmer regions. They see land birds flying overhead and smell the fragrance of plants growing. There grows within them the hope of finally reaching shore. It is no wonder, then, that one fruit of the Holy Spirit is joy, for that is what Jesus is offering us in this age. It is a fruit that we should and can cultivate more. We have the hope of this word from Jesus, that there will be not only an end to the winter of this age, but the arrival of summer, the season of new life, of abundance, of healing, of comfort, of rejoicing and love forevermore.

Whenever you feel the bitter bite of the winter season in your soul, whenever you feel that it will never end and is full of endless days of cold and separation from others, reflect on this phrase:

"summer is near." Winter will not always reign; summer is surely on its way. The signs of its approach are sometimes great and sometimes small, but they are there, if we but look. And in that season we will live with Jesus and with our brothers and sisters who will come from all lands and tribes, and we will live together forever. Let that thought warm your heart and bring hope and joy as well as give you strength to endure the winter of this age. "Summer is near..."

WATCH THE SUNRISES

February 8, 2024

My wife has gotten me to start watching sunrises, and I've decided it reminds me of our life in this age. The sunrise is a harbinger of the sun approaching our world to give light and warmth. And our life is like that in a way. Every day is an opportunity to reflect the glory of God and show the hope of the return of Jesus before a watching world. But one thing I've also noticed is that it's not much of a sunrise without clouds being present. I think we best reflect God's glory and that hope as the clouds do the approaching sun. Those clouds remind me of the troubles and cares we face in this life. As God brings them into our life—as Hebrews 12 reports about God's discipline—he is yet giving us another opportunity to grow in grace as we handle them. Discipline, as the writer of Hebrews says, is sorrowful, not joyful, yet when we allow ourselves to be trained by it, we receive the "peaceful fruit of righteousness." You will grow more and better reflect his glory like the sunrise in those clouds as you submit to them and trust him.

But they are hard to endure. So. Very. Hard. But the writer exhorts next, "...strengthen the hands that are weak and the knees that are feeble..." (Heb. 12:12). I have seen this need repeatedly in my life in the last three years. And as I have asked for help from the Lord, in dealing with my discipline, I have seen my brothers and sisters in Christ respond to strengthening my hands that are weak and my knees that are feeble. Thank you for that help and in being the answer to my prayers for that help. It means more to me than I can say, and praise my Savior for the care that comes from his body! I encourage you to do likewise as you face your own acts of discipline. You won't regret it, but will be glad to receive that answer to your prayers for wisdom and help.

CONTENT WITH WEAKNESSES

MARCH 1, 2024

Because of the surpassing greatness of the revelations, for this reason, to keep me from exalting myself, there was given me a thorn in the flesh, a messenger of Satan to torment me to keep me from exalting myself! Concerning this I implored the Lord three times that it might leave me. And he has said to me, "My grace is sufficient for you, for power is perfected in weakness." Most gladly, therefore, I will rather boast about my weaknesses, so that the power of Christ may dwell in me. Therefore I am well content with weaknesses, with insults, with distresses, with persecutions, with difficulties, for Christ's sake; for when I am weak, then I am strong.
2 Corinthians 12:7–10

I AM NO APOSTLE Paul, who suffered worse than I have and for a greater cause. Nonetheless, I think Paul was taught an important principle. There are sufferings that come from God even through a messenger of Satan, sufferings that no amount of prayer will remove. I have always believed that this cancer and its treatment and side effects were discipline for me to endure (as discussed before per the explanation of discipline in Hebrews 12). Paul never tells us what the thorn in the flesh is, but it is interesting to note that once Jesus explains the general principle of suffering (in v. 9), Paul embraces his sufferings and broadens them to include all manner of things (in v. 10), such as insults, distresses, etc. Yet Paul concludes: "...for when I am weak, then I am strong."

I think the natural response to suffering, like a terminal disease, is immediately to seek relief. And Paul does just that, as he mentions in v. 8. He implored Jesus for the removal of his torment, yet the answer was "No." As I say in the appendix on healing, no healing is guaranteed. The answer might come back as "No" in spite of how much we implore because Jesus also teaches us to pray, "Thy kingdom come, thy will be done." And in those cases, God wants us to see that his power is perfected in our weaknesses: "...when I am weak, then I am strong." In those moments, we will see Jesus's power at work in us to help us have the opportunity to grow stronger and boast in that weakness. We will know that God's grace is truly sufficient in a way we may have never known without that suffering.

Because of this principle, I intend to try to be well content with my weaknesses, for it is then I hope to grow in Jesus's strength and grace. Amen, Lord. May you help me make it so.

BE OF GOOD COURAGE

MARCH 28, 2024

> We are of good courage, I say, and prefer rather to be absent from the body and to be at home with the Lord.
>
> 2 Corinthians 5:8

As I've mentioned before, my wife and I pray regularly to be filled with the Spirit and ask that the fruit of his presence be seen, and then we verbally list those fruit (Gal. 5:22) in our prayer. But we have recently added a trait to those fruit. Paul mentions that character trait here in 2 Corinthians: *courage*. Courage plays such a large role in our Christian lives for a number of reasons, but especially as we face adversity. Here Paul gives one reason for our ability to have courage: because one day we each will die, when we will be absent from these decaying, increasingly painful bodies and go on to be with the Lord. I use that thought on days when I struggle to find joy. This life is only temporary, and the suffering we undergo here will be gone. We will then know the permanent joy we will never find here. And that's because unending joy will be found only when we're at home with him.

Don't let yourself get discouraged, much less despair, as we have yet a race to run, one that he will help us to endure, and in the end be granted the blessings and benefits of completing. And we will find that those blessings far outweigh what small troubles now nag, distract, and afflict us. As Paul ends his first letter to the Corinthians: "Be on the alert, stand firm in the faith, act like men, be strong" (1 Cor. 16:13). In other words, he tells them (and us) to have courage!

IN WHATEVER CIRCUMSTANCES

April 24, 2024

> I have learned to be content in whatever circumstances I am. I know how to get along with humble means, and I also know how to live in prosperity; in any and every circumstance I have learned the secret of being filled and going hungry, both of having abundance and suffering need. I can do all things through him who strengthens me.
>
> Philippians 4:11–13

In v. 11, Paul gives us a general principle of suffering. He applies that principle in the verses that follow for having contentment in various economic situations (which would be a good meditation for any culture, but especially in ours).

But I think that principle could be applied to our health as well. Our health is like our wealth—it may be better or worse, and it's something we earnestly want to improve or prevent from declining. Though, as with wealth, we should act with prudence in regards to its possession, we should learn contentment with whatever it may be today, even when what's happened is completely outside of our control.

That approach is a hard discipline to learn, or at least it has been for me. Mine took a sudden and dramatic turn for the worse three years ago, like a stock market crash, going from virtually no health issues to a terminal diagnosis, from being health "wealthy" to health "poor" overnight. From feeling well virtually every day to feeling badly every day. But it has taught me the need each morning not to rely on my health for my joy, but on the only one who can give joy and contentment in these circumstances. And it has also shown me the importance of loving and caring for others in their sufferings, even when that suffering is the result of their behavior.

Actually, in one sense, all suffering is "our" fault because the curse came on us not because we were born guiltless, but because we all are a part of a sinful and thus suffering humanity. Jesus as our high priest suffered in this age as we have. And that suffering he underwent without sin, in no way deserving it. So, now we can trust him to help us when we suffer. He is no distant God, afflicting us as One who is untouched by our pain. Rather, he's a Savior who has lived also under the burden of the curse, and he did it because he loved us and cared for us. That's what I want to learn: not only not to complain in my sufferings (again, following his example), but to stop thinking of my sufferings so much, and to see how I can help others bear their own as he did mine with his life. May God grant me grace to continue to improve in my ability to do just that.

FINAL UPDATES AND PARTING WORDS
May–July 2024

MAY 30, 2024

I MET WITH MY oncologist last Tuesday (May 28, 2024) to review my status CT scan, done on Monday, May 20. He confirmed what I had told people privately—that the cancer has been virtually unchanged (in size or number of nodules), and that there has been no sign of metastases. As the oncologist said: "I was surprised when I saw no growth after four months of no chemo." Him and me both.

So, what next? A few things.

1. He stated, "You have earned yourself another three months without chemo." My next status CT scan will be August 14.

2. He says it's gotten so on the CT scan that it's hard to tell the difference between scarring and CA. And if you look back on the last several radiology chest reports for the CT scans, you will see that he (same radiologist) mentions that the area looks like a lot of scarring. Previous radiologists, however, measured the nodules (seeing the nodules as the cancer; they were what was originally biopsied by needle in April, 2021) and compared them to see if they

had increased in size or number. If not, the radiologist reported no change in the cancer.

Because of this emphasis on scarring in the recent radiology reports and the lack of CA change, the oncologist is sending me to a pulmonologist to see if he can increase my lung function. Count me among the skeptics, as I think that lung scar tissue is too stiff to stretch (unlike scars in soft tissue such as skin, ligaments, etc.). Nonetheless, knowing how ignorant I am of lung scar tissue, I am more than happy to visit the pulmonologist to hear what he has to say. Maybe there is something that can be done. That would be nice.

3. He wants me to continue to try to decrease the amount of prednisone I'm taking. On February 7, my most recent chemo tx, I was on 15mg/day. He told me, as I've mentioned before, that his experience is that when you hit 20mg/day (of prednisone), you're functionally immunosuppressed and more apt to get illnesses. Since then, I've lowered my intake to 10mg/day. Though I was able to go down 1mg/day every two weeks initially without too much trouble, in my drop from 11mg/day to 10 mg/day, I'm having a lot more trouble. Now I'm feeling very weak, and shaky at times. This last drop has been much more difficult than all the others. I'm not sure why. It could be that as I get down further, the change of 1mg/day becomes a larger percentage of the total. I was so tired yesterday that I finally broke down and took a thirty-minute nap. It didn't help much. I feel better when sitting and resting, but I don't want that mode to become a lifestyle. I spoke with a PCP (primary care physician) today, and he suggested another strategy for lowering it. He told me, as I've heard many times, that stopping chronic prednisone use is extremely difficult. He is so right. But I'll try his new approach and see if that helps.

4. I have another problem that I would never have guessed: my gout. When the podiatrist performed the PNA (partial nail avulsion) on my right great toe, he inadvertently set off a constant low grade attack in that toe. It will on occasion wake me at night from

the pain, but not every night (none last night, but twice the night before). I had no idea how much colchicine to take, since MDs and most reputable online sites (like Mayo Clinic) warn against taking too much. I spoke today to a PCP (the same one as suggested a way off the prednisone) who told me to try half a tablet of colchicine (they're 0.6mg tablets) in the morning and one in the evening to get the toe to calm down. And I went ahead—at his prompting—and sent a message through MyChart to the podiatrist about the gout problem. I hope when the toe completely heals from the PNA, this gout issue will disappear.

Still, all these problems are minor compared to the plain fact that after four months without chemo tx, my cancer has been unchanged. God is very good. I am not—nor ever will be—cancer free. Nonetheless, as of today, I am experiencing relief from the CA growth and unrelenting chemo tx. I could die of the CA by the time of the next status CT scan. But I am grateful for God's kindness in extending my life these last three years.

Let me just encourage you not to lose sight of the wonderful things that God does for you no matter what problems you face. As the apostle Paul said:

> Therefore we do not lose heart, but though our outer man is decaying, yet our inner man is being renewed day by day. For momentary, light affliction is producing for us an eternal weight of glory far beyond all comparison, while we look not at the things which are seen, but at the things which are not seen; for the things which are seen are temporal, but the things which are not seen are eternal.
>
> 2 Corinthians 4:16–18

What could be a better or more important view of life?

June 12, 2024

I have three good things to report:

1. My blood pressure (BP) has dropped from 150/90 in the morning at my last chemo (February 7) to 125/85 daily—an amazing change. My heart rate (HR) is still tachycardic (>100bpm), but at least the BP is much better. I'm continuing the Losartan (the lowest dose, 25mg) as you cannot just stop the medication. You have to be tapered off (much like steroid). If I continue at this BP level, I may talk with the PCP to see about doing just that.

2. My itching is basically gone. I can't tell you what a relief that is.

3. My gout attack (on my right great toe) is gone. The tophus no longer hurts, though it looks funny. Regardless, another blessing, for sure.

The only bad thing I have to report is my breathing. My 02 saturation throughout this time of treatment of the esophageal cancer in my lungs has always been normal—upper 90% (97–98%). Even when I was exercising in the garage using dumbbells, it almost never dropped below 90%. Now it regularly sits in the low 90% (91–93%), and when I do curls or lunges with dumbbells, it has—in the last three sessions—dropped to 85%. That percentage is the level I was taught as a PT to stop exercise, since it was at that point that many people would pass out. Yet, first, mine doesn't stay at 85% for more than a few seconds. Second, I've been completely asymptomatic (other than being short of breath, SOB). So, I've just ignored the level up till now. I have increased slightly the time between sets to permit better recovery. But if I get symptomatic, or the SOB gets worse, I'll have to let the oncologist know. Of course, at the last appointment the oncologist had said he wanted me to get in to see a pulmonologist, but I've heard nothing yet about that appointment (and I did message him in MyChart several days ago, which would have been exactly two weeks since my Status Review appointment).

And, as always, the prednisone dose (as I mentioned above) is an ongoing problem. The last PCP's suggestion was to go from 10mg to 9mg by alternating for a week (10-9-10-9, etc.), then finally dropping to 9mg. When I get the nerve, I'll try that and see if I can avoid the "slug on the couch" syndrome. It's hard; trust me. But "...we do not lose heart..."

JULY 2, 2024

It surprises me that I have so many symptoms of my chemo. They are still there, e.g., the lethargy. My lung scarring is worse, as I say below. But my gut is somewhat better. In fact, the nurse practitioner at the primary care office told me to stop the Losartan—no more high blood pressure medication. She also checked my chem report: sodium, potassium, alkaline phosphatase, etc. They were all normal. So, it would be untrue to say that all my chemo symptoms have disappeared (and my hair—such as it was—has mostly come back, so I don't look so sick). But I'm still very sick and short of breath.

My three biggest issues are still shortness of breath (SOB), for which I often have to take Budesonide (the corticosteroid confined to my gut), my generalized itching, and the gout in my toe (large right one). I know I said the latter two were gone, but I was mistaken. All three come and go. I don't understand it but just treat them when I have to. I'll see what the pulmonologist says about my lungs on August 8th.

I do have one piece of good news, and then will give a brief meditation. The good news is this: As usual, I was going through my library, book by book, morning by morning. This time I picked up an old Merck Manual (2006, which was bought when I was in PT school). I read some entries, one on my cancer, esophageal CA, and on several other diseases. Then it mentioned the website: merckmanuals.com. I thought it was probably dead—just some old website. But, far from it, it was alive and active. The print edition is expensive: $79.95 for the 20th edition (last printed 2018). That's too expensive for me, plus it's already outdated. So, I looked at the mobile app on the website, and I was stunned: it's absolutely free! I couldn't believe it! So, to get it, go to the App Store (for Apple iPhone) or Google Play Store, and choose either the Professional Edition (if you have a medical background; it's designed for MDs or health professionals) or the Consumer Edition (same info as the Professional version, but written so any layman can understand). Anyway, the point is the Merck Manual is absolutely free (well worth the little bit of work it takes to install it).

MEDITATION

> But he, being compassionate, forgave [their] iniquity and did not destroy [them;] and often he restrained his anger and did not arouse all his wrath. Thus he remembered that they were but flesh, a wind that passes and does not return.
>
> Psalm 78:38–39

We have a string of Christmas lights going from our living room to the dining room. And I noticed a week or so ago that half the string was burned out. And I thought to myself: "That's exactly how I feel: more than half burned out." And as the psalmist tells us, that's how God looks at us: we are but flesh, a wind that passes and does not return. If we may speak of it this way (and the psalmist does), God is surprised, in a manner of speaking (since he is all-knowing and is not truly surprised by anything) by the brevity of our life span. Like a string of Christmas lights, we burn brightly for a short time, then go out, never to return.

Except in my case, I'm not a fully lit strand; half of my lights are gone, never to return; I'm almost done. But in God's eyes, we all so quickly reach seventy or eighty or ninety years. They are nothing to someone like him who has seen many thousands of years (trying to use time to help us to understand eternity).

Don't waste your shortened life striving after the things of this age. Our life is but preparation for an expanse of time (eternity to us) that we cannot now conceive. God gave me a few "lights" to warn me, and to prepare me for death, to indeed embrace it. You will not return, as psalmist says. So, the Scriptures warn us as well. But Jesus *will* return, and so we must be ready. He died for creation, but primarily for us, for his people. *People* are the most important part of anything—not science, philosophy, languages, land, machine, possessions. All these things are important, but they can distract us and cause us to forget who Jesus primarily died for. We have little time and should use it wisely. We will not return. But remember that he died for *us*.

JULY 22, 2024

Well, I finally did it: I joined hospice. I had my brain MRI on Wednesday night (taken over to the place by my daughter, who is a surgical RN). Thursday morning my oncologist called to tell me I have a brain tumor. (It wasn't on MyChart, so I didn't know for sure.) My oncologist said there are three treatment options: *the chemo route*, which doesn't work too well because of the blood/brain barrier. Nix on that. *The surgical option*: just cut off parts of my brain that they don't think I'll need. Hmmm—I don't think so. Even if they could get at the metatheses in the head, where did this mass come from (my chest or esophageal CA)? Then *the radiation option*: really trying to shrink the tumor (before surgery, for instance, or just help with the nausea/dizziness). Well, no thanks to getting radiation before attempting surgery, but I appreciate the mercy via the chemical means. So, that's where we went—just radiation treatment. He ordered the dexamethasone (16mg/day) to help get the nausea and vomiting down. The vestibular symptoms would disappear. Unfortunately, the increased dexamethasone (another corticosteroid) joins forces with the corticosteroid I'm already taking: prednisone. Do I need both? I've been on prednisone for three years for side effects coming from the chemo. But the side effects of the chemo are nothing compared to the (lingering) effects on my adrenal glands. So, it's a tradeoff: the dexamethasone was—by the oncologist and the hospice nurse—not to be stopped. Of course, the weight gain is not till I eat the food!

You would think after six years of home care I would know, but hospice is its own service. They become your PCP (primary care physician), over your oncologist. Are the scans for body and brain—CT and brain MRI—going to take place? I don't know. And will the pneumatologist's consult still be legitimate and covered come August 8th? Even this morning, we found out that allopurinol (to prevent gout attacks) and ipratropium (the prescription version of Flonase) would not be covered! But the Medicare is behind all this. To be sure Medicare will pay for this cure: is the care palliative or curative? Anyway, so we found the hospice group on Friday morning. Yet it turns out the head of the church home group will be the head MD of the hospice group this weekend. And my (step) uncle is a retired orthopedic surgeon. He is still very helpful with the meds. What a blessing to have such good help!

Plus, I worked with Carilion health hospice, and our spiritual needs will be met by *you*, the church. They were fine with that—no problem.

So, we can only guess at how fast the tumor(s) will be growing. Who knows?

The Joyous Mystery

Bach's cantata is a favorite of mine (I'm writing like a drunken man, and I hope my typing is a little better!). He came after the Reformation and so was a staunch Lutheran. He was moved to hear the "Sleepers, awake" cantata in the Lutheran's pastor's repertoire. He moved that song into the (virgins') call for the sleepers' awake. But I'm reminded of 1 Corinthians 15:51–52, "Behold, I tell you a mystery. We will not all be asleep, but we shall all be changed, in a moment, in the twinkling of an eye, at the last trumpet. For the trumpet shall sound, and the dead will be raised imperishable, we shall be changed."

What a great hope we have! That trumpet will sound, and those who sleep will awaken. We will be changed; we brush off the imperishable and put on the imperishable. The brain tumor, the lung metastases, the esophageal CA mean nothing to me. What matters is that statement: *"We shall be changed"!*

"Sleeper, awake" is our cry, our hope, our joy. And a great joy it is!

Appendix 1: On Healing

December 2021

I developed an compelling interest in the topic of healing when it was discovered that I have a tiny primary tumor in my esophagus that metastasized to my lungs, where it exploded into a cancer that filled them with what was diagnosed as stage IV (esophageal) cancer (there is no stage V). My prognosis is "treatable, not curable," meaning there's no way to kill or remove the cancer, but they can (and have) put me on chemo drugs to kill some or much of the cancer. So, as someone who was diagnosed as dying from cancer, I listened and thought and, of course, prayed with others in the hopes of being healed. I had much support from my church. But even those outside my church, both Christians and non-Christians, were most kind. From one believing friend, I received several books on supernatural healing. I knew also that my church (a conservative Presbyterian denomination) practiced anointing with oil as is mentioned in the book of James (5:14–15). The following little study grew out of my interest because of my condition but also as result of reading particularly one of the books on healing I had received.

Two Views on Healing

There are two views that seem prevalent among Protestants today that I want to look at. I will go through my thoughts for each one. Of course, these are my own thoughts, not my church's or my denomination's, though I don't believe they would find much, if any, of this material to be objectionable.

The first view is what I call simply "Supernatural against natural healing." This view emphasizes primarily a supernatural healing by God for serious illness as opposed to a more natural role as played by traditional medicine. I think of it as some version of what is popularly known as the "health and wealth gospel" (obviously in this study, I'm dealing only with the *health* aspect).

The second view is what I call "Natural against supernatural healing." This view emphasizes primarily the natural role for healing an illness as played by traditional medicine rather than the thought that healing might come in a supernatural manner through the Holy Spirit. I think of this view being the one seen in most evangelical churches in our country.

I realize I'm painting with a broad brush here, but I'll use one of the books on (supernatural) healing I received—called *Christ the Healer* by F.F. Bosworth—as an example of what might typically be taught by the "supernatural against natural healing" view. For the "Natural against supernatural healing," I'll use my own observations as a guide, since I have been a member of a number of churches where I think most of the members would tend to follow this perspective.

Supernatural against Natural Healing

I will summarize what I understand this view to be teaching, namely, that God guarantees healing to every believer for any sickness, provided the person follows some specified method, usually involving first the patient's faith (being practiced as specified), followed by praying using the correct words. Without following this "method," it is unlikely the person will be healed.

As mentioned, it seems common with those who hold this view that to be healed, the patient must follow a particular method. Let's look at some of the hallmarks of this method. Again, I'll be using Bosworth's book as a guide in outlining it, in addition to referencing passages of Scripture. We can begin with Proverbs 4:20–22 (KJV).

> My son, attend to my words; incline thine ear unto my sayings. Let them not depart from thine eyes; keep them in the midst of thine heart. For they [are] life unto those that find them, and health to all their flesh.

According to Bosworth, this passage is the "most comprehensive instruction as to how to receive healing" (19). He writes, "The flesh of thousands today is unhealthy flesh because they have failed to 'find' and 'attend' to that part of God's Word that produces healing" (20). In other words, we are to locate the promises of healing in the Bible and believe them to be absolute. "Your symptoms may point you to death, but God's Word points to life, and you cannot look in these opposite directions at the same time" (22). Thus, "[m]any have failed to receive healing simply because they have not followed this method" (20). There are several things to note here.

Now, it makes sense from this starting point that Bosworth would encourage and warn his readers of several things.

First, we should always thank God in advance for our future healing when we pray for that healing. "When we ask for healing, we are to say on the authority of God's Word, 'I thank Thee that Thou hast heard me'" (p. 140). "The reason thousands are not getting what they pray for is that they are keeping their blessing in the future tense. This is only hope and not faith, which [faith] takes the blessings now" (14).

Second, he warns against the phrase, "If it be Thy will." Many sufferers have prayed for healing for years without success. This is because they have prayed the faith-destroying phrase, "If it be Thy will" (177). We are to remember that "Every time you confess doubts and fears, you confess your faith in Satan and deny the ability and grace of God" (153).

Third, "The second step toward being healed is to be sure you are right with God. Our redemptive blessings are conditional...Until a man squarely faces and settles the question of obedience to God, he is not on believing ground. 'If I regard iniquity in my heart, the Lord will not heal me'" (97).

The atonement guarantees that God will heal the believer. "Isaiah 53:4 ('Surely he hath borne our sicknesses, and carries our pains') cannot refer to disease of the soul, and neither of the words 'sickness' and 'pain' have any reference to spiritual matters but to bodily sickness alone" (35).

QUESTIONING THE VIEW

Now we need to examine this view against what the Scriptures as a whole say. First of all, the certainty of the patient's faith, especially as it is reflected in certainty for healing in his prayers is, I believe, a misunderstanding of the nature of our petitions we offer in prayer. Jesus teaches us how to pray in what Protestants usually call "The Lord's Prayer" (e.g., Matt. 26:9–13). Note especially the first petition He teaches us to offer: "Your kingdom come, your will be done..." Here we have a petition that precedes all the others and also frames the following petitions. Our desires and requests are bounded by and encompassed in the will of God. All that comes to pass is because of God. We can request that his revealed will be changed, for instance, as shown in the way that some part of our life is going—such as finding a job, or buying a home, or the presence of terminal illness in our body. But we dare not usurp God's right and claim to oversee our lives and fortunes.

We can see how this petition molds Jesus's own prayer in the Garden of Gethsemane just before his arrest, trial, and execution. If anyone had the right to demand that his petition be guaranteed, it surely would have been the sinless Son of God. But that is not how he approaches his heavenly Father in his petition. Listen carefully to his request: "My Father, if it is possible, let this cup pass from me; yet not as I will, but as you will" (Matt. 6:39). "Abba! Father! All things are possible for you; remove this cup from me: yet not what I will, but what you will" (Mark 14:36). "Father, if you are willing, remove this cup from me; yet not my will, but yours be done" (Luke 22:42). Jesus requests that the cup of God's wrath pass him by, but he frames the request using the language he had taught his disciples earlier: that God's will takes precedence, even over his request.

And this approach has become the one I pray, and have asked others to pray for me—that I would be healed of my cancer, but framed as Jesus taught us to prayer. So, I pray: "Please, Father, take this cup of cancer from me; nonetheless, not my will but yours be done."

Bosworth's catalog of God's promises to bless and heal us are most useful as reasons for God to heal when asking that your sickness be taken from you. But in the end, it is God's prerogative to answer as he wills, and his answer (as he told Paul as reported in 2 Corinthians 12 when Paul requests three times to remove his thorn in the flesh) was steadfastly "No."

Let me give an illustration of a failed healing that seemed to check all the boxes of the method that Bosworth advocates, but with a different view of our status before God in our petitions. In 2 Samuel 12:15–23, David's infant son from his adulterous act with

Bathsheba was afflicted with a serious illness: "Then the Lord struck the child...so that he was sick" (v. 15). But David "inquired of God for the child and David fasted and went and lay all night on the ground" (v. 16). David had already confessed his sin of adultery when he was confronted by the prophet Nathan (v. 13). David fasted and prayed for his son for seven days; nonetheless, the child died (v. 18).

This sickness and death of the child do not fit Bosworth's paradigm. In fact, it is very much against the outcome he guarantees from following his method. But listen to David's response to the death of his young child: "He said, 'While the child was alive, I fasted and wept; for I said, "Who knows, the Lord *may* be gracious to me that the child *may* live"'" (v .22, italics mine). David's remarks indicate that he obviously did not seem to follow Bosworth's application of David's own Psalm, 50:14–15, with Bosworth believing that David there writes of an absolute promise of healing. Further, David is not recorded as thanking God in advance for a healing of his child, as Bosworth insists must be done. Instead, we see that David, as Jesus later teaches his disciples, submits his will to God's. The answer of "no" to David's petitions—despite his unceasing prayers, fasting, confession of sin, and humbling himself in prostration day and night before God—was still "No." Nevertheless, David, to the surprise of his servants (v. 21), was at peace with God's decision. "Your Kingdom come, your will be done" was a principle that David obviously believed and practiced.

In the NT, we see another application of subsuming our will to God's in our petitions. It comes in a healing that Jesus performs, recorded in Mark 1:40–45. There a leper comes to Jesus for healing and says *not* (as might be expected if he followed the method): "Heal me, as I know you are able and willing to do, and I thank you now for this healing that has already taken place, since I know it is guaranteed you will grant this healing petition." No, instead the leper petitions Jesus to heal him with these words: "If you are willing, you can make me clean!" This phrase "If you are willing" is almost an exact statement of one that is anathema to Bosworth. Bosworth reports that the phrase "If it be Thy will" is a "faith destroying phrase" (177). And for the leper to have used it should have elicited a rebuke from Jesus. But, far from being rebuked by Jesus, we find Jesus is stirred: "Moved with compassion, Jesus...said to him, 'I am willing; be cleansed.'" Different from Bosworth's condemnation of this phrase is Jesus's attitude, for he is stirred to pity and grants the man's healing. This example is yet another concrete instance of a healing that violates the method, especially in the understanding of our stance before God as we make our petitions.

WHAT ABOUT ATONEMENT?

What of this idea that the atonement guarantees our present healing? Bosworth quotes an Old Testament passage to show that Jesus was predicted in Isaiah 53:4 to remove all our illnesses: "...our illnesses he carried."

First, it is clear as Bosworth suggests that the atonement here in this passage gives us the right to petition God for our healing. But, as I believe I have shown above, that petition should not be taken as an absolute right.

Second, I don't think Isaiah 53:4 should be isolated from the sentence that follows it (v. 5). The link is clear if you notice the word "but" at the beginning of verse 5: "Surely he hath borne our griefs, and carried our sorrows: yet we did esteem him stricken, smitten of God, and afflicted. *But* he [was] wounded for our transgressions, [he was] bruised for our iniquities: the chastisement of our peace [was] upon him; and with his stripes we are healed" (KJV). The importance of this link is simple: whereas Bosworth is able to show that v. 4 refers to physical healing in Matthew 8:17 (and it surely does), he ignores the verse that is certainly linked to v. 4, namely, v. 5, which also refers to our healing via Jesus's atonement. What

Bosworth leaves out is the use of the verse in the NT. Peter in 1 Peter 2:24 uses v. 5 in quite a different way than physical healing: "And he himself bore our sins in his body on the cross, to that we might die to sin and live to righteousness, for by his wounds you were healed." Peter is clearly quoting Isaiah 53:5, where the atonement is linked our healing, but Peter indicates that our healing is not only physical. My point is not to dispute Bosworth's claim that v. 4 refers to physical healing—it certainly does. What I dispute is that the healing, when mentioned in connection with the atonement, is only physical. It certainly is not. Our healing from the atonement is also a spiritual one, and, therefore, no absolute guarantee of physical healing.

Further, I believe that Bosworth makes an important mistake: he confuses the certain hope of our future existence with our current situation. Let me illustrate what I mean. For example, Paul says that there is no male or female in Christ (Gal. 3:28), but that is clearly not the current reality. Paul obviously relies on Jesus's statement that there will be no marriage in heaven (Matt. 22:30), indicating that the roles of male and female will be radically altered. But Paul also gives elsewhere instructions to wives (females) and husbands (males) (in Eph. 5:22ff) about their current responsibilities. Clearly, if we believed that the first statement about there being no male or female was absolute, we would conduct no more marriages. But that statement by Paul is only a partially realized one. As he shows in the Galatians passage, that future reality informs our current belief that we are all one in Christ, and all equal heirs of the promises. But it does not rescind our current need to continue to act as males and females.

Bosworth, then, is correct that the atonement opens the way for our present healing (why else would we see the healings of Jesus and those in the book of Acts?), but what he misunderstands is that the full, complete, and final healing for all believers will occur only in the age to come, in the new heavens and earth. What healings we have now are only partial or the beginnings of the final healings in heaven. Jesus raised people from the dead, such as his friend Lazarus, but Lazarus would die again because that resurrection was a resurrection to life only in this age. Lazarus's final resurrection (and complete healing) would come only when Jesus returns and raises our bodies to be like his: a new, unending life-filled one.

SIN AND HEALING

Now, what of Bosworth's belief that we cannot be in sin and expect healing? I am inclined to agree with that view for the most part, but we will discuss this aspect more later when I talk about anointing with oil, as mentioned in James 5:14.

We would also be well served by looking at some of the many healings in the Scriptures. It is always tempting to take a few verses and make them *the* biblical view of a subject. But here we can look at the actual healings performed in the Bible. Do they follow Bosworth's method? The answer is simple and clear to me: none of them follow his method.

Look first at the healing of King Hezekiah in 2 Kings 20:1–7 (remember that Isaiah's statement in Isaiah 53:4 was taken by Bosworth as an absolute guarantee of healing). Here Isaiah comes to Hezekiah to report that God is going to cause Hezekiah to die. When Isaiah leaves, Hezekiah prays for healing with a simple prayer and not one that Bosworth would commend in the method, I think: "Remember now, O Lord, I beseech you, how I have walked before you in truth with a whole heart and have done what is good in your sight" (v. 3). There is here no thanking God in advance for a healing, no reference to atonement for sin, nor reference to a guarantee of healing (such as he might done with Ps. 50:14–15, from David who predeceased Hezekiah as king, if the passage were intended to be taken as Bosworth interprets it). Yet this prayer, not in the form required by the method, moved God to extend Hezekiah's life by fifteen years through healing him.

Look also at the healing/raising of a son for a widow by Elijah (in 1 Kgs. 17:17–24). The mother's response to her son's illness and eventual death is not one of belief, but of unbelief: "So she said to Elijah, 'What have I to do with you, O man of God? You have come to me to bring my iniquity to remembrance, and to put my son to death'" (v .18). Elijah responds by praying to God, "O Lord my God, have you also brought calamity to the widow with whom I am staying, by causing her son to die?'" (v. 20). Again, virtually none of the steps of the method Bosworth advocates are followed—no confession of a sin (at least not that Elijah mentions to God in his prayer), no thanks presently for future healing, no mention of healing guaranteed by atonement, or any belief in the promises of God for healing. In fact, just the opposite: the widow is angry and unbelieving, thinking that Elijah is an evil prophet, bringing only death to a widow who has shown hospitality to Elijah. And yet Elijah is able to raise the son who experienced a sickness unto death by God's power (v. 22).

Finally—though we could examine quite a number of other passages—look at the healing of Naaman the Syrian in 2 Kings 5. Though Naaman comes from Syria to seek healing in the land of Israel from the prophet Elisha, Naaman balks at the command to dip in the Jordan River (v. 10). Naaman is "furious" (v. 11) and initially refuses, but is finally persuaded by his servants to at least try the prophet's command as long as he is there near the Jordan. Naaman does as he was told and is healed, and only then does he state he now has faith in the God of Israel (v. 15): "...now I know there is no God in all the earth, but in Israel...." In other words, Naaman is healed as an unbeliever, and as a result becomes a true believer in the God of Israel! This is an example of a healing in which every step of Bosworth's method is violated. The man is not even a believer before the healing, probably the most surprising part of this healing.

OTHER EXAMPLES OF HEALING

There are many other examples of healing in the Old Testament and the New Testament (we will look at some more later), none of which follows Bosworth's method.

Though for the most part Bosworth holds to the view that sickness is an unmitigated evil, he does finally admit that sickness may be an affliction from God, and well he should. Job is the principal example in the OT—a faithful man and yet one who lost all that he had, including his health. His affliction of physical sickness of boils was not because of his sin, but because something that was a part of God's plan that was outside of Job's ability to foresee or understand. Thus, Job's physical suffering was not subject to healing until God was ready for it.

Further, for Bosworth, God's love is equated with healing. But Bosworth misses the description of the love of God given in Hebrews 12:5–11: "For those whom the Lord loves he disciplines, and he scourges every son whom he receives" (v. 6). Scourging is a strong word, not intended to convey that God might lightly rap you on the wrist. It was intended to signal a difficult discipline. Sickness, especially as a terminal illness, is not an easy discipline, as I can attest, but it is one any believer should be able to bear, knowing that God through that discipline is helping him to grow (as I also can attest). Discipline in whatever form—including sickness—is an indicator of God's love, not necessarily the devil's control.

We must also wonder why the gift of healing (e.g., 1 Cor. 12:28) was needed and exercised throughout the NT, if, from Bosworth's perspective, we all essentially have the gift of healing within us. Nor do the accounts of many of these healings—such as the way Jesus healed using mud, or spit (in the Gospels), or in Acts (touching a handkerchief or having a shadow fall on them)—follow the method at all. As Bosworth believed that this would have been in accord with New Testament practices, it is curious to think that Paul would feel the need to list healing as one of the special gifts of the Holy Spirit and see the gift used in a manner that seems in no way to have regard for any special, detailed method. To repeat, according to Bosworth, all Christians have this ability, and need no one else to help.

It is also unclear to me why there is any need for medications or physicians (MDs) from this perspective. We will discuss in the next section the problem this view creates with using traditional medicine. The Bible quite clearly expects use of natural medications (as opposed to strictly supernatural healing). We can look at several biblical examples that make this point.

One from the Old Testament is a healing we have looked at before when Isaiah reported to King Hezekiah that God had answered Hezekiah's prayer by agreeing to extend his life (2 Kgs. 20:1–7). But there's a surprising detail in the account of this supernatural deliverance that I didn't mention earlier. After Isaiah reports that God has granted an extension of life, he next says, "'Take a cake of figs.' And they took and laid it on the boil and he recovered" (v. 7). Thus, a simple natural remedy was given by Isaiah to Hezekiah and was the means by which Hezekiah's healing was effected. There was no conflict between natural and supernatural healing for Isaiah.

In the NT, we find a similar recommendation of a natural remedy. In 1 Timothy 5:23, Paul says to Timothy: "No longer drink water only, but use a little wine for the sake of your stomach and your frequent ailments." It is clear that Timothy suffered from chronic health issues, especially in his gut. But Paul, rather than what we might expect from Bosworth's position of God guaranteeing healing to every believer by following the method, instead recommends to Timothy a purely natural, common medicine of wine to help with Timothy's stomach and the relief of possibly other issues.

Finally, I feel compelled to mention the possible danger inherent in this view that I personally know of. I was a member of a church in which there was a couple, and the husband received a diagnosis of terminal cancer. The couple believed that God guaranteed healing. They refused conventional medical treatment of chemo/radiation/surgery, instead pursuing only alternative medical remedies (such as herbal remedies), and praying for God's healing. The husband eventually died, as he may have done, of course, with conventional treatments. We'll never know. But before that there was the problem that they may have believed that it was their fault, or worse, his—in their lack of faith, not believing the promises of God for healing, or not confessing enough sins, or not thanking God in advance for the healing. What a great burden to lay on two faithful believers as one is dying, and the other full of concern and compassion! This method may very well lead someone to wonder what they had done that was wrong. Or perhaps leading the wife to blame the husband, or worse, to later blame God for the failure to receive a healing that was guaranteed.

On the other hand, before I finish with this view, I must point out that at least this view values the supernatural, and truly believes that God can intervene in a miraculous, even surprising way in our lives. That is a commendable desire, and one we will discuss more in the next part.

THE NATURAL AGAINST THE SUPERNATURAL

This approach is an overconfidence in traditional medicine. I believe, as I've already shown in the previous section, that God obviously has no objection to us using the traditional medical approach to healing. But I believe that among conservative evangelicals, this reliance has gone too far. I hate to say it, but at times, it begins to resemble Asa's fault: "In the thirty-ninth year of his reign Asa became diseased in his feet. His disease was severe, yet even in his disease he did not seek the LORD, but the physicians" (2 Chr.

16:12).

I believe this problem is a more specific one that arises out of a broader issue: a lack of confidence in supernatural pronouncements and means. The problem is that this lack of confidence leads us to another difficulty. In science, a change in what we expect to see is a paradigm shift (e.g., as discussed in Thomas Kuhn's *The Structure of Scientific Revolutions*). A paradigm is a particular way at looking at the world (or some part of it). It was a term in vogue several years back. What you notice when you read Kuhn's book (it's not very long) is that your paradigm in science or your worldview leads you to see what you expect to see. But, as in science, paradigm shifts for viewing the supernatural occur not only at an individual level, but also in communities. We personally hold to our own paradigm when looking at the world of our experience, but we are encouraged, even pressured at times, to hold to a particular paradigm by the community that surrounds us (as in our extended family, work cohorts, neighborhoods, cities, and all the media—newspapers, television, radio, websites and services, companies we buy from, and so on). Christians for thousands of years were pressured to change their supernatural paradigms from following the one, true, and living God as taught in the Scriptures to some other false god or idol that existed only in the community's imagination.

These days obviously there's none of that kind of pressure. Instead, the community pressures us to change from a supernatural to a purely natural paradigm, i.e., to change from the paradigm as taught by the Scriptures, which views the world in such a way as to believe that there's more to this world than what we can see or measure. There is instead pressure to accept a totally natural paradigm in which the world runs by itself based only on mechanical principles, laws, and forces. I think for most of us, we are unaware of how much we are influenced by the unbelieving community we live in until we say or do something that challenges the community's paradigm for looking at the world.

Maybe an analogy would help. Years ago I took one of my cars to an automated car wash. I pulled into the line and paid the fee, and the attendant pointed to a sign that told me the few things I needed to do for the wash to proceed smoothly. One was to put the car in neutral, which I had done. Another was to keep my foot off the brake. Unfortunately, I had brought some of our children along, since they loved going through the carwash. While I was talking with them, I forgot and left my foot on the brake. In several seconds when the curved pieces of metal under the tires began to try to push the car forward, the brake pushed back. The whole front end of the car began to rise into the air. Startled, I realized my mistake and lifted my foot from the brake and the car moved slowly and smoothly forward. I thought then that I had no idea how much force that chain and curved pieces of metal were exerting on my car until my braking caused the car to resist being propelled forward.

It is similar with our supernatural worldview. All seems simple and easy as long as we put no brake on to holding a completely naturalistic view of the world. But when we begin to resist, we will find enormous pressure pushing us to accept the community's paradigm of believing that there's nothing supernatural at work. Much of the problem could be attributed too closely identification with our surrounding culture. It's understandable given our history of a large Christian population and leaders who often referred to the Bible for help in shaping the form of our government and our laws. But that was a long time ago. Given our recent history of immorality—such as fornication among our youth, adultery, pornography, abortion, the normalization of homosexuality, high rates of divorce and out-of-wedlock births—why would we continue to identify with the general culture? Our government schools, especially our universities, are eating our young alive with the evil they teach and practice, but we pretend not to notice. Not that I think I have all the answers. But it doesn't take a master carpenter to walk into a room and see that the walls or floors are off kilter, even if we don't know how to fix them.

Our citizenship is not primarily of this world. We are citizens foremost of another nation with a king, Jesus, who calls us to listen to him. It is much like trying to deal with our two families. We have a natural family that we are to honor. Jesus showed that in his example while hanging on the cross, when he ensured his mother's care by entrusting her to his best friend, John (John 19:26–27). But there was another side he displayed. When his mother and his siblings came to see him while he taught, and he was told of their waiting for him outside of the room, he pointed to the disciples in the room: "Behold, my mother, and brothers!" (Matt. 13:46–50). Our family is important, as Paul makes clear in 1 Timothy 5:4, when he appoints the care of widows first to their Christian children. But failing their care, it is the church who shows who the widow's true family is when the church takes over her care.

As I write this section, the snow is falling hard outside, now around four inches or so. But when it started hours ago, it seemed so unlikely that it would be a serious factor in our mobility. Now it blankets the entire landscape. We can deny its seriousness, and just add more layers of clothing and encourage others to dress more warmly, but the snow continues to fall. So it is with our culture. The snowflakes of non-Christian culture seemed only a small thing, hardly worth worrying about, at first. But over time our culture has been covered by non-Christian thoughts and practices. We can continue to pretend that nothing has changed by wrapping ourselves in our Christian cocoons. But sooner or later, we will be forced to acknowledge that our lives—and especially those of our children—are being consumed by non-Christian forces.

We don't fight flesh and blood, and we won't escape by retreating. We fight by asking the Holy Spirit to help us be light and salt in a lost and dying world, by living lives that are filled with his fruit, by looking at God's priorities of caring for widows and orphans, the prisoners, the poor and the stranger, and offering shelter and protection as best we can in our communities—first by caring for Christians who are in those categories, and then reaching out to the culture around us, by even challenging the current worldviews of neo-Marxism that are now rampant among our neighbors. But also perhaps recognizing spiritual forces and using such spiritual weapons as God gives us.

TRUNCATED SUPERNATURALISM

What I'd like to do next is give examples of how our supernatural vision has been truncated by the naturalistic view that we have adopted. As I said, the problem with supernatural healing is not just a single, simple issue. I think it is a piece of a broader, more disturbing abandonment of seeing the supernatural at work in our lives and in the world around us. This section is not really a discussion of the continuation of the gifts of the Spirit as seen in the Gospels, Acts, and the letters of the NT, such as tongues and prophesy, though I will make some remarks about those. It is really about supernatural events and beings that most of us would likely not deny the reality of if confronted directly about them.

Satan and Forces of Darkness

Let's start with the forces of evil, such as Satan. The New Testament is filled with examples of warnings about Satan and other forces of darkness. Here are some samples:

- "Be of sober *spirit*, be on the alert. Your adversary, the devil, prowls around like a roaring lion, seeking someone to devour" (1 Pet. 5:8).

- "For our struggle is not against flesh and blood, but against the rulers, against the powers, against the world forces of this darkness, against the spiritual *forces* of wickedness in the heavenly *places"* (Eph. 6:12)

- "And this woman, a daughter of Abraham as she is, whom Satan has bound for eighteen long years, should she not have been released from this bond on the Sabbath day?" (Luke 13:16)

- "Simon, Simon, behold, Satan has demanded *permission* to sift you like wheat..." (Luke 22:31).

- "Stop depriving one another, except by agreement for a time, so that you may devote yourselves to prayer, and come together again so that Satan will not tempt you because of your lack of self-control" (1 Cor. 7:5).

- "So that no advantage would be taken of us by Satan, for we are not ignorant of his schemes" (2 Cor. 2:11).

- "No wonder, for even Satan disguises himself as an angel of light" (2 Cor. 11:14).

- "Because of the surpassing greatness of the revelations, for this reason, to keep me from exalting myself, there was given me a thorn in the flesh, a messenger of Satan to torment me—to keep me from exalting myself!" (2 Cor. 12:7)

- "For we wanted to come to you—I, Paul, more than once—and *yet* Satan hindered us" (1 Thess. 2:18).

These are just a sample of references to Satan and evil forces. Satan has intelligence and personality. He is not just some impersonal force. He tempts, he hinders, he has schemes, he can "sift [us] like wheat," he can disguise himself, and he can torment us. My point is really very simple. Do you ever think that what is happening to you or to those around you, or even in our general culture, is a result of the activities of Satan? I think most of us believe that much of what we see are the result of natural causes, especially people, but Paul's pronouncement in Ephesians should truly give us pause. Look at that list again; he makes it plain that the battle we fight isn't against people primarily, though they are involved and may be acting purposively with evil forces. Instead, we are trying to rescue humans from Satan's control. Judas acted as he did because of Satan: "After the morsel, Satan then entered into him [Judas]. Therefore Jesus said to him, 'What you do, do quickly'" (John 13:27). Jesus even calls Peter Satan! Very surprising: "But turning around and seeing his disciples, he rebuked Peter and said, 'Get behind Me, Satan; for you are not setting your mind on God's interests, but man's'" (Mark 8:33).

And Satan is active in the lives of unbelievers, most notably when hearing the gospel: "These are the ones who are beside the road where the word is sown; and when they hear, immediately Satan comes and takes away the word which has been sown in them" (Mark 4:15).

Satan is clearly active in our world. You may believe that his activity was heightened because of the ministry of Jesus and the apostles, but it's hard to believe that it has ceased. In fact, there may be a case to be made that it has increased. But that's another discussion. The question simply is: do most conservative Christians ever discuss or show concern for the influence or activity of Satan? I think that would be the exception rather than the rule.

Angels

Next, let's look at the interesting topic of angels. Angels in the Scriptures are God's army, his divine troops, which is one of the reasons people are usually frightened at their appearance. They were not bike messengers of the supernatural world. They were more military messengers from headquarters bringing a word to someone from the Commander-in-Chief. They expected, in fact, *demanded* acquiescence to their words with no debate. And yet, paradoxically, they are a race of beings who closely resemble humans. Thus, Jesus can say that there will be no marriage in the new age, but rather we humans will be "like angels in heaven" (Matt. 22:30). There is some correspondence to humans, which we can clearly see also in several other examples.

The first example is from Acts 12:10–16, where Peter is rescued unexpectedly from prison by an angel. Once outside, Peter goes to the house of Mark's mother and knocks on the door. Rhoda, the servant girl, answers the knock but doesn't open the gate. Instead, she runs to tell the other disciples that Peter is outside. Their response is more than a little surprising and very telling about their worldview. First, they say that Rhoda is out of her mind. But then they switch to this point: "It is his angel" (v. 15). What they meant exactly I'm not sure, but I doubt seriously any modern Western Protestant would have such a thought flit through their mind, much less express it out loud. They might possibly be remembering Jesus's comment: "See that you do not despise one of these little ones, for I say to you that their angels in heaven continually see the face of my Father who is in heaven" (Matt. 18:10). Here Jesus says that the children coming to him shouldn't be looked down on. Why? Because their angels in heaven see the face of God. I don't remember anyone warning me recently about being careful of child care because the child's angel in heaven has the Father's attention.

Another even more surprising example would be the exhortation of the writer of Hebrews: "Do not neglect to show hospitality to strangers, for by this some have entertained angels without knowing it" (13:2). Again, it strikes me as most improbable that any of us could believe that we might bring an angel home with us when opening our home to hospitality (though my wife and I discussed whether we had entertained an angel when we fed what appeared to be a homeless person on the back stoop of our apartment).

Why are angels mentioned so frequently in the NT? I think it is because of what I discussed above. The New Testament writers believed we are in a literal spiritual war in which we are always in danger (as Peter mentions in 1 Pet. 5:8, or Paul in Eph. 6:12). Against these spiritual forces of darkness, and Satan himself, we need not only prayer, and the power of Holy Spirit but apparently also angels, who fight beside and for us. What else might the writer of Hebrews mean when he says of angels: "Are they not all ministering spirits, sent out to render service for the sake of those who will inherit salvation?" (Heb. 1:14). The writer might also have in mind the image given in the Gospels: "Then the devil left him; and behold, angels came and *began* to minister to him" (Matt. 4:11). Apparently, they minister not only to Jesus, but also to us!

And, remember, too, then when Jesus returns it is not alone: "For the Son of Man is going to come in the glory of his Father with his angels, and will then repay every man according to his deeds" (Matt. 16:27).

Dreams and Visions

How about dreams and visions? In the OT, we see examples of even unbelievers having dreams from God. For example, God preserved Abimelech from sin in regards to Sarah when Abraham told him that she was only his sister (Gen. 20:3–7). A dream also came to Pharaoh from God that he needed Joseph to interpret (Gen. 41:25). The same is true of Nebuchadnezzar, as he called Daniel to interpret his divinely given dream from God (Dan. 2:28).

More examples abound. In the NT, Pilate's wife had a divine dream and warns Pilate to leave Jesus alone (Matt. 27:19). The magi, too, are warned about Herod by God in a dream (Matt. 2:12). In the OT, Belshazzar sees the hand sent from God writing on the wall and calls for Daniel to interpret the words written (Dan. 5:24). And, of course, in the New Testament we have the vision of Cornelius, a gentile Jewish convert, who saw an angel in a vision who told Cornelius to call for Peter (Acts 10:3–5). These things remind us of Peter's pronouncement at Pentecost:

> But this is what has been spoken through the prophet Joel: "And it shall be in the last days," God says, "That I will pour out my Spirit on all mankind; and your sons and your daughters will prophesy, and your young men will see visions, and your old men will have dreams; and even on my male and female servants I will pour out my Spirit in those days, and they will prophesy. And I will display wonders in the sky above and signs on the earth below, blood, fire, and vapor of smoke. The sun will be turned into darkness and the moon into blood, before the great and glorious day of the Lord comes. And it shall be [that] everyone who calls on the name of the Lord will be saved."
>
> Acts 2:16–21

Thus, the expectation was that not just prophets and apostles would be recipients of divine communication, but that all God's people, old and young, men and women, would receive those signs. Again, you may believe that prophesy ended with the apostles, but with something like dreams and visions that came to even unbelievers, it seems possible that they may continue on (and, yes, I've had several dreams over fifty years that I thought were divine communication for my situation).

Vows

How about vows? Though vows are permitted by the WCF (Westminster Confession of Faith, Chapter 22, "Of Lawful Oaths and Vows", sections 5–7), I've never heard of anyone actually making one (though it's possible they have and didn't announce it to anyone), especially in regard to healing. I can testify, though, that I did take a vow to effect healing, and I believe it worked.

When my wife and I had moved away from our hometown in order for me to earn my doctorate in physical therapy, she began to have regular sinus infections—at least once a month—that required her to go on a steady stream of antibiotics. Finally, after a year or so of this pattern, she said she could stand it no longer and went to see an ENT (ear, nose, and throat) MD. He ordered an x-ray and found that she had a serious sinus infection that remained even after many courses of antibiotics. The only recourse was for him to bring her into the hospital, push a needle up her nose and break through sinus bone and rinse the infection out. He scheduled the procedure for a week or so later. The following Sunday afternoon I was sitting on the deck at the back of our house, and expressed my concern in prayer. But instead of just praying for God's protection and healing of my wife's disease, I made a vow: that if God would heal my wife, I would complete something in return. There may be some who feel this is a coarse attempt to bribe God, but it was an accepted practice in the Old Testament and NT. Let's see just a few examples.

"Jacob also made a vow, saying, 'If God will be with me and will keep me on this journey that I take, and give me food to eat and garments to wear'" (Gen. 28:20). Jacob's vow was to tithe his possessions to God.

Of course, in Leviticus we have a votive or vow offering, again to acquire a granting of a request by God. And there's the Nazarene vow that Hebrew men or women could make, devoting themselves to God for a time.

Then in the New Testament we read: "Now Paul, when he had remained many days longer, took leave of the brothers *and sisters* and sailed away to Syria, and Priscilla and Aquila were with him.

Paul *first* had his hair cut at Cenchrea, for he was keeping a vow" (Acts 18:18). Though Paul does perform this vow in the temple, he is encouraged by the church to do so as they have four men who are also taking that vow.

Again, the idea of a vow is so foreign to us that I doubt most of us would ever even consider performing such a thing. Anyway, to finish my story from earlier, I said nothing about my vow to my wife. But on Monday morning, she awoke and reported that she felt much better. She called her ENT MD and asked to have a repeat x-ray. He agreed and she did, and all the infection was gone. Her sinus was completely clear. Needless to say, I fulfilled my vow with a very glad heart. Think what you will, but I believe God answered my vow request in a very clear and remarkable (and gracious) way.

Casting Lots

Now, another supernatural practice would be casting lots. We see lots cast in a number of places, but most notable is the example in Acts 1:15–26, where the replacement for Judas Iscariot as apostle was replaced. The apostles chose two men who were both qualified as they were among those who had followed Jesus during his earthly ministry. But instead of just voting to decide who should be Judas's replacement, they cast lots. I think they did it because they so believed in the sovereignty of God that they were sure that whichever man was chosen by casting lots—when accompanied by prayer asking God to make his choice known—would be the same as Jesus calling Peter or Matthew or John when he was present in the flesh on earth. While I don't recommend using this method in a frivolous manner, I do believe that there are times when we may need to make an important decision, but even after much thought, prayer, and counsel, we are unable to make that decision.

For instance, in a "Letter to a Friend" by Andre Rivet in the book *Faith in the Time of Plague* (edited by Stephen M. Coleman and Todd M. Rester, Westminster Press, 2021), the pastors in Geneva in one of the many plagues suffered around the time of the Reformation wanted to visit plague victims, but didn't think it was safe for each pastor to go to plague and non-plague victims. So, they decided which of the pastors would go to plague victims by casting lots, which was an act accompanied by prayer for God to make the choice. I'm hard pressed to believe that many of us would literally make a life or death decision based on prayer for God to choose using a coin flip, but that's exactly what they did.

Plagues

This next example may seem somewhat strange to our modern sensibilities, but it certainly wasn't for the Reformers. I'm referring to a plague. The Reformers felt that a plague was not just a medical issue; it was also likely an instance of God's divine intervention in history. Our temptation would be to ascribe such a thought to the ignorance of the 1500–1700s, when medical knowledge was minimal. But I think that would be a grave error. First, because the Reformed community did not believe that their plagues were miraculous, i.e., without secondary causes. They firmly believed that the many plagues they suffered through (on average one every ten years or so, with a mortality rate of 25%) were contagious, and, therefore, operated through secondary causes, though they had little idea how. Second, because they believed that God did intervene in their lives and so was likely telling them of their need for repentance.

Once again, my point is simply that we as a Christian community have reached a point where we see what we expect to see as conditioned by the non-Christian culture around us: that what occurs in our lives is almost exclusively from secondary causes, and that we would not expect God to intervene to cause such a thing as a pandemic to call us or our surrounding culture to repentance.

Miraculous Gifts

But for some, the question really becomes: Have all miraculous gifts and other wonders ceased? They accompanied the coming of the Holy Spirit at Pentecost in Acts 2, and were certainly given to the apostles to establish their authority, as is made clear by the writer of Hebrews 2:4. But they were given also to ordinary believers as Peter predicted at Pentecost, and as seen in Paul's prescriptions for their use in the time of worship as well as his encouragement of their use (e.g., 1 Thess. 5:19–21).

Though by and large I think miraculous gifts seemed mostly to have faded early on in the church, nonetheless, I think the church continued to believe in supernatural occurrences in the lives of ordinary believers in, for example, dreams, visions, angels, demons, and Satan. And it would appear to me that this supernatural work continues even today with healing. I think it's certainly possible that other supernatural activity may occur as the need arises for God's people. Believers around the world testify to such events. It's only in the rationalistic West, who have countries filled with people who would not believe in the supernatural even if they saw someone return from the dead (note God's comment to the rich man who refused to help Lazarus the poor man at his door, Luke 16:30–31).

On the other hand, I believe that supernatural healing has been institutionalized in the church as related in James 5:14–16, in the commission to elders to anoint with oil accompanied by prayer. That is the reason I called for the elders, asking for their anointing within a week of my terminal diagnosis, and only two days after the first visit to my oncologist who confirmed that diagnosis. It was that important to me.

Calvin disagrees with me (see his commentary on James 5:14), as he believed that this anointing by the elders was a symbol only for the time of the apostles. He thought that the gift of healing had ceased, so the symbol of that gift should cease as well. But I believe that Calvin was overly swayed by his disagreement with the Roman Catholic Church over the use of this passage to justify the sacrament of extreme unction (i.e., anointing of the dying with oil). And I agree with Calvin in that respect. Why anoint the dying if there is no expectation of healing, which is the point that the passage is commending? But I believe Calvin has missed several important points (if I may venture to disagree with him). First, I think that what was happening in the early church was the institutionalization of a supernatural gift. Second, it is hard for me to believe that if the gift of healing were present at the time of James writing, why would James tell the person to call for the elders? Why not call for the person who has the gift of healing? Third, it is also difficult for me to believe that only elders in all the churches would be the ones who had the gift of healing.

Instead, I think the elders are called by the sick for anointing as well as to hear their confession of sin, if necessary, and for the prayers of the elders. This idea leads me to ponder further that there may be the institutionalization of other such gifts within the office of elder: preaching may institutionalize some aspects of prophesy and tongues (which look to me like unintelligible prophecy until translated/interpreted) as well as words of wisdom and of knowledge (1 Cor. 12:8); laying on of hands for commissioning as well as to confer gifts (e.g., see 1 Timothy 4:14: "Do not neglect the spiritual gift within you, which was bestowed on you through prophetic utterance with the laying on of hands by the presbytery"); and the sacraments. First, of course, is baptism (tied to Pentecost and the baptism of the Holy Spirit, as occurred in Ephesus with Paul):

> It happened that while Apollos was at Corinth, Paul passed through the upper country and came to Ephesus, and found some disciples. He said to them, "Did you receive the Holy Spirit when you

> believed?" And they [said] to him, "No, we have not even heard whether there is a Holy Spirit." And he said, "Into what then were you baptized?" And they said, "Into John's baptism." Paul said, "John baptized with the baptism of repentance, telling the people to believe in him who was coming after him, that is, in Jesus." When they heard this, they were baptized in the name of the Lord Jesus. And when Paul had laid his hands upon them, the Holy Spirit came on them, and they [began] speaking with tongues and prophesying.
>
> Acts 19:1–6

It's clear that John's baptism was only one of repentance, but the baptism into Jesus carries the clear expectation of receiving the Holy Spirit and his gifts.

Second is the Lord's Supper (with Christ's supernatural presence and power being present, prompting Paul's warning about eating unworthily in 1 Cor. 12:27–32, resulting in weakness and death for some (v. 30). Note the use of the verb "sleep" to describe their death. To me that indicates that these people died in Christ, so that even by sinning at the last, Christ absolved them, not condemned them in discipline, in Paul's view).

Deacons, too, may have had certain gifts and functions attached to their office as a part of this process of institutionalization. I'm thinking here of functions such as caring for widows, as well as certain gifts such as service, giving, and mercy.

Thus, I believe the supernatural gift of healing continues in the church today, institutionalized through the office of elder. So, in our culture, I think we have neglected to use this gift not because we believe God can't heal us, but think that God heals us primarily through MDs and our personal prayers for these elders or for our healing. The admonition of James plays no part in most of our thinking. But if I'm anywhere close to being correct about James 5:14, then we should see ourselves as being offered the opportunity to use the gift of supernatural healing, with oil and prayers (particularly for forgiveness, if warranted). I might mention that I don't believe the oil (contra Jay Adams, if you know who he is, and siding with Calvin this time) is medicinal in nature, but instead is like water in baptism—a symbol of God working through a physical item, in this case, the oil representing his healing hand.

By not calling for the elders, we lose a wonderful opportunity for God to act. It is not a guaranteed result, but it is nonetheless important and can be a source of great hope for us as we pray for healing to petition God that he may remove our cup of sickness or death (just as Jesus prayed in the Garden of Gethsemane). Paul and James, I think, were preparing the church for the loss of the apostles, part of the preparation or institutionalization being the inscripturation of the apostles' teaching and acts (see, for example, Peter's comment in 2 Pet. 1:12–15). So, the Scripture of the New Testament was not only to educate then living or current believers, but also to inform future believers who will not have the benefit of ever knowing any of the apostles personally, men who had been taught by Jesus himself. To likewise enable the church to keep from losing many of these spiritual gifts that accompanied the apostles' ministry, they worked to institutionalize them, especially attaching them to the offices of elder and deacon.

Conclusion

So, where does this little survey leave us? I hope it reminds us of the spiritual war that rages around us every day. Paul repeatedly mentions the influence or danger of Satan in the lives of ordinary believers and, of course, unbelievers, so that we are not to make room for the devil (as Paul warns in Eph. 4:27), and pray that the god of this world who blinds the minds of unbelievers may be stopped. Of course, there is the danger of being obsessed with angels, dreams, visions, and Satan, as we are warned about by Paul, because Satan is an angel of light (2 Cor. 11:14), and so may deceive us as he did Eve (2 Cor. 11:3). Nonetheless, I doubt seriously that any one of us is being tempted in those aspects, but rather the temptation is in the direction I mentioned initially in this section: to discount or completely ignore the supernatural work of God around us. Believe me, it can be done. How many ignored the many miracles that Jesus performed, or mocked speaking in tongues at Pentecost as being a product of drunkenness? (Acts 2:13) Look to see the supernatural works of God, and the dangers and deceits of Satan. And think about asking for supernatural help, especially the anointing with oil by the elders, whenever the need arises.

I would mention, though, that there is one problem with the way most Protestants use the James 5 passage. Certainly it commends calling for the elders and having them anoint with oil and prayer. But it also makes very clear that the sickness might come from sin in the sick person. It, therefore, recommends that we also confess any sin(s) that might have brought about this discipline from God on us. The elders, then, should ask the one who called them if they know of any sin that might be bringing God's discipline. The person doesn't need to confess every sin they know of; just the one or ones that particularly come to mind with respect to the sickness.

I believe we see this same pattern in the Gospels with Jesus healing the paraplegic (Luke 5:17–26). The paraplegic's friends lower him through a hole in the roof to reach Jesus, obviously for healing. But Jesus's approach is quite surprising. We would expect him to simply heal the man. But instead he forgives the man's sins! At first we might think it was done solely to score a point off the Pharisees. It is clear, however, from Jesus's words to the paraplegic that that was not the case. "Man, your sins are forgiven you" (v. 20). Of course, this pronouncement is what angers the scribes and Pharisees. But Jesus's order in this account may not have been chosen simply because of the Pharisees. Perhaps the principle of James 5 may have been at work: repentance *then* healing, not the other way around.

We know from elsewhere that Jesus disavows the view that all evil that comes on us is a result of our personal sins (e.g., first of all Job is the paradigm. But, we see the principle spoken by Jesus in John 9:1-3), but even so he expected repentance of all, even those whose personal sins had not been responsible for the evil come upon them (e.g., Luke 13:1-5). We have noted before that there were instances recorded in the Scriptures where even unbelievers were healed. Nonetheless, I believe those to be the exception to the rule as James outlines it: normally, it's repentance *then* healing. It is possible, then, that our sickness is the result of our sin. It's yet another reason to call for the elders and for them to solicit a confession, if needed, in order to effect healing.

So, I simply encourage evangelical believers to take seriously the statements of the New Testament on the presence of the supernatural—first in our everyday lives, and then in the possibility of a supernatural healing as explained by James 5. Jesus can and does have the power to heal—with, through, and even against all natural means. But James 5 and other passages seem to indicate that even in our current time, God is willing to use supernatural means to heal us. We should avail ourselves of such a gracious offer.

APPENDIX 2: REFLECTIONS ON CANCER TREATMENT

TREATMENTS HAVE SIDE EFFECTS

I HAVE PEOPLE ASK about my treatments, so I thought I'd spend some time discussing those with this caveat: there are many forms of cancer and obviously the treatments are suited to the need. Common ones are chemotherapy, radiation therapy, and surgery. But there are others as well, so I am reporting only what was chosen for my treatment. A neighbor of mine about my age during the time I was diagnosed with my cancer was diagnosed with some kind of neck or throat cancer. He's a cigarette smoker, so I suspect it was likely related to that, but he's had a much harder time with his treatments than I have. He now has a tracheotomy, a PEG (a tube that goes into his stomach through which he receives liquid food), and chemotherapy and radiation therapy, one of which has made his tongue swell to the point where it protrudes from his mouth—a terrible thing, I'm sure. And, as a home health physical therapist, I saw quite a number of cancer patients receiving various treatments, but most did not tolerate PT very well.

My Treatment Regimen

Having said all that, let me talk about my treatments and how they have affected me. My biggest problem is the metastatic cancer in my lungs. There's no discrete, defined tumor there that they could remove with surgery. You'd have to take out both my lungs to get rid of the cancer. The cancer in my esophagus (the source of the primary tumor) is apparently very minor. And, since both cancer growths (esophagus and lungs) are essentially the same, they're treated in the same way. My treatment is solely chemotherapy, no surgery, no radiation, nothing else. I'm on a regimen they call Capox, which refers to the two chemo drugs I receive: Capecitabine, which is the oral drug I take twice daily, and Oxaliplatin, which is the medication I receive by IV once every three weeks. I qualified also for a clinical trial of an IV treatment that is a form of immunotherapy. The treatment "drug" (for lack of a better term) is Opdivo. When I say "qualified," what I mean is that there are several tumor markers that are checked for in the cancer, since the Opdivo is designed to specifically direct your immune system to attack tissue with those markers. I had one of the two markers, so that was good enough. I receive the Opdivo on the same day as I receive the IV dose of Oxaliplatin. So, once every three weeks I go to the oncologist's office where there's a large room full of recliners with IV poles, where I receive three treatments: the IV drugs (chemo and immunotherapy), and a take home bag with the oral chemo pills in it, which I take while I'm sitting and receiving the IV drugs and carry the rest home to finish over the next two weeks. It takes about four hours for the two IV meds, and I also receive a cocktail of drugs before the chemo drugs are administered: a steroid (to prevent allergic reactions) and an anti-nausea medication for obvious reasons.

SOME OF THE SIDE EFFECTS

So, I usually tolerate the treatments okay, though the first day is kind of rocky. Nausea is a never ending problem for most chemo treatments. The Capox regimen uses drugs that sound old school to me: sort of like using a sledge hammer to kill the cancer cells. The drugs kill any fast growing cells, and cancer is made up of fast growing cells. But there are plenty of other fast growing cells in your body, cells that need to be replaced constantly, e.g., your gastrointestinal cells lining your gut (hence the nausea), hair cells (I'm almost bald, so not a problem for me), and so on. The other problems with these two chemo drugs are a cold sensitivity in your hands, so they warn you not to remove things from the refrigerator at first. The cold sensitivity usually lasts several days and is never very severe for me. The other place you develop cold sensitivity is in your mouth and throat. So, it's usually a number of days before I can eat anything really cold like ice cream. But the one that is the most disturbing for cold sensitivity are the laryngospasms (an involuntary contraction of the vocal cords making it difficult to breathe). The laryngospasms result from the IV chemo med (Oxaliplatin). I've experienced it a number of times, always on the day I receive the IV med. The first time was pretty scary, as it wouldn't quit recurring every minute or so. I finally found if I shut my mouth (always a good idea for me—ha!) and breathed through my nose to warm the air entering my throat, the spasms would stop. Unfortunately, that trick worked only the first time I experienced the laryngospasms. The next time (three weeks later when I received my next IV treatment cocktail), it didn't help, but what fixed it that time was my wife making me a quick cup of hot tea in the microwave that I sipped on and waited for the spasms to fade away. The next time it happened, it could be relieved only by drinking hot tea. It usually dissipates after about twenty or thirty minutes and ratchets down as time passes during that period.

A Bigger Problem with Another Side Effect

The big problem with these chemo drugs (the Capox regimen) is that one set of fast growing cells that they attack are the cells in your bone marrow, the cells that produce red cells, white cells, and platelets. As the drugs beat down these cells, eventually the bone marrow produces less of them, so as the red cells diminish you become anemic (making you tired and short of breath), as the white cells diminish you become dangerously susceptible to infections, and as the platelets diminish you can have bleeding issues as platelets help form clots. The bone marrow can withstand this hammering only so much, so at some point if the Capox regimen is not halted, those drugs will kill you. My oncologist told me that most people can't tolerate more than about seven or eight cycles of Capox treatment. Around cycle seven, usually neuropathy shows in the hands or feet. Neuropathy is a sign of peripheral nerve damage (meaning outside of the central nervous system—i.e., the spinal cord or brain). It shows up as burning, tingling, pins and needles, numbness. It's a very bad sign that the nerves are starting to reach a point where they'll be damaged so much that they won't recover. At that point, they stop the chemo.

I'm on my third week (my week off from treatment) of my fourth cycle and go Monday to start cycle five. When I go in, they draw blood to check my hemoglobin (the red substance in your red cells that carries the oxygen you need), my white cells, and my platelets. My hemoglobin had dropped about 2 gm/dl to about 12 gm/d when I was tested at my IV session for cycle four. Normal men's hemoglobin is around 13 to 17 gm/dl. That probably indicates my bone marrow is starting to give out, but how fast that will occur is hard to say. I don't know exactly how low they'll let my hemoglobin go before they stop. They don't just give you blood whenever your hemoglobin gets below the normal range, since transfusion of someone else's blood has risks of its own. As a rule of thumb, I think a unit of packed red blood cells (prbc) usually bumps your hemoglobin up about 2 gm/dl. In the hospital I noticed that a hemoglobin of somewhere around 6 gm/dl was sort of the trigger that occasioned a transfusion, but that probably depends on lots of factors. So far my white cells and platelets haven't shown any decline.

IMMUNOTHERAPY SIDE EFFECTS WERE THE WORST

I had a host of other side effects, but the worst by far came from the immunotherapy drug. I didn't receive it during my first IV session, and so I actually didn't feel too bad; even the nausea was fairly mild. The next cycle, I received the two Capox drugs and the immunotherapy drug. My thought was that it would be easier on me than the old school (if that's what they are) drugs. Boy, was I ever wrong. The side effects of the immunotherapy were way worse (I have to mention that during one session I sat in my recliner next to someone who turned out to be a home health PT patient of mine. She was also on Opdivo, but suffered zero side effects from it, so nothing like mine. Your mileage may vary, as they used to say when I was a kid). I thought the immune drug would stimulate my immune system to kill the cancer cells, which I assume it did. The problem was that the drug also revved up my immune system to attack *me*, even my good cells, even those I needed (i.e., it attacked my own body, not some "foreign" cells such as bacteria or viruses). It produced a sort of autoimmune response that was really hard on me. And, unlike the other chemo drugs, the effect of the immuno drug didn't fade away the further I got from the day it was administered. It seemed to get worse—severe nausea and gastrointestinal (GI) issues, all of which make you simply miserable.

I know you would think the anti-nausea meds would fix that, but they didn't. Ginger is a favorite treatment, and ginger ale and ginger beer help with queasiness and mild nausea, but not with severe nausea. A friend brought me crystallized ginger, and that actually helped some. By far the "drug" that helped the most was the California product. Of course, I'm referring to cannabis (marijuana). Why on earth lawmakers can't distinguish between the recreational use and medicinal use as they do with morphine, oxycodone, and fentanyl is beyond me. I used a cannabis tincture (it's basically an oil that cannabis has been dissolved in and is used sublingually, i.e., you put a drop under your tongue). It did help, though of course it didn't eliminate the GI symptoms. And then a bunch of other problems: light headed/dizziness, spacey/fuzzy minded, muscle cramps in my legs, swelling (called edema) in both my legs around my knees and ankles as my joints were attacked—I was forced to wear compression stockings and keep my legs elevated. I also had skin drying out on my hands and feet to the point that I had to put lotion on them regularly (and I wore socks most of the time to keep the lotion on my feet). Also, my eyes felt as if I had had the drops you get in the ophthalmologist's office before an eye exam, so I couldn't take bright lights, a fan blowing on me (as my eyes were dry), and I couldn't focus well enough to read. And finally my favorite side effect and one that my oncologist said he had never seen before: loss of my fingerprints. I first noticed that when I tried to use touch ID on my iPhone and it kept rejecting my right forefinger print. It accepted my left forefinger fingerprint for several more days and then rejected it as well. I tried re-reading both forefingers, but the fingerprints were so faint I guess that the phone simply couldn't read them. Several of the apps on my phone were not happy with that development.

Some Principles for Recovery

Let me segue into what I'll call "Brian's dictums." These are just a series a sayings that I often repeated to patients in home health to help them understand or maybe remember some physical therapy or medical principle that they should know. Of course, any one of Brian's dictums is just a rule of thumb. I had professor who had saying about a rule of thumb: "It's only good thumb of the time." I used to tell the patients that dictum as well! They loved it.

I might as well say it up front: these are sayings or principles that I have tried to live by in the course of my sickness as well. I believed them when I taught them to patients, and I see their value even now as I go through this trial of cancer, so these are not ideas that are unrelated to my condition, but a part of my personal treatment regime.

Dictum #1: *For* You and *To* You

Here's the first dictum that I often repeated: "If a medication can do something *for* you, it can do something *to* you." That meant if you are taking a medication regularly (I'm not talking so much about a limited course of a drug like an antibiotic for a sore throat or a steroid for some allergy you have), then you need to know the side effects of that medication and watch out for them. Plus, a corollary to this dictum was: "If you're taking a drug whose effects can be measured by you, then you should be measuring them." So, if you're on oxygen (which in the medical world is treated as a drug), then you should have pulse oximeter (which does exactly what it says—it measures your pulse and your oxygen saturation). If your O2 saturation is consistently getting low, then the MD will likely want you on oxygen at home. You can buy a pulse oximeter on Amazon for around $20. If you're on insulin or some other blood sugar lowering drug, you'll need a glucometer to measure your blood sugar.

The drugs I had the most trouble with in home health were blood pressure medications. I found that people took one or a number of these drugs regularly for years, but often rarely measured their effects. Your body changes over time, which means that the effect your blood pressure (BP) medication has on regulating your BP may change as well. And the problem is that when you go to your Primary Care Provider (PCP), or whoever is prescribing your BP meds, they get usually only one BP reading. That is to say, your PCP gets a snapshot, and what he'd prefer is a movie of your BP. The one reading at the PCP is the snapshot, but you recording your BP reading daily at home and then taking those readings with you when you go to see the PCP is the movie. Those series of readings enable the PCP to see how your BP has varied over time, not just when you are at the MD office (and may be suffering from white coat syndrome).

I suggested that the patient take the BP at a consistent time each day, probably in the morning before taking the BP meds. Why would I suggest that? Well, for several reasons. First, if you take the BP before the meds one day, but an hour after taking them the next day, you're comparing apples and oranges because you've introduced the effects of the BP in your readings in an inconsistent way. Second, and more important for me, was the fact that I often received patient referrals for patients that were falling. I would do a history and find that the patient had problems with dizziness, being light headed. So, I did several things: initially, I'd tell them that when they first stand, they should wait for a few seconds to be sure they didn't immediately experience any dizziness. Then, I would have them walk with me. One lady experienced dizziness as we walked, so I had her bend over and put her hands on her knees. Her dizziness disappeared, which told me that it was likely her BP dropping. I've actually had patients whose BP I would take when I arrived at their home and find it was something like 90/60 (normal is 120/80. Below 100 on the top is a red flag that the systolic BP—the top number—may start to cause symptoms, such as dizziness, especially when changing positions). I would ask, "Did you take your BP before taking your meds?" Invariably the answer was no. So, I'd give them Brian's dictum and tell them that if their BP is anywhere near 100 for the top number, they needed to call their PCP to decide if they should take the BP medication.

Something interesting I had a number of patients tell me earlier this year was that their PCP had changed pretty dramatically the way the patient's BP was managed. In the past, MDs pretty much had the rule that everyone's BP, whether you were twenty years old or ninety, should be 120/80. But now patients have told me that that rule was no longer in effect. If the patient's age was eighty or above, the patient was told that a systolic reading (top number) in their BP could 140, 150, or even 160. The MD didn't explain why, but my guess is that the number of falls and serious injuries from those falls have reached a point where the falls are much more dangerous than the elevated BP. I could only say, "Finally!" I had a ninety-year-old patient who was a retired engineer and said it made sense to increase blood pressure for the elderly. It had something to do with fluid mechanics. If you wanted more blood to reach the brain when you stood and you couldn't change the blood vessel diameter to increase flow, then you would have to increase pressure. I walked out thinking maybe the blood pressure med people need to consult someone who understands fluid mechanics!

The point of this long example is that your meds are not completely benevolent. They may have benefits that you need, but I can just about guarantee that they have side effects that you don't want, and nowhere is that more true than with cancer meds, and the host of other meds that you take to fight the cancer meds side effects. But there's no escaping the need to constantly monitor and report your effects to your MD.

Dictum #2: What's in Your Gas Tank?

Here's another one of Brian's dictums: "Everyone has a gas tank. When you have surgery (e.g., knee replacement), a serious injury or illness, most of the gas in your gas tank is used to heal you. There ain't a whole lot leftover for everything else." So, you may feel pretty good one morning and get up thinking, "I'm going to do some chores for a change," and begin to try to do some work. Then you find after a short while you're thinking, "I need to sit down and rest for a while," or maybe even, "I need to lie down for a while." But the good news is that as you heal, you need the gas in your gas tank less for healing and more for other activities.

This one certainly applies to cancer therapy as the cancer may sap your energy (I tell people I'm eating for two, except the second one is like Rosemary's baby, an evil presence in me). But, in my case, the problem is the side effects of the cancer drugs that constantly make me feel weak, unsteady, and just plain tired. I have very low endurance, and, of course, because of the cancer in my lungs, get short of breath very quickly, which also makes me want to sit and rest. I do what I can, but I have to accept that a lot of the gas in my gas tank isn't just used by the cancer, but in dealing with the chemo treatment drugs side effects and that won't change until I'm off of them.

Dictum #3: Make Those Deposits

Here's another dictum: "If you have been exercising regularly, you've been making deposits in the exercise bank. So, when you get the bill that's labeled surgery, serious injury, or serious illness, then you have something to pay that bill with. But if you haven't been making those deposits, you're going to have a heck of a time paying that bill." Of course, I'm not talking about a financial bill; I'm referring to your body's ability to accept and heal from one of those three attacks. The best way to prepare for such an assault on your body is before the assault occurs—that is, by exercising regularly and controlling your weight (being significantly overweight creates a whole host of health issues, e.g., hypertension, diabetes, joint pain, breathing issues, and on and on). I rarely talked to patients about their weight, since I assumed they'd heard it all before, unless their weight was 400 lbs. or above. In that case, then I told them that their problem wasn't PT (they just needed to get up on their feet and quit sitting so much like most people). My feeling was that their eating problem wasn't going to be solved with the right diet. They needed to treat their overeating as an addiction like alcoholism. They needed therapy but not the PT kind. And most of them had an enabler. They could no longer drive, so someone was buying all that (usually junk) food, and so that person needed to help and not hinder their "recovery."

I'm not talking about becoming a body builder, but I am talking about some form of regular exercise. I can't count the number of people who retire and decide that they worked hard their whole life and that they're due for some rest, so they come home and sit in front of the television most of every day for years after they retire. I've had people who literally didn't get out of their recliner except to eat or go to the bathroom. Those are the people who had the most difficulty dealing with one of those three health issues (surgery, injury, or illness) because one of the things that will contribute to trouble with recovery is being sedentary (sitting). One of the PT directives I gave those people was to not sit more than one hour before they got up on their feet and stayed up for more than a minute. I get that they didn't feel well, or were in pain, or were weak, but it would only get worse if they continued to sit (most of them understood and agreed, but years of habit is hard to break). I used to tell patients that the TV is many people's drug of choice, since it really does seem to me to become an addiction that people just can't let go of even when they know it's bad for them.

Dictum #4: It's Up to You

Here's another dictum: Remember the referee's warning when the two boxers enter the rink: "Defend yourself at all times." When you enter the health care system, and I don't care where you are—you could be in the best system in America—don't forget this dictum. First of all, doctors have tunnel vision. They try to watch what other docs are doing, but nobody can keep up with everything. When you are in a hospital, the hospitalist (an MD that is like a general contractor when you're building a house), will try to keep track of all the MDs who are involved in your hospital stay: for me, it was pulmonology, radiology, and gastroenterology. But no one can watch every test, every med, every injection, pill that you receive or are subject to. I tell everyone: get a notebook and write down every MD who enters your room, and record what he said, what you asked, what tests are coming up and meds are to be added/changed/deleted, etc. Keep track of appointments, tests, and don't expect others to do that for you.

You must be involved. You don't have to be abusive or angry or accusatory, but you can politely ask about tests, meds, diagnoses, and so on. I went for a CAT scan, and the tech was going to do the scan on my leg rather than the arm I knew the MD had ordered. I merely asked if she was sure that was correct, and when she checked and saw that I was correct, she was very apologetic. She wasn't lazy, or careless, or incompetent. She just misread the order, and was glad for the help I gave her to prevent a mistake. Know your tests, write down your meds, and know who your MDs are. You will be glad you did at some point.

Dictum #5: Don't Sit Long

The next dictum is a sort of a repeat from a previous one, but it's so important that I'll say it again: "Don't sit more than one hour. Get up and stay on your feet for more than one minute." Try to find chores you can perform no matter what your strength and endurance are. Of course, you don't want to overdo it, but under-doing it is just as big a problem. Get some guidance from your physical or occupational therapist. No matter what you're suffering from—serious surgery, serious injury, or serious illness (like cancer)—you need to continue to practice some form of regular activity, preferably exercise.

I have had numerous patients with any of the above (surgery, injury, illness), and invariably the ones who do best are the ones who push to remain active. You will feel better in the long run if you continue to remain active rather than giving in to what you feel like doing, which is sitting or lying down all day. Don't yield to that feeling. Try to participate in normal daily activities as much as you can: attend worship, go to the grocery store, visit the library, visit friends and family or encourage or permit them to visit you. Again, in the long run, you'll be glad you did, and it will pay not only physical benefits, but also social and emotional ones as well.

Here's a suggestion for an exercise: the best exercises are what PT's call functional ones, i.e., ones that are molded around an activity that will help you do something that you perform regularly. So, I almost always assigned one called simply "Sit to Stand." The exercise is exactly what it sounds like: you are to stand up from a sitting position. You should do a stand up and sit down exercise in repetitions starting out, using your hands as much as you need to. Then try to work your way up to ten repetitions. Do this two to three times a day at a minimum, more if you can. And here's how I suggested progressing this exercise (i.e., making it more difficult):

try to stand using only one hand to help. And, with the elderly, I reminded them to perform it using proper technique: scoot forward in your seat, then lean forward, putting your "nose over toes" to get your center of mass (COM) over your base of support (BOS). Otherwise, physics is against you. I can't count the number of times I've had an aide or family member tell me that they have to practically pick grandma up to get her on her feet because grandma can't do it without a huge amount of help. I then said, "Let me try." I coached grandma through proper technique with me simply urging her to push when time to stand and—surprise!—up she popped, usually with me barely or not touching her at all.

The next step is begin trying to do the sit to stand without using your hands (yes, no hands at all). I usually had people cross their arms over their chest (if this sounds easy to you, then try it. If it is easy for you, then you are an exception unless you are young). If you have to use your hands to perform a sit to stand, then your thigh muscles are weak and need strengthening. I once had a patient who couldn't do the sit to stand from her wheelchair without using both hands and pushing on them with a lot of force. I kept warning her that doing it that way was very risky because she might not always be able to use both hands. Sure enough, I came one day to her home for a PT session, and she had one arm in a sling. I asked her, "Mrs. Smith, how are you able to stand up from your wheelchair with only one hand?" "I can't," she replied. She reported that she had injured her shoulder getting into the transport service van to go to an MD appointment. I spent the rest of the session working on her shoulder to help her shoulder feel better so she could use both hands to stand up. When I left, I told her, "Now you see why it's important to practice sit to stands to reach the point where you can do them without using your hands." "I know," she said. Of course, knowing is one thing, doing is something else.

The Gift of Foreknowledge

> We think about mortality so little, these days, except to flail hysterically at it with trendy forms of exercise and high fiber cereals and nicotine patches. I thought of the Victorian determination to keep death in mind, the uncompromising tombstones: "Remember, pilgrim, as you pass by, as you are now so once was I, as I am now so will you be…" Now death is uncool, old fashioned.
>
> Tana French, In the Woods

Dealing with death is exceedingly difficult, not just for the patient, but also for family and friends. Knowing that you are going to die is a great gift. I'm grateful that my mode of death is cancer spread over the course of months. I've had friends who died instantaneously and unexpectedly. That meant they had no time to prepare themselves for death, no time to prepare their families, no time to set their affairs in order. That to me is a terrible way to go. I know it seems much easier on the patient, but as a Christian, I would rather have time to examine or to prepare for all aspects of my life: my personal stance before God, my family relationships, my financial affairs, etc. My first thought when I found out I had a terminal disease was a concern that I would have enough time to get all the income sources started up: my Social Security income, our fixed index annuity, and my pension from the hospital system. I am so grateful that I have been granted enough time to do just that. It's such a relief to know the income stream has now been set up for my wife.

It also gave me time to let all my children know about my

likely impending death, to give them time to prepare and to have an opportunity to discuss with me any unresolved issues. Is there something they need to get off their chest? Something they've had against me, but had never felt there was a good time to discuss? Thankfully they've had that time to talk with me about any such feelings.

The same applies to friendships. My situation gave me time to let all my friends know so they can prepare. We were able to let each other know that we love and care for one another and have been very grateful for our friendship.

Lastly, my wife and I have had the opportunity to discuss the funeral arrangements. At some point several years ago, when my mom died, we purchased two burial plots next to my parents, my brothers, and my grandmother (on my mother's side). But with the cost of funerals these days, we've discussed selling the plots, and electing just to have cremation. I know there may be some Christians who have scruples about cremation as opposed to burial, but I am okay with that option. And, of course, the price is literally about half of the cost of a burial. We're "shopping" now with the cemetery and several funeral homes about cremation services.

The point is that if you have time to live before you finally die, don't waste it on just treatments and meds and side effects and frantically searching for a cure. Take time to also prepare for death and let others help in that preparation.

My Brain (not Brian) Problem

I thought I'd take just a few words to speak about "chemo brain." I always wondered about it as I heard patients mention it to me, but didn't know much about it. I think it's sort of a wastebasket term, a catchall for mental problems you suffer as you undergo chemo treatments. It usually refers to difficulties with word recall, memory, etc. My feeling is that it's another central system effect of the chemo treatments, so I lump a number of my problems under chemo brain.

The Never Ending Checkout

I'll give several examples of things I call "chemo brain." I was at Kroger yesterday and went through the self-checkout line. I had to check out three times. Yeah, you read that correctly. The first time the attendant had to come over to say I was over twenty-one for some Pumpkin ale I had purchased. I closed out my purchase and then found when transferring my purchases back into the grocery basket that I had left some yogurt and a container of nutmeg in there. So, checkout #2. Then I left the line and was putting up my cart at the entrance to the store and found a digital thermometer in the cart that I hadn't paid for. Back to the self-checkout line for checkout #3.

Seeing Is Not Believing

Another example: Some time back, my wife and I were in worship when I began to see a dog coming up to me and touching my leg. Of course, I kept fading in and out, fighting my grogginess, and so I wasn't alarmed by the incident, but I leaned over and whispered to my wife that we needed to move out to the chairs that the church has in its large foyer where I felt that I could fade in and out of attention to the worship service without risking disturbing anyone else, and where it would be easy to leave if I got too bad. I've hallucinated only once more in my life that I can remember, and that was when my fever as a young adult went to around 103 degrees. Anyway, the point is that chemo brain can be a cause of hallucinations, but also of just disturbing forgetfulness as I've had patients report to me. I've also noticed more problems with word choice, sometimes having to get on Google to find a word that I should know, but just can't recall. And trying to remember things can be difficult, even things my wife just told me.

But the big problem is trying to multitask. I find that if I focus on just doing one thing, I can do it fairly well. But if I let my mind wander, then I can't keep both the task I'm doing and the thoughts I'm having stay on track for very long. So I try to limit what I'm doing to one task at a time. If I'm speaking with someone, I tend to stop whatever else I may be doing and focus on just the conversation. Some days are better than others and may be easier to do some multitasking. I was always a list person, but now I need to keep a piece of paper and pen in my pocket to write things down when I think of them (like changing the AC filter) because it's unlikely I'll remember the thought later. As I've said before, my side effects change from day to day, and sometimes from hour to hour. My wife said recently, "I used to ask you how you're feeling today. But I changed to asking how you are right now, since how you were an hour ago may not be relevant." Very true.

The Fog

There is a constant issue with memory. My wife will tell me something, and five minutes later, I can't remember what she said. Also, I sometimes think I did something and find I didn't. It makes for an awkward situation with my wife when I tell her I did something but didn't. Fortunately, she gets it and is patient with my foibles. Of course, the opposite is also true: I do something and then forget I did. Sheesh. Of course, then there's the regular issue of losing things that I just had in my hand. Or going to a room and forgetting before I get there why I was going. None of these are major problems, but they are a steady source of irritation, not to mention disorientation.

APPENDIX 3: A SERMON FOR BRIAN'S MEMORIAL

Delivered by Doug Hart on September 18, 2024

My name is Doug Hart. I count it one of the great joys and honors of my life to be Brian Zimmerman's friend and a friend of the family. I have known Brian for forty-five years. Karen, Justin and Becky, Madeleine and Josie, Chris and Elyse, Sarah and Adam, Artemis, Winnie and Idabelle, the rest of the family too, we only understand a little bit of how much you miss Brian. There are many friends here, some of fifty years and more are here today. The grief that we all share is that Brian is absent. He's not here. That reality presses in on us, but he's present with the Lord.

What a blessing it is to have known him! Brian was such an interesting friend—one of the rare friends whom I never got tired of talking with. We could talk for hours about a lot of different books and subjects, and it was always interesting. I never wanted it to end. But if I begin eulogizing Brian today, I won't have time for the job that he gave me to do.

Today I want to very simply and clearly remind you that there is good news. The gospel is truly good news because it is the answer to death. I want to direct your attention to a few verses in 1 Corinthians 15. The Corinthian church was troubled by the death of the saints in their midst, and some of them began to lose faith in the resurrection. They began to lose faith that the Lord was going to take care of them even in and through death. And so Paul wrote this letter to the Corinthian church. And in the longest chapter—chapter 15—he spoke to this very issue, the answer to death.

He wrote to remind them to bring into their memory the gospel that he preached to them, the good news that he evangelized them with. So, beginning with verse 3, let's read from 1 Corinthians 15.

> For I delivered to you as of first importance what I also received, that Christ died for our sins in accordance with the scriptures, that he was buried, that he was raised on the third day in accordance with the scriptures, and that he appeared to Cephas, and then to the twelve, and then he appeared to more than 500 brothers at one time, most of whom are still alive, though some have fallen asleep. Then he appeared to James, and then to all the apostles, and last of all, as to one untimely born, he appeared also to me.
>
> 1 Corinthians 15:3–8

I want to point out three elements or aspects of this good news that are indispensable, that make it the good news. And then, lastly, I want to point out what Paul says about why we can believe it, how we can trust it, how we can know it.

But first, a brief story. My family moved from Virginia to Queens, New York, when I was little. And we spent five years in Queens, New York. My parents, in their wisdom, decided to send my older sister and me, when I was in the first grade and the second grade and she was in the fourth grade and the fifth grade, to Flushing Christian Day School.

It was a great blessing to be sent there, but it necessitated that my mother put us on the city bus in the morning to go to that school. We rode together. And in the afternoon, we left school and went down the street a few blocks to the train station, got on the Long Island Railroad, and rode it back home where my mother would pick us up.

The plan worked flawlessly until one day my sister was sick and had to stay home. So I was charged to travel with my friend Billy, my classmate, and we would leave school that day and go get on that train and get home. Well, I have thought about it a lot, and I think what must have happened was we walked out the front door of that school and turned the wrong direction. I realized later that I had always only followed my sister, and I had no real idea of where that train station was. And so Billy and I are trudging around the streets of Flushing, New York, the shops, the restaurants, the crowded sidewalks, cars parked on the street, more and more lost at every moment—completely lost.

And just when I thought nothing could be worse for a first grader, Billy found a large rock on the sidewalk, and he picked it up. And for some unknown reason, the devil maybe—the idle mind was the devil's workshop, right?—he picked up that rock, and he threw it through the windshield of a parked car. Now we're not only lost; we're criminals, trudging along with our book bags and our lunchboxes.

And all of a sudden, I heard a voice. It was my name being called, and I looked through the parked cars and, double-parked, a familiar blue car with its side door swung open. My mother said, "Get in." She had all the means and the knowledge and the ability to get me home. I was just as lost as I ever was, but I'd been found.

And that's why the gospel is good news for us today. The right person has come. The *right* person has come.

You know the world is made in a personal way by a personal God, the triune God in three persons—Father, Son, and Holy Spirit—made everything. And it's his personal space. And it's so bad that we forget that so easily and just live in an impersonal world. But God made it personal. And the way he rescues his people is he sends someone. And he did that over and over again, didn't he, in the Scriptures? He always sent someone, his representative, his ambassador, his prophet, his priest, his king was sent to rescue his people whenever they were in trouble.

And the gospel is good news right there in the beginning because it starts with the word *Christ*. That Christ, that's what makes it good news. It wouldn't be good news if it wasn't the right *person*—the person you and I really need in the face of all our troubles, and even death itself.

Now, one of the things that we've learned from the Scripture is that God always sends the right person, but it's usually not the person everybody expects, or they don't come in the way people would expect. It's often the child of the infertile couple, or it's the youngest child, or it's the person from a despised part of town, or it's the person without the right credentials the world might expect.

So, point one of the good news: the right person, the person of Jesus Christ, the Son of God, has come in the flesh, has come for us, and he's given a name—the Christ, the Messiah, the Anointed One. He has come. That's what makes it good news.

Secondly, it's truly good news because the gospel is all about what someone else, this person, this right person, Jesus, has done for us. Now you and I have learned to be cynical, and so when we get an incredible offer on the internet or in the mail, we look for the fine print, right? This is too good to be true. Or we might expect that we would have to do something to qualify for this, and that's the way our minds work. And so often we don't grasp the goodness of the good news because we can't believe that someone, the right one, would do everything for us.

Spurgeon in his little book called *All of Grace* said, "I'm not going to ask you to do anything," as he presented the gospel, and that's true. Why? Because someone else has done it for you.

That's what makes it really good news, and to be qualified for it, the only qualification that the Scripture presents is that you know you're not qualified. You admit that you're not qualified to receive this wonderful gift that Christ has come to give you. And if you're willing to admit that and open your hands like a little child receive the gift that Christ has worked for us, you receive a *finished* work. Christ's work is finished, and it's described here by Paul in 1 Corinthians as Christ's death—but it doesn't end there.

First of all, Christ obviously lived for us. He came and lived the perfect life that we could not live. Born under the law, he fulfilled the law completely—all God's righteous demands, he fulfilled for us, and he died. He suffered, and he died, and he was buried. What does that mean? It means that he was really dead. He went into the full experience of death itself, and he was not just resuscitated or revived, but God raised him up declaring his victory over sin and death. He did it. He defeated death. And so we don't have to. And that's why it's good news. It's good news today. It's good news that someone else has done it. That's point two of the good news.

Thirdly, I want to point out very simply that not only has the right person come, and not only has he accomplished all that you and I needed to have done for us, but he did it for *us*. He died in our place. It would be a wonderful grand demonstration if he'd lived a perfect life and sacrificed himself nobly. But no, more than that, what makes it good news is not only that it's for others, but for us. He did it for us.

In John's Gospel, we learn that greater love has no man than this: that he lay down his life for others. Jesus did that for us. That's what makes the gospel good news. It's not an impersonal event.

You say, "Well, you know, it happened a long time ago. How

could it be for me?"

The Scripture says very clearly he died for our sin. When he was placed on that cross, our sins were laid upon him. And before he was raised from the dead and vindicated, having faced the judgment and wrath of God, the whole earth turned dark for three hours under the wrath of God as he was dying on that cross. And he cried out, "It is finished." He did it for his people. He did it for us. How else could we be rescued?

You know, it's a wonderful thing to have a substitute when you really need them. And that's the way God works. He would send a substitute, and whenever he did this over and over again in the Old Testament, he did it so we would understand how he's going to ultimately save us with the good news of the gospel: he would send a substitute. He would send a representative. He would send someone to stand in the place of his people and do *for* them what could not be done *by* them.

David was a champion. The Israelites were faced with Goliath, the greatest enemy, the greatest warrior, the most dangerous man, and who did God call but little David, the shepherd boy? And he was the champion, and he stood by faith and won the victory, foreshadowing what Christ has done for us. And all of Israel enjoyed that victory. Why? Because their champion, their representative, had defeated the enemy.

So when Christ was raised, he was raised for all who trust in him. He was raised as the first fruits of the life that we now have by faith in him. By the power of his indestructible life, he defeated death, and he brought about the new creation, the new heavens and the new earth. He's the first fruits of this new creation, his resurrected body. We will be like him. All who are in him will be raised with him because he died and was raised for us. What wonderful good news!

The Heidelberg Catechism puts it, "not only for others, but for me also." That's what faith is—being able to say that. He died for our sins; he died for *my* sins.

If this didn't happen, we would face judgment. As the author of Hebrews says in Hebrews 9:26–27, "but as it is he has appeared once for all at the end of the ages to put away sin by the sacrifice of himself and just as it is appointed for man to die once and after that comes judgment."

The reason that this is very good news is because each of us have that appointment. Someday you and I will be the guest of honor at a service like this, won't we? Today we remember and honor our brother Brian Zimmerman, but our day too will come; we have that appointment. And Paul said if this didn't happen, if this good news is not true, the good news of the gospel of Jesus Christ, then we will all die in our sins. Eat and drink, for tomorrow we will die; our preaching is in vain, he said. Our faith is futile (1 Cor. 15:17). We are of all men most to be pitied (15:19) if Christ hasn't been raised, for we also are to die in our sins. If we are not to be raised, then Christ has not been raised. The good news is that Christ *has* been raised.

It's interesting to me, and Brian and I would talk about this, how Paul flips the argument around in 1 Corinthians 15. We didn't read that far, but you can go down further where Paul makes the argument. "Look, Corinthian church, if you're not going to be raised, then Christ wasn't raised."

You'd think he would make the argument the other way around. He would say, "Well look, Christ has been raised, so you will be raised." That's the other way of putting it. It'd be fine to make it that way. But Paul turns it the other way, and he says, "Look, those of you who have trusted in him, those of you who have looked to him, those of you who have received this gift of grace and of salvation that he has accomplished—you are so tightly connected to him. You are so much a part of him and he of you. He has joined himself to you in such a way. You are so united with him that if you're not raised, then he wasn't raised." I love that. I love that assurance. And Brian and I used to just shake our heads together as we talked about. What a wondrous promise that is.

Lastly, that's the good news, and why it's good news, just briefly. But how can you believe it?

Well, there's two phrases there that I want to draw your attention to. Christ died for our sins *in accordance with the Scriptures.* He was buried, he was raised on the third day in accordance with the Scriptures. How do we know? Well, we have 500 eyewitnesses or more. That's certainly valuable. Paul was one of them. What a testimony in his life of seeing the resurrected Christ! His life was changed. It really happened. He was convinced. He went from one day wanting to kill Christians to the next day being willing to die for the resurrection truth.

When he was placed on trial later in his life, Paul stood before all the people and said, "I am on trial for the resurrection from the dead. That's what I'm on trial for. I will go to the executioner's block for the truth of the resurrection."

In other words, Paul is saying to us that if this isn't the good news, if this didn't really happen, if it's not really true, then there is no good news. There is *none.* This is such good news that any other good news has to be connected to this good news.

So, how do we know it's true? Well, we have 500 witnesses. We have Paul when he was on trial with King Agrippa. He said in Acts 26, "to this day I have had the help that comes from God. And so I stand here testifying both the small and great, saying nothing but what the prophets and Moses said would come to pass, that the Christ must suffer and that by being the first to rise from the dead he would proclaim light both to our people and to Gentiles."

Did you get that? Paul is saying, "I'm not—even though I've seen the resurrected Christ with my own eyes—I'm not telling you anything that's not in this book. It's been there for 2,000 years. God has been proclaiming it. God has been foreshadowing it in every detail, in every story, in every person, in every event. He's been pointing forward to this great culmination, the resurrection of Jesus

Christ, the defeat of death."

It's all in the book. That's why we call it the word, and that's why it's the word of God: it's God-breathed; it's God's explanation to us who are hard of understanding.

How can this be? How can it be for me? This is his explanation in his word written by holy men who were moved by the Holy Spirit, for us, that we might know. Two thousand years he spent telling the story over and over again and working it out in history so people would get it. But guess what? It's still hard for us.

We have the whole Scripture; it's the word of God, and it all speaks of him, and it won't be my word or any human word that will convince you. It has to be the Holy Spirit speaking through his word to your heart and to your trouble and to your need today.

And the Spirit uses the word to speak, and when he speaks, you'll know that he's called you. His sheep hear his voice. He lets you know through his word, by his Spirit. The good news is for you.

I'm going close with Brian's words. Brian wrote a blog I commend to you. Bobby Dobyns, who's here, I think suggested it, and Mike Moffitt as well. They said, "Brian, you should write a blog. You've been teaching us your whole life, you're such a great teacher. Now you have the opportunity to teach us how to die." And he did, and in his last meditation on the last entry of his blog Brian wrote something after he looked at the following passage:

> Behold, I tell you a mystery, we will not all sleep, but we shall all be changed. In a moment, in the twinkling of an eye, at the last trumpet. For the trumpet shall sound, and the dead will be raised imperishable. We will be changed.
>
> 1 Corinthians 15:51–52

Here's what Brian wrote:

What a great hope we have. That trumpet will sound and those who sleep will awake. We will be changed. We will brush off the perishable and put on the imperishable. Brain tumor, the lung metastases, the esophageal cancer mean nothing to me. What matters is that statement, we shall be changed. "Sleeper, awake!" is our cry, our hope, our glory, our joy, and a great joy it is.

Amen and amen.

www.ingramcontent.com/pod-product-compliance
Lightning Source LLC
LaVergne TN
LVHW041742060526
838201LV00046B/885